OUR WAR

An Account of the Civil War in Bedford, Virginia

*For Jane —
Enjoy!
June*

Annotated by
June B. Goode

June B. Goode

Our War
*An Account of the Civil War
in Bedford, Virginia*

Copyright 2003
Avenel Foundation

ISBN: 1890306479

Library of Congress Control Number: 2003109110

No portion of this book
may be reproduced in any form
without the written permission
of the author.

The original spelling from quoted material
has been retained.

Warwick House Publishing
720 Court Street
Lynchburg, VA 24504

CONTENTS

PREFACE v

CHAPTER I Prewar Liberty 1

CHAPTER II Lettie's Journal 12

CHAPTER III Feeding Traveling Soldiers 31

CHAPTER IV A Call For Help 52

CHAPTER V An Outbreak of Typhoid 80

CHAPTER VI Death of Maria 101

CHAPTER VII Fan's Wedding 121

CHAPTER VIII Ladies' Hospital Association 143

CHAPTER IX "So Much Excitement" 154

CHAPTER X Confederate Hospitals in Liberty 170

CHAPTER XI Medical Correspondence 185

CHAPTER XII The Diary of Henry C. Sommerville 199

CHAPTER XIII County Court
and Central War Committee 210

CHAPTER XIV Hunter's Raid 223

APPENDIX A Samuel Harris and His Gun 263

APPENDIX B Court Orders 265

BIBLIOGRAPHY 275

INDEX 279

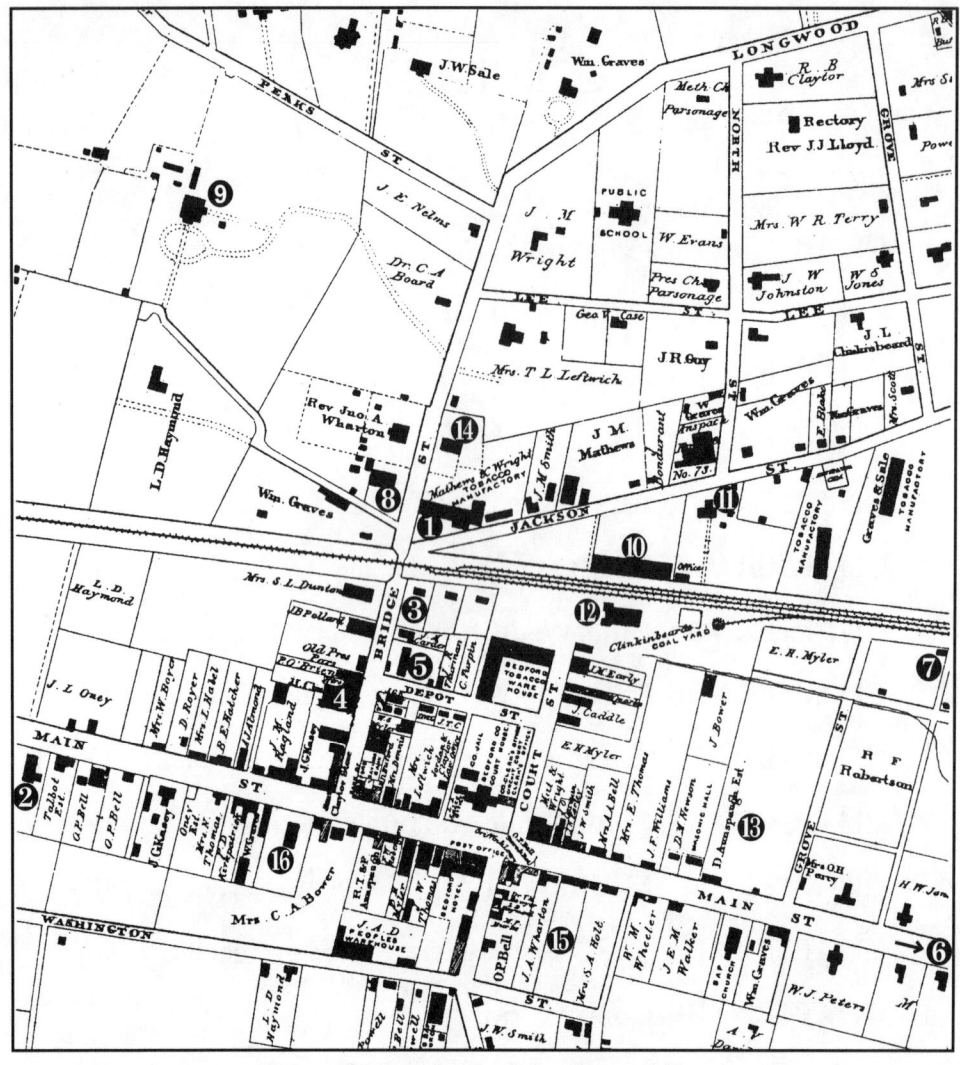

Map of Liberty, Virginia, circa 1876

Buildings Used for
Confederate Hospitals
1. Campbell's Tobacco Factory
2. Crenshaw Tobacco Factory
3. Micajah Davis Tobacco Factory
4. Toler's Furniture Factory
5. I.N. Clark Carriage Factory
6. Piedmont Institute
7. Reese Warehouse

Other Buildings
8. St. Paul's Episcopal Church
9. Avenel
10. Hewitt House
11. Jesse T. Hopkins home
12. Railroad Station
13. Aunspaugh Estate
14. Baptist Church
15. Sentinel Office
16. Presbyterian Church

PREFACE

This book is a story of the Civil War in Bedford, Virginia, as seen from local diaries, letters, newspaper clippings, local stories, and other sources. While Hunter's Raid has been the most well known important historical happening in Bedford of that period, it is noteworthy and of no less importance to recognize Bedford as a hospital town during that time. Once the hospitals were established, the affect on the town and its inhabitants is clearly seen through the eyes of sources in this book.

In 1986 Dr. Peter Houck of Lynchburg, Virginia, published his findings relative to the Confederate Hospital Center there, and this provoked my interest in the establishment of the hospital unit in Bedford County. The research done, it was put on hold until after retirement when family and friends urged me to publish it.

The journal of Lettie Burwell of Avenel was written during this time period and is such an absorbing one that it is printed in its entirety. Many of her friends and relatives are footnoted for easier identification. Excerpts from the diary of Henry Sommerville, a doctor who served at Piedmont Hospital, are descriptive of Bedford and its people. Excerpts from the diary kept by David Hunter Strother, nephew and namesake of General David Hunter, as he rode with the General, are interesting. When they are compared with the diary of Thornton N. Hinkel, a correspondent from the Cincinnati Gazette riding with the same group, the eyes of each saw and reported different findings, as they could have been miles and hours apart.

There may be omissions as well as errors in the book for which I ask your indulgence. I wish to express my appreciation to the many generous sources of assistance: Jones Memorial Library, Mrs. Sydnor Walker Hayes, the Bedford Museum, the Bedford Library, Alderman Library, Avenel Foundation, Dr. Peter Houck, the Virginia State Library, Darrell

Fisher, Mrs. B. J. Strong, Mrs. George Parker's Scrapbook, and her History of Bedford County. If, by error, I have omitted your name I am very sorry but remain very grateful for your assistance.

June B. Goode

CHAPTER I
Prewar Liberty

Liberty, the county seat of Bedford County, Virginia, lay quietly nestled beneath the mighty and beautiful Peaks of Otter. Because it was the most populated area in the county, Liberty housed the necessary businesses to make life convenient for its then 1200 citizens. (Daniel, 1985, 3) A closer look at this little town reveals that Main and Bridge Streets were both defined but the streets were paved with poor material and only for short distances, keeping mud, dust and ruts a frequent problem. (Graves, 1903, 7-8) Streets were continually cluttered with such nuisances as dogs and hogs, which ran rampantly in the road already cluttered with horses, necessary for transportation. (Daniel, 1985, 3) And we think Interstate 81 is bad!

Three newspapers documented the news of Liberty in 1857—the *Sentinel*, *Bedford Democrat* and *Bedford Bulletin*. All carried interesting advertisements of locally available merchandise. Stores were wooden, inconvenient, and lacked heat, but each carried a variety of stock. (Graves, 1903, 7-8) To mention a few: Samuel C. Whitesides, located on Main Street one door below Samuel Hoffman, advertised clocks, watches, and jewelry and claimed to be a mathematical instrument maker. William Gish advertised new goods for ladies and gentlemen, while Tyler C. Jordan carried shoes, dry goods and groceries; J.F. Gregory offered clocks and watches for sale. (*Bedford Democrat*, 1857)

Bedford House, the most prestigious hotel in Liberty was located on the corner of Market and East Main Streets across from the courthouse, where the First Citizens Bank now stands. Bedford House, then operated by Charles Phelps, replaced the old Bell Tavern, which was dismantled in 1856.

E. J. Buckwalter and J. F. Stone, a tailoring partnership was located in the basement of the Bedford House. The only drug store, operated by Dr. J. A. Otey, was also located opposite the courthouse. One could purchase diverse items at the drug store...perfume, paint, oil, ice cream freezers, fresh salmon, lobster, and sardines. (*Bedford Democrat*, 1857)

The first bank in Liberty was known as Bedford Savings Bank of which Micajah Davis was cashier. This bank, however, was closed as the war years approached. (Parker, 1954, 23)

There were no livery stables in town as people owned but few carriages and most walked to their destinations. The town had only one butcher who might ride out in the morning, buy a small beef, drive it home and butcher it about nightfall on the lot of Col. Daniel Aunspaugh. The next morning about four o'clock all who wanted beef would go there and purchase it. The market would close by 6 A.M. to be open no more until the butcher went out again to the country and returned. (Graves, 1903, 7-8)

Conveniences we now take for granted were non-existent in 1857. Water came from the well, heat from the fireplace, and light from the lantern. There were no water works, no telephones, and no electric lights. "When the moon did not shine we took our lanterns." (Graves, 1903, 7-8)

Campbell House on North Bridge Street, formerly the Baptist Meeting House

Parents had many school choices for the education of their children. Sydney L. Dunton operated a girls' school in 1857 called Bedford Female Institute in the Campbell House on North Bridge Street. By 1858 the school advertised its location near the home of L. A. Sale. Campbell House operated from the building originally known as the Baptist Meeting House across the street from the former John Wharton House on North Bridge Street.[1] (DAR, 1976, 30, 72)

In August 1857, Dunton placed the following ad in the *Bedford Democrat*:

BEDFORD FEMALE INSTITUTE

The next session of the Institute will commence on September 15th and will continue ten months with no intervening vacation except the holidays in December and at Easter. The principals, Mr. and Mrs. Dunton, divide their attention to the requirements of the Institute and they will be aided by competent assistants.

TERMS:

Board for session of 10 months	*$130*
Tuition in Primary English	*$20*
Tuition in more Advanced English classes, Mathematics, and natural science	*$30*
Tuition in Music, piano, and guitar	*$40*

Each boarder will supply herself with toilet napkins. Payments to be made in advance, half on September 15, and half on February 15.

S. L. Dunton, Principal, Liberty, Bedford County, Virginia.

In 1861 Dunton purchased the property on the west side of North Bridge Street, just south of the railroad, now a parking lot, and continued to conduct his school there until 1871 when he became Superintendent of Bedford County Schools. (DAR, 1976, 68)

---

[1] By 1850 the Baptist Congregation moved to a new home on East Main Street. In September 1842, Deed Book 30, pages 8-9 show deeds of a portion of the church property transferred to the Trustees of the Bedford Female Academy from the Trustees of the Liberty Baptist Church. In 1847 the remainder was transferred to Vinal Smith.

The Reverend H. S. Osborne, Principal, and Professor A. Sloat who served as Assistant Principal, advertised in the *Bedford Democrat* in 1857 that Piedmont Institute, an academy for boys, would open on September 3 for a five-month session. Piedmont Institute was built in 1847 and had operated since that time under the leadership of various individuals. Professor Osborne advised that the following terms prevailed:

TERMS

Board in the Institution	
including necessary light, fuel and washing:	$75
Tuition as follows:	
Primary English	$12.50
Higher English Classics	$17.50
French, German, Philosophical Lectures,	
Mathematics with use of apparatus	$1.00

Each student will be required to pay 1/2 of his tuition on entering the Institute and the balance at the close of the session.

Mr. S. A. Harris, Teacher.

Also in 1857 Albemarle Military Institute advertised its school in Charlottesville. The English and Classical School at Timberidge, near Lowry Depot, advertised that it was operated by J. M. Lowry. The Virginia and Tennessee Collegiate Institute was advertised in Bristol, Virginia. In 1860 the Reverend Alexander Eubank, a Baptist minister advertised that the 2nd session of his school, Sunnyside, would commence on October 1, 1860. This school was located on the Dickerson Mill Road. (*Bedford Democrat*, 1857, 1860)

Though tobacco had always been the chief money crop cultivated in this and surrounding counties, no warehouse for the auction of tobacco was opened in Liberty until after the Civil War. Micajah Davis, Col. John B. Crenshaw, and W.T. Campbell would manufacture tobacco for a few months in the spring and summer. During the winter they would visit the farms and buy tobacco as it hung in the houses at so much a hundred. Frequently Col. Crenshaw could be found in the counting room of William Graves who did a large mercantile business at the corner of Main and Bridge Streets. (Parker, 1954, 19)

There were actually eleven manufacturers of tobacco in Bedford County at the close of the antebellum period in 1860. They employed 308 men and 29 women. The monthly salaries for men ranged from $10 to $14.28 for an average wage of $12.30. The monthly wage paid women who comprised 9.4% of the labor force varied from $5 to $10 with an average salary of $9.41. Eight of the eleven enterprises employed some women. Five of the tobacconists represented capital investments of more than $15,000 each. These were Moorman & Peters, Matthews & Wright, Stewart Brothers, Miller & Wilson, and John Crenshaw. (Daniel, 1985, 86)

The largest operation was that of Matthews & Wright. They employed fifty-three persons including nine women and reported an annual business of nearly $42,000. The Bedford manufacturers produced plug and other forms of chewing tobacco, smoking tobacco, and processed stems. (Daniel, 1985, 86) John Mays Wright of Matthews and Wright, was born near Stewartsville in 1836. While still a young man, he became associated with James M. Matthews, his brother-in-law, in the manufacture of tobacco at Stewartsville and soon both moved their families to Liberty where they erected a large factory on the northeast corner of Bridge and Jackson Streets. Here they continued to manufacture tobacco until the death of Mr. Matthews. Mr. Wright then became a partner in the firm of Newsom & Wright and conducted a warehouse for the sale of tobacco for a number of years. Late in his life he moved his family to South Boston where he established and operated a hardware business until his death. (Ackerly & Parker, 1981, 630)

Such was life in Liberty when rumblings of discontent began to be heard here. The militia here was organized into companies but the thought of war was very threatening to the way of life, principles by which the people lived, and the foundation upon which their economy rested. Perhaps this threat was becoming more real, for as early as December 2, 1859, the *Bedford Democrat* carried the following notices, showing more activity in the militia:

MILITARY BOUNDARIES

The last Regimental Court laid off the boundaries for two new companies, viz: The boundary of the first commences at Claytor's Mill; thence along the road by Timber Ridge Church to Lowry's Old Shop on the Forest Road; thence along Forest Road to Main Street in Liberty; thence across said street, and down the alley between John F. Sale's and Mrs. Aunspaugh's to Back Street on Regimental Line; thence down Regimental Line to Claytor's Mill, the beginning.

The boundary of the second company commences at Wilkes's Mill; thence along Big Otter to Hardy's Mill; thence along the road to Centerville; thence along Ridge Road to foot of Allen's Mountain; thence to the top of Thomas's Mountain; thence a straight line to Patterson's Mill; thence along the road to Patterson's Merchant Mill; then along the road to Lisbon; then along the turnpike road to the fork of the road below Robert Jones; thence along the road to Stiff's on Regimental Line; thence down Regimental Line to the alley between John F. Sale and Mrs. Aunspaugh; thence along said alley to Main Street; thence crossing street to Forest Road and down Forest Road to Wilkes's Mill, the beginning.

All persons living in the bounds of the above companies and subject to military duty will assemble in the town of Liberty on the second Saturday in December for the purpose of electing officers.

Jesse S. Burks, Col. 91st Reg.

ATTENTION OFFICERS

At the request of the Officers of the 91st Regiment and a portion of the 10th Regiment, I will commence a Monthly Drill in the town of Liberty, on the first Saturday in December. The Officers of the above Regiments are requested to attend in full uniform and all others who may desire are invited to attend and participate in the drills.

Jesse S. Burks, Col. 91st Regiment.

According to the custom of the times anyone who wished to do so might raise a company and so it was that T. C. Jordan, James O. Hensley, both attorneys, R. B. Claytor and R. T. Aunspaugh, merchants, secured the names of persons in Liberty and Bedford County who signified their willingness and intention to be organized into a military company. (Graves, 1903, 7-8)

Tension mounted between the industrial north and the rural south throughout the 1850s and into the 1860s as talk began in the south of secession. The war aims of the two sides were different but simple. The Confederacy would fight for independence and the North for re-establishment of the Union. So far, slavery was not an issue. In February 1861, the Confederacy was formed with Jefferson Davis's inauguration. Lincoln was inaugurated in March of 1861, and on April 12, Fort Sumter was bombarded.

Five days later, by April 17, 1861, the Richmond Convention passed the Ordinance of Secession. The services of three Bedford companies were the first in the state to be tendered and accepted by Governor Letcher. After the call for troops, nine companies were in the field before the end of May 1861, namely: The Rifle Grays, Captain Thomas Leftwich; Clay Dragoons, Capt. William R. Terry; Old Dominion Rifles, Capt. Thomas M. Bowyer; Bedford Light Artillery, Capt. T. C. Jordan; C. R. Rifles, Capt. William L. Wingfield; Southside Dragoons, Capt. James Wilson; Rifles, Capt. McG. Kent; C. F.

Rifles, Captain Augustus L. Minter; Bedford Rangers, Captain Radford. Of these, some retained their name and organization through the war, others retained their organization but were attached to regular regiments and became companies in them, while others were disbanded, and the men re-enlisted in other organizations. Capt., later general, Terry was the only one of these officers who had a good bit of military education. (Hardesty, 1884, 393)

When the Civil War began in the spring of 1861, VMI had provided a reservoir of trained manpower to Virginia. Shortly after Virginia seceded, almost all the cadets then enrolled at the Institute were sent to the camps of instruction at Richmond to assist in training the newly organized units. Virtually all of these men then went directly into the southern army. In addition to the alumni and the 1861 corps, men from the large wartime classes left the Institute all during the conflict to join the Confederate Army. It was estimated that a total of 1,796 VMI cadets and alumni were in Confederate service in 1861. Eighteen of these became rebel generals, 95 colonels, 65 lieutenant colonels, 110 majors, 310 captains and 221 lieutenants. What this reservoir of trained manpower meant to Virginia is illustrated by the case of a company which was organized on April 26, 1861 at Pierceville, Virginia, in the Goode, Bellevue vicinity of Bedford County. (McMurry, 1989, 101, 102)

After the men were assembled there, the question arose as to who might instruct them in the complicated maneuvers of 19th century drill. Dr. James McGavock Kent, who had attended VMI for about six months in 1840/41, was unanimously chosen as Captain and the men began to drill twice a day under his tutelage. This company, originally called the Bedford Letcher Grays, became Co. F of the 28th Va. Infantry. Later Kent left the company to become a Confederate surgeon, but the presence in the community of a citizen whose education had provided him with enough military knowledge and experience to train his comrades had proved of great value to the unit in its earliest days. (McMurry, 1989, 101, 102)

PRE-WAR LIBERTY

The Old Dominion sent fifty-six regiments and battalions of infantry and heavy artillery into Confederate service in the early months of the war. Twenty of them were commanded by VMI men. Two of the eight cavalry regiments organized in 1861 also began their service under the command of VMI alumni. Virtually every Virginia unit included several men who studied at VMI. Many of the VMI alumni living outside Virginia in 1861 also wound up fighting for the Confederacy in the Old Dominion in units from other states. (McMurry, 1989, 101, 102)

The county lost no time in organizing to meet wartime needs. At the May 1861 term of the county court, with about thirty justices present, and without one dissenting vote, $50,000 was appropriated for arming its militia and another appropriation was made to purchase supplies of coffee, flour, bacon, sugar, and corn for the destitute families of absent volunteers. At a meeting of citizens the following were appointed a Central County Committee: Jesse T. Hopkins, Elbert A. Talbot, O. P. Bell, Abner Fuqua, William Bush, A. B. Nichols, Wilson Wheeler, Dr. J. A. Otey, Col. T. P. Mitchell, and Col. Richard Crenshaw. This committee appointed a subcommittee composed of gentlemen from each magisterial district for distribution of supplies:

District 1: Charles W. Gill, Caleb D. Parker, John Crenshaw and Richard Crenshaw.

District 2: James M. Matthews, Josiah H. Nimmo, Fielding H. Jeter, Robert E. Jones.

District 3: George Johnson, Thomas W. Robertson, S. P. R. Moorman, William A. Wingfield.

District 4: Elijah C. Cundiff, August L. Thurman, Alexander Leftwich, William M. Fields.

District 5: Spottswood Brown, Samuel I. Wade, George W. Shelton, William I. Bell.

District 6: Hector Harris, David W. Kyle, John M. Anderson, John W. West.

District 7: Samuel M. White, Benjamin N. Hobson, Lewis C. Arthur, William O. Hurt.

District 8: Robert N. Kelso, John P. Hurt, William L. Wilkerson, John C. Hopkins.

District 9: William Reilly, Theophilus Scruggs, George P. Luck, Jesse R. Gibbs. (Hardesty, 1884, 393)

S. A. Buford, a Bedford resident, wrote in an undated newspaper article that the winter following the election of Abraham Lincoln for president was full of excitement all over the country and the little town of Bedford partook of the commotion and shared in the martial spirit:

"With the drilling of the companies, the preparations for their equipment and the passing of thousands of Southern troops through the town, our people were wild with excitement and grief. At any time in the morning when notice had been given that a train bringing soldiers on board would pass through, our housekeepers would put the cooks to work to prepare breakfast for them, and great trays and baskets, bearing steaming pots of coffee, cooked meats, breads, etc., were cheerfully borne to feed them. The soldiers were gay with enthusiasm and sometimes the train was held here long enough to permit those who wished to walk through the streets, and we heard many words and songs of praise for the good cheer and hearty welcome given them, and we had the pleasure of admiring the gallant soldiers in their handsome uniforms. As soon as our soldiers began to equip themselves for service in the field, the ladies of the town of all ages, except the infirmed, assembled at the courthouse to make their uniforms, which had been cut by the tailors. Perhaps all the ladies, and certainly the younger ones, did more hard work on the sewing and pressing of these uniforms than they had ever bestowed on anything before. There were always smiles for their soldier friends when they came to see how the work progressed, or perhaps for some other reason. But every heart held its own bitterness at the thought of the parting hour."

How could one imagine the fear, hardship, exhaustion and deprivation which the future would bring to this small town of 1200 and to the carefree, easy pace of those who called "Liberty" home.

In the events of the following chapters we see how pride, perseverance, and a great determination of spirit would give way to strength and endurance to face whatever must come; to rise above that which was cast upon us, not only in Liberty, but also in Virginia and across the Southland.

CHAPTER II
Lettie's Journal

Letitia McCreary Burwell of Avenel was about twenty-five years old when the war began. Her journal begins on April 19, 1861. The original manuscript is at the Alderman Library in Charlottesville, Virginia. It has been transcribed by Bowyer Campbell who added a few notes of identity of the persons mentioned. The journal is reproduced here as written with minor changes in sentence structure for clarity. Lettie, as she was known, appears at times to be writing rapidly, as if in haste. As she says, paper was scarce and she must write in a laconic manner, expressing much in as few words as possible. Toward the end of her journal, the dates of some entries are out of sequence, which was confusing. An 1861/1862 calendar was consulted and dates correctly changed for better sequential order. Despite the fact that she

*Frances Steptoe Burwell,
wife of William Burwell*

*The Honorable
William McCreary Burwell*

does not always use verbs, she expresses herself so well that her meaning is quite clear.

The family at Avenel consisted of her parents, William McCreary Burwell and Frances Steptoe Burwell and their four living children: Lettie, the eldest girl, Kate, referred to as "Sister," Fan, and Rosa. A boy, James, died early in his life and is not in the home at this time.

William and Frances Burwell began construction of their handsome brick home in Liberty in 1835. It was completed in 1836 and named "Avenel" for the white lady of Avenel, a character in the popular novel, *The Monastery* by Sir Walter Scott.

Avenel, home of the Burwell family, was built in 1836. This picture was taken after the war (from Old Virginia Gentleman, *by Bagby).*

At that time Avenel Plantation embraced the land now bound by Bridge Street, West Main Street, College Street, and Peaks Street in Liberty, Virginia. A long tree lined drive from what is now North Bridge Street led to the fine house of William Burwell.

Even though some sense of intrusion accompanied the decision to print the private thoughts of Lettie Burwell, thoughts which she probably intended for no eyes but her own, she paints a colorful picture of life in Bedford as she knew it and in doing so introduces us to many of its citizens. Her opinions and feelings give us an important sense of the times, which cannot and should not be measured by today's standards. Her strength and courage in the face of the Yankee enemy are vividly shown and the sadness and grief with which she nursed her terminally ill servant are described as if they happened today. Her acute sense of loss at the death of her sister, Fan, was such that she wrote no more in her journal and thus it ended. All of these are a part of Lettie and will with much feeling and sympathy live in your heart for her as you read.

OUR WAR, A JOURNAL
APRIL 1861–AUGUST 1862
by Letitia Burwell

APRIL 19, 1861

For several days great excitement. Virginia has seceded at last. Seceded which it ought to have done long ago, and old Governor Letcher has waked up sufficiently to telegraph the different volunteer companies throughout the State to hold themselves in readiness in case of fighting.

The telegraph yesterday brought news that Mr. James Allen had made an effort to secure the arms at Harpers Ferry, but his brave company had been defeated by Mr. Lincoln's troops who came over from Washington. I hope this is not true. No news from there today. Mr. Allen is a brave and sensible man and it was so gallant of him to try to seize the large store of arms at Harpers Ferry, as soon as he got the news that Virginia had left the Union.

But what a sad time is before us! The only thing we poor women can do is to weep when we think of the gallant lives that may be lost, and to pray without ceasing for them.

Very busy today packing Sister and Dr. B.'s[1] trunks in case of a dispatch from Richmond calling Dr. Bowyer's company. Sister has determined to go with them. She would be miserable up here. Papa is going too, although he is fifty years old. So Mama, Rosa, Fan and myself will be left alone. Cannot help hoping there will be no fighting although I feel so anxious the northern fanatics shall have proof of the bravery of the South they have been abusing so long. I feel that the South should come out boldly now before the world and assert her independence. She should make such a brave stand for her rights and institutions that hereafter the civilized world will tremble and turn pale whenever it dares assert that the slave owners of the south are a set of villains and murderers. We should declare in Europe and every place to which "our northern brethren" have had access, that it is time now for our people to come forward and put down this wide spreading sentiment even with the force of arms. This is very natural, if "our Northern Brethren" find so much fault with and abuse us so heartily that we should desire to set up a government for ourselves,

---

[1] Dr. Thomas Michie Bowyer was a son of Henry Bowyer and his wife, Sarah Preston, former mistress of East Greenfield plantation, in Botetourt County. Thomas Bowyer married Kate Burwell, daughter of William and Frances Steptoe Burwell in June of 1859. The Bowyer family was connected to the Breckenridge family through a marriage of Matilda Breckenridge to H. M. Bowyer of Fincastle. (Robertson, 1979, 10).

Thomas Bowyer graduated from University of Pennsylvania and was educated as a physician but mustered into service as Captain of Co. C, 28th Va. Inf., and later transferred to artillery service commanding Bowyer's Battery. In 1863 he was promoted to Major of the Artillery and assigned to staff duty in southwestern Virginia where he continued to serve until the end of the war. After the war he served as Mayor of Liberty from 1871-1879. He had an established medical practice in Liberty for a number of years. (Fields,1985, 50)

especially as we have all of the resources requisite. This might be done peaceably, but the Northerners do not like the idea of losing so much good Southern money.

How strange to think we are in the midst of a Revolution. Who would have thought that in our time there would be such a thing?

A note from Sis Wingfield. Mary is at home at last, first time since she was married. Wish I could go to see her, but the weather is so disagreeable and we are helping Sister to get ready, so I don't expect I will see her.

Dr. Bowyer's company drilling in lot opposite our front gate. Such a fine looking set of men. He is quite proud of them. Commenced reading Froissart's *Chronicles of the 15th Century*. But so many things going forward in my own time I cannot confine my attention to Froissart and his times. Telegrams coming and going.

Papa, Dr. Bowyer, and Sister all packed to go to war. The village rampant with troops. Three companies drilling all the time. The country people riding in, in great excitement to drill and hear the news. The ladies busy making flags. Dr. Bowyer came in to supper and told us he had just heard through the telegraph that the Baltimoreans have seized the Northern troops, 800 men, who were on their way to Washington to be sent by Mr. Lincoln to reinforce Harpers Ferry and Fortress Monroe. Great rejoicing over this news. Papa sent up immediately for Mr. Davis and all to come down and hear it. What a brave thing of the Baltimoreans, especially as their Governor had declared he would not help us.

Nine o'clock at night. Telegraph said they were still fighting at Baltimore and the "Plug Uglies" had torn up the railroad each side of their city and thus imprisoned the Northern army, the 7th Regiment of New York had killed 200 men, only sixteen Baltimoreans killed. I wonder if this is true.

Mr. Berry[2] and Tom Davis[3] came in after supper. Talked over the exciting news and rejoiced over the telegram from Baltimore. No definite news yet from Harpers Ferry. Mr. Berry tried to cheer Sister. She is much distressed because of the suddenness of Dr. Bowyer changing his peaceful profession for one so opposite. But he is so brave a man he should have had a military education. However, natural bravery will make up for educated bravery.

Nannie Davis[4] sent us down some handkerchiefs to hem for her brothers. Hemmed them in a great hurry, stitches so long they can see something to remember us by.

---

[2] William Wallace Berry was born in 1837 and married in 1856 Mary Annis Davis (Tom Davis's sister). He was a "circuit preacher" being assigned different churches each year. Rev. Berry was serving a church in Buckingham County, Virginia, at the outset of the war when he decided to join the men of Bedford County, Virginia, and mustered into the Old Dominion Rifles, an infantry company attached to the 28th Virginia Volunteers with his brothers-in-law, Lt. John M. Davis and Private Samuel P. Davis. They saw their first action at the Battle of Bull Run on July 21, 1861. William Berry's efforts to be commissioned as a Regimental Chaplain took several months, since there was no official recognition of chaplains by the Confederate Government nor any orderly procedure for entering the service. When he was commissioned in November of 1861 he found that he was allotted the pay of a non-commissioned officer, given quarters of a second lieutenant, yet allowed no commissary privileges. Although generally considered to be a Captain, he had no rank, no uniform, and no insignia. It was not uncommon for commanding officers to feel that religion had no place in battle and therefore opposed the work of Chaplains. The Chaplain, while a non-combatant officer, often stationed himself near the front and accompanied the surgeon to minister both physically and spiritually to the wounded and dying. Chaplain's work also included visiting the sick and prisoners of war, prayer meetings, conversions, and sermons. When the war was over the Methodist Church assigned him to Hanover County. He returned to Liberty in 1868, when Judge Davis purchased the *Bedford Sentinel Newspaper*. Berry became the editor of this paper. In the fall of 1875 he was elected to the House of Delegates for a two-year term. A man of many talents, he was a gifted orator and an attorney. (Berry Family Papers)

[3]Thomas Edward Davis was born in 1835 and died in 1917. He graduated from the University of Virginia in 1858. Subsequently he studied

SATURDAY, APRIL 20, 1861

News from Baltimore confirmed. Governor Letcher dispatched to Dr. Bowyer he will not have to go down today which will give Sister more time to make her arrangements.

Dr. Bowyer thinks Papa will find the camp life harder than he anticipated. I think they will all find it so, never having been accustomed to anything of the sort.

I wish the Yankees would go home and let us do as we please with our own Southern States. We must have been a great source of revenue to them that they are so enraged at the prospect of our setting up for ourselves. The ladies in town are busy today finishing uniforms for Dr. Bowyer's company. I never heard of such a mania for fighting. I be-

---

medicine and law but did not practice either. He joined the Confederate Army in May 1861 and became Major, Adjutant of the 21st Virginia Cavalry. He fought in numerous engagements and at the close of the war removed to Montana where he was engaged in mining. He later moved to Galveston, Texas, and from there to Houston, Texas, where he met and married Mary Evelyn Moore, daughter of Dr. John Moore in 1874. He entered the field of journalism in 1876, founding the *Houston Telegram*. In 1879 he joined the staff of the *New Orleans Picayune* and became its editor in 1884, remaining there until its sale and consolidation with the *Times-Democrat* in New Orleans in 1914. Two children were born of this marriage, Thomas Davis and Mollie Davis.

Tom Davis was the son of Micajah and Ellen Phillips Davis. Micajah Davis rode as Sheriff of Bedford County for 15 years, served as Justice of the Peace for 10 years, as tax collector under the Confederate Government for 3 years and as County Coroner for 12 years. For 12 years he also held the position of County Judge. He had seven children and lived at Chestnut Hill, a short distance from Avenel on the road to the Peaks.

The Micajah Davis House on what is now Peaks Street

[4]A sister to Tom Davis was 20 years old at this time. In 1862 she married Dr. Marcellus P. Christian of Lynchburg. At that time he was a surgeon in the service of the Confederacy. See later references to him.

lieve if Dr. Bowyer and some of his company are not allowed an opportunity for fighting some Yankees in a few days they will go crazy. I am certain Sam[5] and John[6] Davis will go wild so intense is their desire, and so impatient are they to shoot some Abolitionists and Yankees. The idea of a Union of people who so cordially hate each other! How could such a union have lasted so long!

SUNDAY, APRIL 21, 1861

Mr. Berry preached an excellent and eloquent sermon (at the Methodist Church) to the soldiers who have prepared to answer the summons of the Governor. The Presbyterian Church, too, was thrown open on this occasion. At both churches the military companies all appeared in uniforms, their captains at their head, all marching in and taking their places by word of command. The churches very crowded...benches placed along the aisles and every space that could be stood up in. Mr. Berry's sermon was very impressive and brought tears in every eye, even of the bravehearted soldiers who have so nobly responded to their Country's call.

Mr. Berry's sermon was everything it should be, patriotic, earnest and delivered with the faith and conviction of one who really believes, as everybody must, that this war is brought upon us by a base and unchristian people who endeavor to overthrow our social institutions, murder our in-

---

[5]Sam Davis was a brother to Tom and Nannie Davis. He was 23 at this time. He served the confederate army as a private in the State Line. He married Laura Virginia West in 1867 and died in 1872 in Bellevue, IL.

[6]John Micajah Davis was also a brother to the Davises mentioned above. He being 18 was the youngest boy in the Micajah Davis family. He married in 1866 Virginia Phinney Phillips and served as a lieutenant in the 28th Virginia Infantry CSA. The Davis family lived at Chestnut Hill on Peaks Street, so were very close neighbors to the Burwell family.

nocent inhabitants. The Southerners, in resisting and fighting these vile Yankees are doing God a service. For He has given our slaves to us for some wise purpose to protect them and our rights.

I cannot help thinking that when the Yankees reflect how unjust is their attack and are awakened to a sense of our earnestness in resisting, they will leave us to ourselves....

Mr. Tom Davis came by in the evening from the depot and brought the papers. All a mistake about the victory at Baltimore, the northern troops passed through the city with only a skirmish. The citizens who determined to fight could get no weapons. The Governor had ordered the police to lock and guard all the arsenals. So the brave Baltimoreans, who would have taken the Northern troops if they had only had arms, were obliged to resort to brickbats, knives and anything they could pick up. But with these they managed to kill a good many and tried to throw the train from the track but the police removed the obstructions. What a pity these bold Southern spirited men could not have had arms.

No order yet for Dr. Bowyer's company and we are beginning to hope that they will not be ordered at all, but I believe it would nearly kill him not to have the pleasure of shooting a Yankee and going into a fight after all his drilling.

MONDAY, APRIL 22, 1861

Such a beautiful day. I would have gone to see Sis Wingfield[7] but the village was so full of people I could not. A great crowd in town for besides being Court Day, a great many people came to hear the news about the war. Met Sam

---

[7]"Sis" Wingfield is thought to be Miss Charlotte Wingfield, daughter of Judge Gustavas Adolphus Wingfield and Charlotte Griffin Wingfield, who were married on December 14, 1831, in Bedford. The children of this family will be listed since there are many references to them throughout the journal. Mary E. married Robert Allen, Col. of the 28th Va. Infantry, who was killed leading his regiment in the charge

Davis as we were walking on the bark road, directly after breakfast. He looks so well in his uniform. He gave us some consolation by saying that he thought they would not have much fighting to do.

Oh. It is terrible to be in such suspense! In the evening we heard a tremendous shouting over on the street and learned afterwards that it was on account of a dispatch, which Dr. Bowyer received and read out on the courthouse steps. The dispatch from Richmond told of the certain overthrow of the 7th New York Regiment by the Baltimoreans. The dispatch said that the New Yorkers finding Baltimore in such a commotion turned back and attempted to cross through Maryland at Annapolis. Then the Baltimoreans made haste to meet and attack them there and "cut them in pieces." But we hear so many conflicting reports one hardly knows what to believe.

In the evening we were walking and Sister seeing Mr. Tom Davis passing the gate hurried to meet him and ask the

---

of Pickett's Division. William Lewis Wingfield raised a company of volunteers at the outbreak of the war and these were attached to the 28th Va. Infantry, Pickett's Division. He received a promotion to the rank of Lt. Col. of the regiment succeeding Col. Allen as its commanding officer, after Gettysburg. He married Jericho Kasey. Charlotte, Katherine S., Nannie, and Sarah were unmarried. Samuel G. was a cadet at VMI during the war and participated in the Battle of New Market. He married Sallie Alexander and served as Clerk of Court and Mayor of Lynchburg. James Frank married Lucy Dillard. Judge G. A. Wingfield attained much distinction in public affairs. He was a member of the Virginia Legislature in the 1840s and 1850s. He served as Judge of the Circuit Court of Bedford County from 1861 to 1887 and later was first president of the Court of Appeals in 1872. His home was located on what is today Roberts Lane, but was dismantled in 1985. The area of his estate encompassed all of Wingfield Mountain on which the house was located over to South Street, all of Reservoir Hill and the bypass at 122 South. (Peaks of Otter Chapter, 1976, 33) In her journal, Lettie Burwell refers to Judge Wingfield's home as "Belleview" on the outskirts of Liberty.

news as he generally gives us a more cheerful view of things. But he said he thought Dr. Bowyer would be ordered on the field in a day or so which set Sister to crying again.

Dr. James Bowyer was up today. He also is much excited and is getting up a guerilla company to be commanded by his cousin Carlton Radford, to harass the enemy if they attempt an invasion through the mountains on the Pennsylvania side.

After tea Mr. Tom and Sam Davis came down, also Mr. Donald[8], who with Papa and one or two others were appointed by the Court today to go to Richmond and buy arms

---

[8]Benjamin Donald was a son of Andrew Donald, a Scotch merchant in the county. At the time of the Revolution a number of Scotchmen were living in New London with mercantile stores there. Many refused to take the Oath of Allegiance and as a result were called Tories and left the country. One firm there was owned and operated by Robert Donald & Co. whose members were James Donald, Robert Donald, Sr., Thomas Donald, Jr., Alexander Donald, Jr. & Sr., James Buchanan, and Andrew Donald of the City of Glasgow, Scotland, Merchants and Partners. Andrew Donald remained loyal to his adopted country and settled at the foot of the Peaks of Otter where he purchased a large boundary. His home, built here in 1780, was later known as Fancy Farm.

Benjamin married Sallie Camm of Amherst County and in the early 1800s they built a home, which they called Otterburn, about two miles from the village of Liberty. They had no children and after their death the home passed out of the family. Benjamin Donald was a presiding justice and active in all county affairs.

Benjamin Donald

Sallie Camm Donald

for the Bedford Volunteers. They were waked at three o'clock and took the night train. His friend, Mr. Stevens[9], Vice President, is down there.

TUESDAY, APRIL 23, 1861

I have a headache today, from excitement. We are beginning to think that Sister had better not go if Dr. Bowyer's company is ordered for they may have to be stationed at Norfolk or some place she would not like to stay. Coz[10] (Miss Charlotte Mitchell), and Sis (Miss Charlotte Wingfield) came about one o'clock and spent the day. We were very glad to see them. At dinner we got very much excited about the war and the defenseless condition of our State. And Sister

---

[9]Alexander H. Stephens of Georgia was elected Vice President of the Confederacy. As time wore on Stephens harbored a good measure of wrath against Jefferson Davis and his conduct of the war. Stephens absented himself from the Capitol for long periods of time, and when he did assume his duties as presiding officer of the Senate, he frequently used his position to criticize Davis.

[10]"Coz" as Charlotte Mitchell is called here, was the only child of Harvey Mitchell by his first wife, Elizabeth Griffin. Harvey married Elizabeth on July 22, 1828, (M.B.1, Pg. 33, Lynchburg) and she died shortly after the birth of her daughter, Charlotte, in 1829. Their daughter, Charlotte Mitchell, married Col. William Harvey. The connection between the Mitchells and the Wingfields appears to be the Griffin family. Gustavus Wingfield married Charlotte Griffin, thought to be the sister of Elizabeth Griffin.

Harvey Mitchell was born in 1801, a brother to Robert Mitchell and to Katherine Mitchell who married James C. Steptoe II. Their daughter, Frances, married William Burwell. This made Mrs. Burwell a niece of Harvey Mitchell and Lettie a great niece. Harvey Mitchell attained some notoriety as an artist and portrait painter. He lived a roaming life visiting with his family members. He owned no land and traveled about the country stopping wherever he had commissions to paint. His second marriage was to Jane Wood Johnston, a sister of General Joseph E. Johnston, in 1832. (Buck, 1989, 1-17) There were three children by Jane Johnston: Mary Louise, Sue Henry, and William.

and I said a great deal about the Union men having been the cause of it and that they would have to answer for the lives it would cost Virginia now to defend the country without good arms. If it had not been for the Union men who controlled the Legislature and Convention, we the secessionists, might have had time to have sent to Europe before the Northerners blockaded our ports and gotten arms. Now it is too late and our men just have to do the best they can with the present supply. This wounded Sis's feelings as her father had become a unionist and member of the Legislature. I am so sorry we became so excited and said so much, for there is no difference of party now. In the afternoon, Mrs. Donald came in to stay with us till Mr. Donald gets back.

Otterburn, the home of Mr. and Mrs. Benjamin Donald. This is located on the east side of Route 122 North, about two miles from the city limits. Presently Otterburn Home for the Aged is housed on the premises.

Mr. Tom Davis came down to give Fan and myself a shooting lesson and says he will leave his six-shooter with us if he is called away to fight. But I am so stupid, I don't think I shall ever learn to shoot, no idea I can. Dr. James Bowyer came again today, in the night train. We were busy making lint[11] this evening for Dr. Bowyer to carry.

I slept or tried to sleep in the room with Mrs. Donald but we both got to thinking so much about the dreadful troubles and excitement that we could not sleep hardly at all. I still pray there may be no fighting, although the Yankees ought all to be killed. Yet to think that some of our brave young men, of the best families and the flower of chivalry, may be killed by these miserable, low bootblacks and hotel waiters that the Yankees have to send down here.

WEDNESDAY, APRIL 24, 1861

When I think of the dreadful events, which may follow in a few weeks, it fills me with grief so that I would just have to go to bed. But that would be wrong. We want all courage and encouragement now that we can give each other. And especially our sex should control their grief and do all to cheer up our brave hearted men. O! The bravery of our men! Was there ever anything like it! Each man, each boy, seems to be thrilled with a spirit to resist the enemy and fight them to the death so that I can but think we are to be victorious under God, who by His right hand and His holy arm will get himself the victory. If ever there was a righteous cause, a holy cause, in which men had to fight, it is for their homes and families, their honor and their rights. The ladies offered to make up the undress uniforms for the Old Dominion Volunteers while they were out here this afternoon drilling. I wrote the offer of the ladies and sent it down to them. It was read aloud and tremendous cheers rent the air for the ladies.

Too much excited all day to sew, and felt badly on account of loss of sleep. In the afternoon I went with Mrs. Donald to Mrs. Sale's. Sue Hobson very busy making red flannel shirts for some of the soldiers. All the ladies very busy.

---

[11]Lint was used to pack a wound after it had been soaked with turpentine. It was then wrapped with bandages and kept wet.

Mr. Davis came again to give me a lesson in shooting. Succeeded a little better. Fired six or eight times and did not hit the mark or anywhere near it but once. No news today. A letter from Papa. He could get no arms for Dr. Bowyer's company. Richmond so full of troops very difficult to get food for them. Still the troops are all flocking there from the country. The trains pass here, extra and regular trains, crowded with brave volunteers who just rush right down to Richmond to see at what points they may be wanted at and give themselves up to the orders of the Governor. Some of these volunteer companies are not armed but are so anxious to lend their aid that they will not remain at home any longer.

THURSDAY, APRIL 25, 1861

Feel much better today; slept more last night. Wish the flannel had come for the undress uniforms. Mr. Munford was here for a few minutes this morning. He seems to think there will be a hard fought battle. I still pray there will not. We have just concluded Papa and Dr. Bowyer ought to take a good servant with them and as Doctor (Godfrey, the carpenter) wants to go, we have determined to fix his clothes today and get him ready. This will be a great comfort to us for Doctor is such a faithful Negro and such an excellent high-tone character; he will be true to his master and will do his duty through everything.

Mrs. Donald, Mr. Bowyer (Dr. Bowyer's father) and myself went down to the gate to look at Dr. Bowyer's men drill. Dr. Gilmore came up while we were standing there. He cannot hold Superior Court: says people are too excited to attend any business.

Mr. Donald returned from Richmond this evening. Says the city is very full of volunteer companies but they are more quiet there since the arrival of Colonel (later General) Lee who has instituted martial law. All was confusion before. Mr. Donald thinks too that the Washington Government has sent a proposition for an armistice of sixty days. I hope our side will not agree to this. The heads of department at Richmond seem to be keeping their plans very secret which is a good thing for this American habit of blazing everything out in the newspapers the instant it happens, sometimes before, will not do for Revolutionary times. Mrs. Donald left us this evening. A letter from Papa, writing very much what Mr. D. told us.

FRIDAY, APRIL 26, 1861

Such a beautiful day. Would like to work my flowers but can't feel composed enough.

Took a walk in the grove in the evening escorted by Ellen and Alice.[12] Got some pretty haw blossoms. Mr. Chalmers came to tea and stayed all night. The last time he was here, about two months ago, he was a warm Unionist and entirely opposed to secession. Now he is ready to fight any day against the Federal Government. Who would have thought the last time Mr. C. was here that the next time he came he would wear a blue jacket and pants trimmed with red and would be all ready to go into service! But he says his company, Wise Troop of Lynchburg, have a very inefficient captain and are not half drilled. I hope they will get another captain directly.

SATURDAY, APRIL 27, 1861

Mr. Chalmers left soon after breakfast. What a curious man he is! We like him so much and feel so much complimented at his fancy for us for we have been very little with him. Don't know his wife or any of his family, and it is curious he should have formed such a friendship for us. Always comes to see us and seems enthusiastic in his admiration of us.

In the afternoon Mr. Tom Davis came by to give me a pistol lesson. I think Mr. Davis likes to come because he thinks

---

[12]Ellen and Alice are two young slave girls who live on the place.

perhaps Fan will try to learn to shoot with me. What a pity he is so in love with her. And how heavy and dark a pall would there be on his heart if he knew of her engagement to Jimmie (Breckenridge).

My heart aches for him, his love has been so beautiful and sincere he cannot soon throw it aside, and when reality bursts upon him that it has all been in vain, what a melancholy hour for him. I am so sorry for we all like him so much and he has always been such a good friend to us. We will miss him very much when he ceases, as he will before long, to come and see and take the old interest in us.

I have seen so many sad changes in my life, old friends, sometimes lovers, whose interest in us was beautiful and had become almost indispensable, grow indifferent from some cause and cease after awhile even to feel like common acquaintances. It is a very sad thought, but I have experienced all its truth. In my early life, when I was about sixteen, many hearts held me dear which have now never a thought of me, and indeed, I rarely remember them now. But how could I have believed then there would ever come a time when those who loved me so much and for whom I felt so warm an attachment, would entirely cease to think of me or I of them.

There were schoolgirl friendships, ardent and sincere, which I believe would have lasted could we all have remained together just as we were then. Then came the breakup of a school; then the separation which bound our hearts more together; then for about two years, letters full of love and devotion, all sincere, then the cares of life falling early upon a few and the pleasures of life engulfing many, the letters from old school mates grow fewer and more far between until at last we are never thought about, and then our name is never breathed by lips that once loved to speak it, unless sometimes when thoughts are roaming after long years, over early trodden paths. The question "I wonder who she married" arises but is soon lost in the chaos of the present.

Then comes the period of every woman's heart when she receives the attention of the other sex. She soon hears that 'somebody' said, "she is perfectly beautiful." 'Somebody' else also that she is "entirely lovely," 'somebody' else that she is "the sweetest creature imaginable," and 'somebody' else that he is very much in love with her. Of course her school–boy beaux, who have thrown her bouquets, written illegible love verses, and in divers ways declared 'love unutterable,' dwindle into nothingness before grown young men with long coats and a profession. When this novelty is worn off then there comes a third period in a woman's affections…devotion is the word, for a woman has no 'affections' but 'devotions.' After the schoolgirl enthusiasms have subsided and the boy lovers in roundabouts[13] have given up their places at her side to tall whiskers, the third period is an immediate settling down of the devotions upon some particular style of admirer or ideal. Having experienced each of these phases, I might write several books!

Well I remember my boy lovers, Charlie Smith and Tonie Robinson, how jealous they were of each other, how little it affected me, how they both talked love to me, how Tonie would beg me to marry him, how I would laugh and tell the girls about it, how Charlie would beg me to kiss him through the window pane, how he was always getting me pretty flowers, all which failed to affect my heart. How strange that the same compliments from grown up gentlemen should have made a greater impression! Wearing the same white dress and blue ribbons in which I had received so carelessly the admiration of my boy lovers, what a different feeling of importance I felt when approached by tall mustached men and how I considered their compliments better worth having! How I know the boys were the most sincere because it was the first spontaneous combustion.

Poor Charlie, he died in California before he was eighteen and Tonie has been in a lunatic asylum since he was

---

[13]Roundabout was a short, tight jacket or coat worn by men and boys.

seventeen, insanity in his family. What a sad fate for these, my earliest lovers! How rarely do I ever remember there were ever two such persons. This is the saddest thought that our hearts and minds are so constituted that we can and do forget our old loves, and what at one time seemed a part of our very existence. It is sad but it is well and ordered wisely by our Heavenly Father.

Although it is sad to remember some things yet it is well now and then to recall past events and different periods of one's life contrasting our present feelings with the past. This may be beneficial, for if we had prayed aright our hearts must grow better everyday, and contrasting old feelings with the new should help us to see whether or not there is that improvement for which we have prayed, and if there is, to be very thankful. If not, to pray more earnestly against so much worldliness and vanity.

What a long digression! And all from the thought of our friendship with Mr. Davis being shortly broken up, and the expectation of his pleasant visits being stopped. It reminded me of so many delightful friends whom once we knew and loved so well, whose loves had long since been broken and pleasant visits discontinued. This is all right, and it would be disagreeable otherwise. Yet to me there has always been something sad in change. Although it would be very wrong not to tell a man you do not love him if you really do not, I never could help feeling as if the dreadful change which must surely follow is enough almost to make one profess a love which is not felt. For, what a change! He from whom we have been accustomed to receive the most pleasant and delicate attentions, in whose heart we have long held second place, now passes our door without even stopping to ask after us. The very heart that but a week before was 'purely devoted' now schools itself to careless indifference. Ah, it is very sad to lose the love of a true heart although we cannot truly reciprocate it.

CHAPTER III

Feeding Traveling Soldiers

SATURDAY NIGHT, APRIL 27, 1861

Mr. Tom and Sam Davis stayed with us till eleven o'clock. I taught Sam the "Mexican Campaign Song." Dr. Bowyer wants his company to learn it.

SUNDAY, APRIL 28, 1861

Mr. Wharton[1] preached and made a very patriotic allusion to the present troubles and condition of our country. Said he thought our cause was just and felt that God would overrule everything to our advantage. We must turn to Him, trust Him, pray without ceasing to Him and He will make our enemies powerless before us. For the first time we omitted prayers for the President of the United States and substituted

---

[1]The Rev. John A. Wharton (Dec. 4, 1810-March 31, 1895) followed the Rev. Nelson Sale as rector of St. John's Episcopal Church in 1858 when Sale died. Wharton was ordained in 1860 and continued as Rector until 1871 when he resigned having been elected to the office of Judge of the County Court. Under his ministry a colored Sunday school was organized. He lived in Liberty across the street from the Campbell House and next door to the Episcopal Church (now the Christian Church).

Home of the Rev. John A. Wharton on North Bridge Street

the President of the Southern Confederacy. This is the first time we have had services in our church (St. John's Episcopal) since the secession of Virginia.

Verily, it does seem that a kind providence is watching and overruling things to our advantage. For in the first place the bloodless victory at Fort Sumter shows the hand of God for there was never such an occurrence before. Then the firing of our Gosport Navy Yard, the matches went out and so did not fire the powder as the M.S. Soldiers expected. So we got all their ammunition. So at Harpers Ferry the fire did not do the work that was intended. Then the sinking of the *Merrimac* which was miraculously preserved under water and on being taken out was found to require only a little repairing to make it as good as ever.

Old St. John's Episcopal Church on Bridge Street, taken from the most recent History of St. John's Church.

Papa returned tonight from Richmond. Had a great deal to tell about the army in Richmond, Colonel Magruder, and General Lee.

MONDAY, APRIL 29, 1861

Today I went out to Mr. Wingfield's[2] and stayed all day. Helped the girls to make some gray flannel shirts for Brother Tom's (Dr. Bowyer) company.

Mr. Allen was there and talked a great deal about the war, is getting up a volunteer company.

Cass Wingfield and I both dreamed there was a regiment of girls formed in Salem. My dream was very vivid and I saw

---

[2]Probably the father of the Wingfield girls, G. A. Wingfield.

Fanny Johnston in command of a large company of girls in a uniform of dark calicos and white cotton long sleeve aprons.

We had a very pleasant day together. The girls walked part of the way home with me. We heard that Cousin (actually uncle) Harvey Mitchell had sworn allegiance to Lincoln. How horrible in a Virginian! And then to send his wife and family into Virginia to be protected by our men.

Found Cousin Armistead Burwell here to stay all night. We sat up quite late talking about the war. I am so excited all the time that I can hardly go to bed. I do not apprehend any immediate danger in our town or anywhere up here, but such an exciting revolution and things happening in such quick succession, forts taken, arsenals seized, troops going through from the south to Richmond, our own troops always drilling, and everything thrown suddenly in such confusion, it is impossible to feel composed. Feel as if I had been looking at a panorama now for two weeks, and am constantly expecting a new and startling picture to be unrolled.

TUESDAY, APRIL 30, 1861

Comparatively a quiet day. Mr. Davis came in the afternoon. We went down into the orchard to shoot. I missed my mark every time. Don't think I will ever learn. Mama's cows in the next field in imminent danger as my powder and balls fly about wildly and promiscuously over the country.

After tea, Mr. Davis came down again. I was so tired I could not sit up till he went away. Felt very sorry for him. He looks so cheerful and so little dreams that Fan is engaged.

WEDNESDAY, MAY 1, 1861

A very cold day for the first of May. Saw in the papers that Mr. Everett (Edward of Boston)[3] has subscribed $100 to a Bos-

---

[3] Edward Everette, a native of Massachusetts, was a well-known and persuasive orator of his day. An imposing figure, he was a tall, trim, white-haired man with a strong voice. (Catton, 1961, 48)

ton regiment in the south. Really felt sad and mortified. Marked and sent him the paper with a card pasted under the paragraph lamenting we had so long been under the same government if this was all we received of love from a good man at the north and one who had received the cordial hospitalities of the south. What are we to expect of the millions there who have been taught to hate us from infancy without ever expecting to see us? I wrote this on the card and signed my name. Wonder what Mr. Everett will think of it? [Miss Burwell had had an extensive correspondence with Mr. Everett on the subject of abolition. Perhaps he even visited at Avenel.]

Heard that the Southern troops, several hundred of them, would pass our depot at six o'clock this evening.

Sam Davis came down and we concluded to send round a Southern Confederacy flag and suggest that the ladies assemble on the balcony of the Hewitt House[4] to bid God-speed to these gallant men who come to defend our homes. But the train was delayed and did not pass until late in the night. Cousin (Uncle) Robert Mitchell[5] took supper here and stayed till bedtime.

---

[4]The Virginia and Tennessee Railroad was opened in 1852 to Liberty and Jesse Turner Hopkins was ready and waiting for it. He had erected a new hotel across the railroad tracks from the depot at the foot of Court Street. The back of the hotel was on the Jackson Street side, but Jackson Street was only an alley then. It faced Court Street and was called Hopkins House. This was reputed to be one of the most well appointed hotels of its time and attracted many distinguished guests. In late 1857 he sold the hotel to Wilson C. Hewitt, (D.B.39, P.362, Bedford Clerks Ofc.) his wife's brother. Hewitt operated the hotel as Hewitt House until 1863 when he deeded it back to Hopkins (D.B. 42. Pg. 324, Bedford Clerk's Ofc.).

[5]Robert Mitchell (1807-1872) married Lucy Phillips, a sister to Mrs. Micajah Davis. He was a brother to Harvey Mitchell and to Katherine Mitchell Steptoe, Mrs. Burwell's mother. This made him actually a great uncle to the Burwell girls. He served as clerk of the Bedford Circuit Court from 1827 to 1845. He represented Bedford County in the General Assembly and served as Senator representing Bedford and Amherst Counties. He made his home at Wheatly.

Wheatly, the home of Robert Mitchell

THURSDAY, MAY 2, 1861

I sewed some this morning, made thread ruffles for Sister. Jimmie Breckenridge[6] came this morning on his way to Richmond to get arms for his company.

In the afternoon we heard that the ladies were assembling at the depot to welcome with their presence some of the Southern troops. We hurried down. Mama, Fan, and I took the large supply of flowers we had collected the day before. The train came soon after we had gotten there. Out jumped a hundred red traveling-capped, blue-coated, brass-buttoned men, screaming and yelling and hurrahing for old Virginia. Then came out one or two hundred gray-uniformed Mobile cadets. A more orderly, gentlemanly looking set, waving their hands, bowing to the ladies and hurrahing for old Virginia and the Southern Confederacy. We threw the bouquets down to them, which they eagerly caught and seemed very proud to get. The eastern train met the southern and the greatest enthusiasm prevailed…ladies throwing flowers, some of them their gloves to the soldiers…drums beating, different companies forming into line and performing mili-

---

[6]Jimmie Breckenridge, son of Captain Cary Breckenridge of Grove Hill in Botetourt County was engaged to marry Fan Burwell. He was a young practicing attorney when the call to war came. He enlisted in Co. C of the 2nd Virginia Cavalry along with his brothers, John, Gilmer, and Cary. He was killed in action in 1865.

tary evolutions around the depot yard...handkerchiefs flying, conductors screaming.

I felt awfully on first beholding this scene of confusion; it looked so much more like war to see so many men dressed in so many uniforms. Their traveling caps of red, white, and blue flannel gave the scene a picturesque and vivacity indescribable. As soon as they had finished their suppers they struck up Dixie and sang some new words written in Alabama: the chorus 'We'll die for old Virginia, we'll fight for old Virginia.' Then one of the gray cadets, being called upon loudly for a speech, which I could not hear, was induced to mount on top of the freight car and make a little speech. I could not hear what he said as I was in a window of the hotel at the opposite end of the crowd which was very great.

Just before the train was about to leave there was a great alarm at the giving away of the lower balcony of the hotel, where the ladies were crowded. We saw it begin to fall. Great screaming on the part of the ladies but the soldiers rushed under and held it up with guns and sticks and some of the cadets instantly mounted upon the shoulders of other cadets so as to reach it. One cadet was caught by each leg and held up by two strong men while he helped support the balcony with his hands and shoulders. The ladies were soon pulled in at the windows and nobody was hurt although it produced great fright. After tea, Mr. Sandy Cobbs and Sam Davis came to learn the campaign song. Sister was sick and could not come down, so I had to teach it to them.

FRIDAY, MAY 3, 1861

Took a walk after breakfast with Sister in the grove. Worked flowers. Wrote words to song and wrote in journal before dinner. In the afternoon read and walked again. Dr. Meredith[7] came as we finished supper. After supper played

---

[7] Dr. Samuel Meredith was the second husband of Dr. Bowyer's sister, Lulie. They lived in Botetourt County.

new songs for Mama. Dr. Bowyer went to Richmond on the twelve o'clock night train to see about getting his company into immediate service. They are all so anxious to fight. Sister is very much distressed.

SATURDAY, MAY 4, 1861

Hearing the ladies were to have a presentation of the flags they have made for two of our companies, Rosa and I went over to the street. But the presentation was not at ten o'clock as we had heard, so we stayed a little while at Mr. Sale's and then came home. The evening was so cold and disagreeable we did not return at three o'clock to the presentation. Put on thick shawls and hoods and took a walk, with Ellen and Alice in the grove. Carried Mr. Davis's pistol, no load in it, so as to show it if we met any strangers!

After supper Papa read President Davis's message to us up in Sister's room. It is elegant, to the point and temperate, and will, I hope, show the Southern States in their proper light and give the civilized world a right view of the justness of our cause.

SUNDAY, MAY 5, 1861

Dark, disagreeable day. Did not go to church, Presbyterian.

A large number of Southern troops passed through on their way to the encampment in Lynchburg. They were very hungry; impossible to prepare breakfast enough at the hotel. Some of the soldiers ran up to Mr. Dunton's and got their breakfast and many others would have been entertained at our private houses if the train had stopped long enough.

William Matthews from Tennessee got permission to stop here a day. He took dinner with us and rejoined the Tennessee regiment at Lynchburg at night. He is a true type of the Tennessean, brave, thoughtful and intelligent. He says any of the men in his regiment can fight the Yankees and kill any number with sticks. "Don't want any guns."

Another long train of Southern soldiers passed in the afternoon. Very hungry. Although I know they found enough to eat in Lynchburg, yet I cannot bear the idea that they should have been hungry an hour on Virginia soil. Mama and other ladies sent down baskets of bread, ham, pickle and some hot coffee, but that could have appeased the hunger of very few. Sister sick all day. I cannot even yet realize that we are actually to have a war although everybody I know has turned soldier and the State is suddenly a military encampment.

MONDAY, MAY 6, 1861

Another dark, rainy day. Went in the greenhouse and moved some flowers and set out verbena slips. Employed myself reading, writing, and sewing a little. Picked up in the Library a pamphlet directed to Mr. Robert Toombs[8], "Meeting and Sermon in Cleveland, Ohio, commemorative of John Brown in Virginia." Very imprudent to have sent it to any Southerner. Got very mad while I read it and thought what a blessing our Union with such people in it is forever dissolved. Stayed with Sister till bedtime. She was quite sick. A letter from Brother Tom who thinks his company will be stationed at Lynchburg.

---

[8]Robert Toombs, born of Virginia parents, was raised in Elbert County, Georgia. He attended the University of Georgia and graduated from Union College in Schenectady, New York. He was admitted to the bar in Elbert County, Georgia, and elected to the U. S. Senate for 16 years. On January 1, 1861, he delivered his farewell address to the Senate from a seceding state. In Georgia he was considered the logical choice for president of the young Confederacy, but finally agreed to become Secretary of State under Jefferson Davis. He was extremely critical of Davis and resigned still at odds with him. The Cabinet did not offer him a place for his turbulent energies so he took a Brigadier General position, a soldier, in spite of his own lack of military experience. He was frequently outspoken in his disgust of West Point and its graduates. He appeared disgusted with the outside world for its refusal to recognize his foreign ministry and its failure to make more prominent use of Robert Toombs. (Catton, 1963, 72)

TUESDAY, MAY 7, 1861

Dreadfully windy. Tried to put flowers out of greenhouse but found the wind would kill them. Marked clothes for Brother Tom. Took long walk in grove with Ellen. Heard train coming; supposed it was full of troops so ran to edge of railroad in Mr. Hopkin's field to look down. Only sheep and cows and no soldiers on freight train. Found some pretty wild flowers.

Dr. Bowyer returned from Richmond. All quiet there, soldiers drilling regularly. Virginians not so well prepared for camp life as South Carolinians and Southerners.

The policy of General Lee seems to be that our people shall not disturb Washington City as General Scott and the Northern Army are hoping he will. So as to inflame more Northerners against us and cause them to send more volunteers. How I wish the war was ended and we were entirely and forever separated from the North.

WEDNESDAY, MAY 8, 1861

The wind too disagreeable again to go out and attend to my flowers. The western train brought five hundred Mississippians this morning about breakfast time. Mama had enough breakfast gotten for a dozen and sent down for some of them to come over. Only four got the message and came. A good many others breakfasted at other houses and some at the hotel, and many got no breakfast at all. The trains are so uncertain it is not possible to provide for the troops regularly.

Took a long walk in the grove in the afternoon. Went through the orchard and had a very private walk.

THURSDAY, MAY 9, 1861

The train came again at breakfast time. Nine Mississippians to breakfast with us. One of them only nineteen years old came back to shake hands with Mama and thank her for her kindness. Said his family were Virginians. Fan, Rosa, and

I looked at them from the upper hall window, but did not go in the dining room. Another windy day. Couldn't go out except to walk in the grove in the evening. Papa went to Lynchburg this morning

FRIDAY, May 10, 1861

Soldiers to breakfast again. One or two thousand stopped in Liberty this morning. I never realized before how many men there are in the world. All the soldiers who have breakfasted with us were very nice looking people, especially this morning. Found out afterwards they were Lieutenant Nelms and several of his privates, 4th Mississippi Regiment. Got ready to go to see Mrs. Winkler but could not for the showers of rain all day. Wrote some verses, "Virginia's Welcome to the Soldiers," as I could not go out. Also other lines in the "Mexican Campaign Song" to make it appropriate for our soldiers.

After nine o'clock Mr. Tom Davis came, but as I had undressed I did not go down. Only Fan saw him. How sorry I am that he is so hopelessly in love with Fan. Ah me! The way of true love never changes, never runs smoothly.

SATURDAY, MAY 11, 1861

Ladies meeting at the courthouse. Fan, Rosa, and I went over, and found a great many ladies there and three sewing machines. Everybody very busy making uniforms for Captain Jordan's Artillery.[9] Found I knew so little about making coats. After talking a great deal to Mrs. Winkler and basting up several seams, I came home. Rained in the afternoon, could not walk.

---

[9]Four sons of Jubal (IV) and Pricilla Jordan served in the Civil War: Alexander, Tyler, William, and John. The first three were Captains and Tyler was later promoted to Major. William was wounded in the war and John, a surgeon, was killed at Yorktown in 1862. (Ackerly/Parker,

SUNDAY, MAY 12, 1861

Heard as soon as I awoke that the patrol, Mr. Chilton, had taken Doctor and was about to put him in jail this morning when he was walking quietly across the bridge. Got very much excited and so provoked that I did not get over it all day. Although Doctor was not put in jail, the idea of such a man as Chilton thinking of disturbing such an honest, gentlemanly Negro as Doctor! Very sorry it happened on the Sabbath as it made me so mad. It was a sin to have had such angry feelings at any time, but especially on the Sabbath. Uncle Tom and Aunt Mildred came home with us from church and stayed until quite late in the evening which kept me from reading and passing the hours profitably.

Mr. Wharton's sermon was partly to the soldiers just about to leave Liberty. His remarks were very touching and caused much weeping. He urged the soldiers not to go forth to battle in their own strength, but in God's. Mr. Ettinger, gone. I had to play. It rained at night, there was no preaching. Felt sad at having passed the Sabbath so badly. Did not read or hear Ellen and Alice read their lessons or anything. Had angry thoughts about the House Guard being so strict about the slaves when they behave themselves quietly and orderly. These thoughts came in my mind during the sermon, when I did not attend at all to the words of the hymns because I was thinking how I was going to play them on the organ. Wish I never had to play the organ on that account, it distracts my attention so. Oh! What a miserable sinner I am.

1930, 663). Alexander commanded Co. E, 34th Infantry and William commanded Co. G, 34th Infantry. William raised and equipped the first company which went from Bedford County, commanded by his brother, Tyler C. Jordan, who entered service as a private and went with that company. William Jordan married in October 1866 Eliza Crenshaw, daughter of Col. John Crenshaw and they lived at Cedar Hill on West Main Street. He purchased it in 1865, one year before Eliza married Jordan. (Hardesty, 1884, 421)

MONDAY, MAY 13, 1861

Very busy all day packing to go with Sister down to Lynchburg Wednesday, with Dr. Bowyer and his company. I am so glad Mr. Mosby[10] wrote us to come. It will be such a comfort to Sister to be near Dr. Bowyer as long as possible and I am always happy to go to Mr. Mosby's. Sewed very hard all day on markers for Dr. Bowyer's company and a red flannel shirt for Dr. Bowyer.

Saw the cavalry go off this morning, Captain Terry's[11] company. This is the first that has gone from our village. And, oh, how sad it was to see them ride off this beautiful morning, some of them perhaps to return no more to their loved ones at home. Mr. Tom Davis belonged to this company. Oh! it was a sight sadly to remember, so many fine manly forms riding away perhaps not to return. Took Alice and walked in the grove in the evening.

TUESDAY, MAY 14, 1861

A beautiful morning. As I was going with my hoe to work my flowers, saw Willie Mitchell[12] coming through the circle. Did not know him and walked by him without speaking. I wish Cousin Harvey Mitchell had not stayed so long with the Lincoln Administration. At night one or two of Dr. Bowyer's company stayed at our house so as to be ready for the train in the morning.

---

[10] Probably Mr. Charles L. Mosby who lived on Federal Hill in Lynchburg. He was an orator and speaker at most important occasions. He was always active in civic affairs and represented Lynchburg in the Virginia Legislature from 1848 to 1865. He was a practicing attorney in Lynchburg and for many years leader of the bar. He died in 1879 (Christian, 1900,326,437)

[11] Captain W. R. Terry (later General Terry) commanded the Clay Dragoon Co. A, which was organized in 1857.

[12] Youngest son of Robert Mitchell.

WEDNESDAY, MAY 15, 1861

This being the day for the Liberty companies, Captain Bowyer's and Captain Jordan's, to leave the village was in great excitement. A special train came up from Lynchburg at nine o'clock. Sister and I were the only ladies with the companies. We took our seats very quietly in the car. The platform at the depot was crowded with ladies taking leave of their brothers and husbands who they may never see again. It was a heart-rending scene, and the strongest men left with a tear in their eyes.

When the train left the depot there was a great shout, and there was a continued cheer from Liberty to Lynchburg, for all the people along the road had some friend or brother or cousin in the companies, and waited on the roadside to wave handkerchiefs, throw bouquets, and bid them God's speed as the cars passed.

After parting with their families and friends the men said the worst part of the battle had been fought. Their natural spirits were gradually restored and they laughed and sang and cheered till we got into Lynchburg.

Mr. Mosby met us with the carriage and took Sister and me out quietly while the companies, which came with us, formed into line and were marched through the street out to the encampment. We came home with Mr. Mosby. Found Cousin Mary, Aunt Judy and Lizzie all well and glad to see us. How sweet everybody and everything is here! It reminds me so of Dr. Bagby[13] and old times to come here.

---

[13] George W. Bagby, a writer, orator and for a time he was editor of the *Southern Literary Messenger*. He was a southern gentleman of refinement, a Virginian to the core, and spent many happy hours at Avenel in close and friendly association with the Burwell family. He was educated at Princeton and at the University of Pennsylvania, he set up a medical practice but writing was his true gift. He was not a novelist, or historian, but a writer of sketches. He had no fixed occupation and probably no fixed income...what money came in must have been meager. He was rather given to wandering about the country writing humorous sketches of life for the press. (Bagby, 1948, xi)

And dear Mr. Mosby, how we love him! He is the perfection of a man.

In the afternoon we rode out with Cousin Mary and Mr. Mosby to the camp. Captain Bowyer's men in fine spirits, pitching their tents. Saw Mr. Tom Davis, his cavalry troop very near the other Liberty companies. Went around to the Fair Grounds where the Tennessee and Mississippi companies are stationed. The Tennesseeans are a rough, undisciplined, uninformed set, but will be great in a fight after good drilling. Talked to a very fine looking Mississippian. Mr. Mosby gave him his card and told him if any of his company should be sick or want anything to apply to him, but did not ask the young man his name—great oversight, especially as the young man talked so well and struck us all as being such a perfect gentleman.

Dr. Bowyer could not come home to Mr. Mosby's with us. Papa came and stayed all night. He slept with Mr. Mosby and Cousin Mary went upstairs. I wish Papa had not enlisted for I do not think he can stand the camp life. He is very hoarse now and I think it would have killed him to have slept in the camp.

THURSDAY, MAY 16, 1861

Directly after breakfast, rode round to the camp. Saw all our Liberty soldiers. Went to the Fair Grounds. Saw some fine looking companies. The Van Dorns from Mississippi are a splendid body; the whole 11th Regiment are elegant looking. Mr. Mosby wanted some of them to come in and take tea with us. Went down on the street and ordered Fan and Rosa's bonnets. The Lieutenant of the Lamar Rifles, 11th Mississippi Regiment, Lieutenant Nelms, came over to see if Mr. Mosby could take one of his sick men. The company had been ordered to Harpers Ferry and Lieutenant Nelms said he could not bear the idea of leaving the young man at a strange hotel as he had promised the young man's mother to take good care of him. Mr. Mosby had no room in his house but promised to find some place for the sick soldier. Went to see them at Judge Wilson's.

In the evening, Mr. Housemann and Mr. Witherspoon, a Presbyterian minister-soldier, in the 11th Regiment, Mississippi, came to spend the evening. Colonel Robert Preston and Colonel Faulkner of Mississippi came too. We were so glad to see them. Also a fat old Mr. Anderson, whom nobody cared to see, came as well. Mr. Housemann was very smart and agreeable. I hope we will meet him again. Sister and I played and sang a great many songs for the company, and the Mexican Campaign song brought tears in every eye, and we had to sing it two or three times.

FRIDAY, MAY 17, 1861

Lizzie Mosby and I very busy fixing up the house in the garden for the sick soldier, George Delbridge, 11th Mississippi Regiment, Lamar Rifles. The room looked very nice and our sick soldier was brought over about twelve o'clock, with him another young man from the same company, Mr. Boon, grandson of Daniel, who had hurt his foot and could not wear his boot. Mr. Housemann and Lieutenant Nelms brought them over.

I sang the "Mexican Song" for Mr. Housemann and he wept, so did Cousin Mary and Mr. Mosby who were in the parlor. Then to my great astonishment Mr. Housemann said that as I had entertained him so much, he would play for me. Whereupon he sat down at the piano and played beautifully. Wish we had known last night that he could play. Gave Mr. Housemann a lunch before he left and I made him a pretty bouquet.

Lieutenant Nelms came in while we were at dinner and took dinner with us, also an Arkansas man who had just arrived and came with Mr. Nelms to see the sick men in the garden.

In the evening Papa brought Captain Clusky, Memphis, Tennessee, to spend the evening. After tea, William Mosby took his violin and Sister the guitar and we went down and serenaded our sick soldiers. As they were both dressed and sitting up, they begged us to come in. Lizzie went in with us and we sang and played a great many songs. They were very much cheered and particularly struck with my secession words to "Wait for the Wagon." And I promised to copy them for them. Miss Ben Rudd came over and spent the evening.

SATURDAY, MAY 18, 1861

Went to the camp again today. Mr. Mosby was not well in the afternoon so William rode out with us. Went to the Arkansas Camp and found the men all drawn up in line, the Captains and the Colonels all speaking earnestly to the men. Discovered the men were becoming mutinous and threatened to go home because the Southern Confederacy could not give them the rifles they wanted to get and had been accustomed to in Arkansas. One very handsome and eloquent man, Captain Crockett, was laboring to explain to them the impropriety of their determination to go home because they could not get the particular kind of arms they expected. He urged them to fight with rocks or anything they could get.

"Yes, gentlemen," he said, "we can fight with our fists and you know every man of you has got a Bowie knife and you can throw one arm affectionately around a Yankee and plunge it in him with the other."

We were struck with the manner and appearance of this man. William inquired his name, introduced himself and then introduced us when the speaking was over. We had become so excited and wanted so much to hear distinctly what was going on that we had gotten out of the carriage and were standing just behind the orators. They, however, whom we afterward knew, were Captain Crockett, and Colonel Fagan, the Colonel of the regiment, and Major Thompson formerly of Staunton, Virginia, and a Lieutenant Gibson.

We liked Colonel Crockett so much that William invited him to come the next evening to spend with us.

No company at night. Mr. Speed and his mother, Miss Ben Rudd and Mr. Henderson sat with us in Cousin Mary's room till bedtime. With the guitar Sister and I sang for them. Sister told Mr. Berry's anecdote about the Irishman and the Scotsman, which amused everybody very highly. Mr. Speed promised to use his influence with Governor Letcher to get Mr. Berry the appointment of chaplain to Colonel Preston's Regiment. Sister told the anecdote by way of interesting Mr. Speed in Mr. Berry's behalf. Mr. Speed said Sister must write the letter to Governor Letcher and he will sign it.

SUNDAY, MAY 19, 1861

Went to Mr. Mitchell's church. His text was "The race is not to the swift nor the battle to the strong." Nobody but Lizzie and I went to church from here, everybody else sick. Sister crying and very low spirited. Met Captain Bowyer as we were coming home from church and took him in the carriage with Lizzie, Mr. Henderson, and myself. Brought him home with us, and he stayed all night.

After supper when we had given out seeing Captain Crockett, and when Mr. Reid had been and spent quite an evening with us, told us good-bye and all, the doorbell rang and in came Captain Crockett, bringing with him Lieutenant Gibson and Major Thompson. Captain Crockett was delightfully agreeable, Lieutenant Gibson rather surly, and Major Thompson, Sister said, is very agreeable and pious, though I did not speak to him.

They asked me to go to see their Colonel's wife who is delicate and could not stand being left in Arkansas.

MONDAY, MAY 20, 1861

Mr. Mosby, Cousin Mary, Sister and I went in the morning to call on Mrs. Colonel Fagan at the Norvell House[14].

---

[14] Norvell House built in 1818 at 11th and Main street in Lynchburg, it opened first as the Franklin Hotel and became Norvell House in 1853. (Lynchburg Historical Society, 1974,95/supplement, p.20)

Found her a very pleasant lady. We asked her to come spend the evening. Called to see poor Aunt Mary Holcomb. Rained hard before we got home, and hailed so as we got to the door that we had to sit in the carriage some time before the storm abated sufficiently for us to get in the house.

We couldn't ride around the camp in the evening. Had a note from Miss Sallie Grattan to whom we had been introduced at church when we delivered Dr. Charlie Griffin's message about making him a fatigue captain.

Notwithstanding the rain, our company came to spend the evening, Colonel Fagan, Captain Crockett, Mrs. Fagan, and Major Thompson. Cousin Mary sent down and got some very nice ice cream. The parlor and library were brightly lighted with the evening and everything. Captain Crockett very fond of music and when Sister and I sang the "Mexican Campaign Song," every one of these strong, brave Arkansans was seen to shed tears. Mrs. Fagan told us she knew the Pikes (General Pike's family) and that Walter's father was trying to get him a place in the Provisional Army.

TUESDAY, MAY 21, 1861

Made fatigue cap for Lizzie's brother. Wrote to Mama. Visit from Mr. Jacob Mitchell who brought his sick soldier, Alabamian. In the afternoon rode out to the camps. All the Tennesseans gone from the Fairgrounds, no troops quartered there now. The Virginia regiment was drilling, dress parade. The companies are fine looking and dressed in handsome uniforms. Brother Tom's company was the best drilled. Found Cousin Lucy Mitchell at the camp. Colonel Preston has taken Papa as his secretary and they have rented a room in a house opposite the Virginia encampment. We went in to see them. Major Robert Allen seems greatly puffed up with a little brief authority.

Brother Tom came in from the camp and stayed all night. Dr. Meredith came after tea. He is surgeon to Colonel Radford's[15] regiment of cavalry.

William Mosby, determined to quiz Bev Rudd, sent a servant over to tell her Miss Mary Eliza said she must come over and spend the evening with some nice young officers. So she fixed up and came over and we introduced Brother Tom as Colonel Brown of the Arkansas regiment. He played his part very well. At about half past nine o'clock William wrote a note and made Jacob ring the doorbell and call for Colonel Brown and hand the note to him. Colonel "Brown" read the note and informed the ladies it was a dispatch ordering the whole Arkansas regiment off that night, excused himself, regretting to leave so abruptly. He told us good-bye and bowed himself gracefully out. The quiz was complete! Miss Bev expressed much admiration for the young 'colonel,' and finding us very dull company without any young gentlemen soon took her departure, leaving us to laugh over our success.

WEDNESDAY, MAY 22, 1861

Thought I ought to go home today. Cousin Fanny Royall came from Richmond this morning. Sister to the camp to stay all day and take dinner with Colonel Preston. Mr. Henderson was so kind as to send me a large basket of strawberries, which we will all enjoy for dinner.

After dinner Cousin Fanny Royall and I rode out to the encampments. Took little Mary with us. Everybody sick at Mr. Mosby's today, Lizzie, Mr. Mosby, Cousin Mary, and Aunt Judy. Carried some flowers and threw them at the Arkansans.

---

[15]Col. R. C. W. Radford was born 1822 in Bedford County and had served in the U. S. Army for 16 years. When the war broke out, he resigned and joined the Confederate Army. He was Col. of the 2nd Virginia Cavalry throughout the war. He made his home at Rothsay after his marriage (Hardesty, 1884, 428).

Sister came home in Cousin Lucy Mitchell's carriage. She was very much distressed at the inhuman manner Major Allen had drilled his men. In order to show himself off on his horse, he had made them run until they were faint, making ten of Dr. Bowyer's men sick. It was outrageous in Mr. Allen. He has turned a complete fool and has made enemies for life already after having held his rank only a week. Sister could not help giving him a little piece of her mind on the subject.

No company at night. We took the guitar in the chamber and played and sang for Mr. Mosby and the family, Mr. Speed, Mrs. Rudd, Miss Bev, Mr. Henderson, and Cousin Fanny.

THURSDAY, MAY 23, 1861

This being the day for taking the secession vote, the soldiers marched down to the courthouse and had no drill at the camp in the morning. Although Mr. Mosby had been quite sick in the night, he rode down too to give in his vote.

Brother Tom came to take dinner with us. I trimmed Aunt Judy's bonnet. Brother Tom came to take dinner with us. Brother Tom rode Dr. Meredith's horse today, which rested him very much. Sister went down and bought him a camp cot, which will also be a great comfort to him.

About four o'clock Sister and I rode out to camp. All the Mosbys too sick to ride, so we took Mrs. Judge Wilson with us. Carried a bottle of milk and a bucket of strawberries for Dr. Bowyer's supper. Stopped at Papa and Col. Preston's room. Found Mama had just sent a trunk of provisions for Papa and Brother Tom. We took out Brother Tom's share, put it in the tray and got back in the carriage with the tray in our laps. Drove to Brother Tom's tent but he hadn't come in from drill, so we drove around to the Arkansas camp with all our provisions on our knees. Found the Arkansas regiment in line receiving orders for the next day. A very raw looking set and very far from being drilled enough to go into battle. Saw Lieutenant Gibson and gave him a cake out of our tray, which he seemed to enjoy. Saw Captain Crockett but did not speak to him.

Returned to Virginia camp. Brother Tom in the tent. Sister got out with all the provisions. Major Thompson and Colonel Fagan of the Arkansas regiment rode up very soon. I invited them to dismount and pay Brother Tom a visit, which they were very glad to do. Papa came up, too, and introduced them to many of our Virginia officers. Sister had to hand around many of Dr. Bowyer's cakes, which distressed her. Gave Colonel Preston's servant, Henry, fifty cents for his kindness to Dr. Bowyer.

FRIDAY, MAY 24, 1861

Directly after breakfast I walked with Cousin Fanny over to Mr. Kirkpatrick's to make a call there, and then went to see Aunt Anne Langhorne in Mrs. Speed's carriage.

Old Dr. Bowyer, Dr. Bowyer's father from Greenfield, Botetourt County, arrived unexpectedly after breakfast. He took Sister out to the camp with him in a hack. They both went to Mr. Edley's to hire a servant for Dr. Bowyer. Old Mr. Edley generously allowed the servant to go and refused pay. Sister and I very busy after dinner making green flannel shirts for Dr. Bowyer.

Nursed Lizzie some. Old Dr. Bowyer and Brother Tom came in the evening and told us Colonel Preston's regiment was ordered to Manassas Gap. It was very sad, but still we expected it and had been preparing ourselves for it.

At night a Don Halsey came to spend the evening. Sister was too much distressed to come in the parlor. William Mosby and I were the only persons to entertain them. I felt sad enough but had to play and sing and talk. I slept in Aunt Judy's room.

CHAPTER IV
A Call For Help

SATURDAY, MAY 25, 1861

Sister and I determined to return home today as we had done everything we could for Dr. Bowyer and Papa and would not see anything more of them by staying in Lynchburg.

After breakfast I walked downtown with old Dr. Bowyer. Bought some red flannel for bandages for Brother Tom and servant and exchanged Rosa's bonnet strings.

Found Brother Tom's company just marching down to the Hall on Main Street to receive their arms. Mr. Bowyer and I stopped and talked to some of them as they stood at the Hall. Then we called at the Norvell House on Mrs. Fagan and told her goodbye. Stopped to see Aunt Mary Holcomb.

Papa and Dr. Bowyer came to Mr. Mosby's to eat dinner with us and take leave of us. We were all very sad and distressed. Dr. Bowyer came to the depot with us. Found a good many Liberty friends coming up, too, on the train. Old Mr. Bowyer got off at Forest Depot to see his son, James, and pay him a farewell visit. James Bowyer is going with Colonel Radford's regiment next Wednesday.

Telegraphic dispatch yesterday—Alexandria taken by the Yankees. We got home again at five o'clock. Everything in the yard so beautiful, it is indeed a fairy spot. But our country is in such excitement and the thought of the war having commenced makes even the beautiful flowers and trees look dreary. We can but hope and pray.

SUNDAY, May 26, 1861

Went to church. Felt very weak and badly. Had to play the organ but could not sing. Was quite sick all day. Saw Mary Wingfield Allen at church.

After supper Rosa and I went to Mr. Davis's to hear the news from our people in Colonel Preston's regiment. Mr. Davis had just come from Lynchburg. He said he saw all of them leave at eight o'clock this morning for Manassas Gap where they expect to have a fight in a few days. What a sad thought!

I do not feel afraid up here. Doctor sleeps in the library and we feel well protected although there is not a gun about the house or a white man. What would the Abolitionists think of that!

We are afraid to walk in the woods because the penitentiary convicts the Governor sent to work on the railroad made their escape and are going about the country everywhere.

MONDAY, MAY 27, 1861

Received dispatch before breakfast saying there was a fight yesterday at Hampton, nine hundred Yankees killed, only fifty of our men killed or wounded. Also a fight at Harpers Ferry, our men victorious there, too. Oh! This is a time for prayer! Incessant prayers this day should ascend to God imploring His aid to overthrow our enemies speedily and let us return to our old peace and tranquility. I suppose they are fighting at this moment, those miserable Yankees.

We were very sad all day thinking they might be fighting at Manassas Gap. I walked out late in the evening. Called at Mr. Goode's[1], saw Mrs. Goode.

---

[1] John Goode, Jr. was born May 27, 1829, in the Goode section of the county. He attended Emory and Henry College and later Lexington Law School. He was admitted to the bar in Bedford in April of 1851. In November he was also elected to the Virginia Legislature defeating William Burwell. He was a member of the Virginia Secession Convention in 1861, and was elected to the Confederate Congress in the autumn of 1861, representing the Bedford District. He was at this time serving in Co. A, 2nd Virginia Cavalry under the command of Captain

Mr. Goode does not believe the rumor about the victory our men are said to have gained at Hampton. He thinks it only a sensation telegram, but I hope it is true.

Our village looks deserted. Almost every man under forty-five and some over that age have gone to war. Wrote a letter to William Mosby. Sister very sad. We, Mama, Fan, Rosa, and I sat in her room till bedtime.

The Honorable John Goode, Jr.

Doctor comes in very early and retires solemnly in the library and we feel confident if anything should happen to disturb us he will protect us the best he knows how.

TUESDAY, May 28, 1861

Slept late. After breakfast worked flowers in my border, and set out some geraniums from the pots. No news from Manassas Station today. I suppose somebody would telegraph us if they were fighting there. Mr. Johnson is going there tonight and we are busy fixing a box of biscuits, chicken, and preserves for him to take to Papa and Brother Tom.

Terry. He remained in the confederate service until February 22, 1862, when he took his seat in the Confederate Congress. In 1856 he purchased from William Gish a lot and house on the northeast corner of Westview Avenue and Longwood Avenue. Today, the lovely home of Mr. and Mrs. Raleigh Worsham rests on this site. The Goode home was dismantled and the present structure was built by the Ballard family, about 1915. In his later life John Goode, Jr. is known to have lived on Hampton Ridge.

Everything looks sad and it is so gloomy to walk out. Sister so distressed that I feel miserably to look at her. In the afternoon walked out toward Mr. Terry's. Stopped to see Mr. Johnson and give him a letter for Brother Tom.

Went up to Mr. Davis and saw Mrs. Davis, Nannie, and Annis. Great excitement against Mr. Allen.[2] His arrogance and inconsideration are insupportable, and all who have brothers, friends, and relatives under his command are distressed to think of his want of kindness and consideration. We became so excited as we talked about him that Nannie proposed that the ladies having brothers, friends, and relatives in Colonel Preston's regiment should sign a petition imploring Mr. Allen either to resign immediately or decidedly to alter his manner towards the gentlemen whom he has the honor to command. I wrote the petition for Nannie to copy, but perhaps we ought not to send it as it might create a great deal of feeling of an ill nature. Moreover, Sister has written a letter to Colonel Preston requesting him in the name of the mothers and sisters and friends of his men not to allow Robert Allen to drill his men so severely again.

Met a young soldier all uniformed on his way to join Dr. Bowyer's company. He, with another young soldier to join the same company too, went to Mr. Davis's to eat supper and stay until the three o'clock morning train. The Davises found one of these soldiers too poor to provide himself the necessary accoutrements. So they went to work and bought gray flannel for a shirt and made it. And also got him a blanket. And we made two haversacks for them.

WEDNESDAY, MAY 29, 1861

Annis Berry came down to see Sister, which cheered her up very much, she had been crying ever since breakfast. I

---

[2]Col. Robert Allen lived at Mount Pleasant, a plantation of 1540 acres off the Peaks Road. Even though he was killed at the Battle of Gettysburg in 1863, the estate remained in the family until 1876.

wish she would not give up so. Heard that the telegram about the fight at Hampton and the seven hundred Yankees killed was all false. No fight there at all.

Soon after dinner Fan, Rosa, and I rode out to Mr. Wingfield's. Saw Mary, Cass, and Nannie. Sis was dressing to go out to Mrs. Allen's and did not come down. Coz did not come down to see us either because we did not speak to Cousin Jane and Lou[3] on Sunday, I expect. I am very sorry but I did not get near Lou Mitchell, (later Mrs. Brinkley), did not see Cousin Jane and did not go out of my way to speak to them. I think they should feel they are in enemy country as their husbands are both in Mr. Lincoln's service and receiving Mr. Lincoln's money. Tried not to say anything that would wound the Wingfield girl's feelings, although we had such hard thoughts of Mr. Allen.[4] So we did not say anything about him at all.

Took a walk late in the evening to Mr. Terry's gate. Saw Mrs. Winkler and Mrs. Goode. Met Nannie Davis and told her we had a nice note from Papa. Came home and as we were looking at the front door, saw a young man walking up. Couldn't imagine who it was as we thought every young man we knew was at the seat of war. It proved to be Jimmie Breckinridge, 2nd Lieutenant, Provisional Army. We were delighted to see him. He was just from Manassas Junction and had seen all our boys and men in Colonel Preston's regiment. Everybody well and in fine spirits. No fighting there yet. I pray there may not be.

After supper Mr. and Mrs. Davis came down to cheer us up a little and talk about the war. They had the news and

---

[3]Cousin Jane refers to Jane Johnston Mitchell, 2nd wife of Harvey Mitchell and "Lou," their eldest daughter who married John Brinkley. Jane and Harvey Mitchell had three children, Mary Louise who married J. Brinkley, Sue Henry who married William Taliaferro, and William.
[4]Robert Allen, Mary Wingfield's husband.

asked what we were going to send our soldiers to eat and remind them of home.

THURSDAY, MAY 30, 1861

Out in the yard all morning walking about and attending my flowers. A letter from old Mr. Bowyer who says Lulie[5] is coming to stay with us some. I am so glad.

I had such a sweet note from Mr. Mosby. He writes that Cousin Mary is in such distress about Leslie who thinks there will be a battle at Manassas Junction, where he is.

In the afternoon walked out to Mr. Terry's gate. Cousin (Uncle) Robert Mitchell came to see us. We got no letters but the Davises sent theirs for us to read. One from Mr. Berry, the other from Sam Davis. They wrote there were two thousand Yankees in Alexandria and two regiments of South Carolinians between Manassas Junction and Alexandria. Sam wrote they had not yet seen a Yankee and he was beginning to fear they would not. Cousin Robert had a letter from Fred. It is so comforting to hear from them. I pray they may all come back to us.

FRIDAY, MAY 31, 1861

Busy all morning setting out slips. I read newspapers a great deal now. All mails stopped now to Yankeedom. I would like to write to Mr. Everett that every man, woman, and child in the south would cut their own throats before they would live again under the same flag with the Yankees.

After dinner very busy fixing box of cakes, biscuits, preserves etc. for Papa and Brother Tom. Mail brought letters from them. Cheerful and no attack from those vile Yankees yet. Mr. Johnson returned this evening. A train of Georgians and New Orleans soldiers came to the village about dark.

---

[5]Lulie is old Mr. Bowyer's daughter and Dr. Thomas Bowyer's sister. Her first husband was Dr. Samuel Meredith and her second husband was a Mr. Douglas.

We had not heard they were coming or would have prepared supper for some of them. I went to the bridge and looked down at the depot[6].

SATURDAY, JUNE 1, 1861

Got up at six. Dressed quickly and went down to help Mama entertain the soldiers whom she had sent for to breakfast. A train of Georgians and Alabamians had just come and we sent the servants down to the depot to invite some up. Eight Georgians came, one major and a lieutenant. They were all honest looking soldierly men and seemed much pleased with our hospitable attention. They wrote their names for us and said they would never forget us. The major was a fine looking man and said the only thing he objected to about going into a fight was being killed by such a class of people. One of the men said, "Well, good-bye ladies, I hope if we all get killed we will leave you to live and enjoy a free country."

Fan and Rosa made them bouquets which we presented just as they were leaving. A very quiet day. Letters from Papa and Dr. Bowyer. No fighting at Manassas Station yet. A letter from Mr. Mosby.

---

[6]Kate Burwell Bowyer, in an article she wrote for "Our Women In The War" states, "In the early days when our storerooms were as full as our hearts, it was the unfailing custom for Southern troops passing through our section of Virginia to be besieged at the trains by the servants from the different households and conducted to our houses in companies of ten, fifteen, or twenty to eat the most sumptuous meals we could prepare. These impromptu entertainments were at that time quite the business of the day. I can well remember how our Avenel front porches would be laid with little tables, wash bowls and towels, wherewith these Southern strangers might make ready after their long journey, to enter our dining room, where one installment after another would be fed. Of course, these moving troops had only an allotted time in which to hurry through their ablutions, refresh themselves with a meal and return to the train awaiting them at the depot."

SUNDAY, JUNE 2, 1861

No preaching at our church today. Did not go to the Presbyterian. Mr. Johnson came over in the morning to tell us about his visit down to Manassas. Said they were all well, in fine spirits and preparing for the enemy. Sister read a sermon in the evening. Very quiet day. Letter from Brother Tom by David Holt. Mr. Davis went down to Manassas Junction tonight. Sent letters by him.

MONDAY, JUNE 3, 1861

Heard the train come in with Southern soldiers. Thought they would stop to breakfast, so got up to dress to receive them, but they did not get off here this morning. Had a letter from Mr. Everett this morning. What impudence for him to write to anybody in the South after he has subscribed a hundred dollars to cut our throats. I do not feel like noticing him at all. Sister has written him a very good letter in reply. He writes that we want more than we ought to have; that we want the Chesapeake and the fort...our forts!! And the mouth of the Mississippi! Yes, we do want and intend to keep everything that God has given us, our beautiful valleys and hills, mountains, rivers and streams, our houses, lands, slaves and everything that is ours, the blue sky that is above us and the ocean that rolls along our coast, all belong to us.

Wrote Mrs. Robert Toombs at Richmond inviting her up here.

TUESDAY, JUNE 4, 1861

Answered Mr. Everett's letter today. Sister also wrote him a letter, which was so good I copied it and sent it to Mr. Douglas in Canada, hoping he may publish it in the English papers. It was a splendid letter, telling Mr. Everett plainly what we all thought of him and the whole North. I wrote and appealed to his feelings, begging him if he had any influence to try even now to stop this unjust, cruel war, assuring him we could never be conquered. We are an independent Confederacy, then why waste and bloodshed. It can result in no good to either section. I wonder if my letter, and Sister's will ever reach this old hypocrite who says he is still a friend of the South and at the same time subscribes one hundred dollars to cut our throats. As Mr. Sale says, "Good Lord, deliver us from such friends."

All mails stopped between here and North. Enclosed our letters to Cousin Tom Mitchell, Danville, Kentucky. The Yankees so busy 'protecting' our property for us on the border, dangerous even for letters to pass that way. Mr. Davis returned yesterday from Manassas. Came over and told us all the news from there. All well and busy preparing for the enemy. General Beauregard there and everything going on finely under his surveillance. I am so glad he is there. His presence lends new vigor to our men.

FRIDAY, JUNE 7, 1861

A train of soldiers at breakfast time. Eight Tennesseans took breakfast here. Very good soldiers and very hungry having had nothing to eat for two days. Fan and Rosa threw them bouquets from the upper front porch as they went away.

SUNDAY, JUNE 9, 1861

Went to church and had to play the organ. Wish I did not have to play, it keeps my attention so much from the services, besides it is very warm and exhausting in the gallery.

Letters from Papa and Dr. Bowyer. No enemy yet to fight at Manassas. Every day they put off fighting there. I hope they will not have a fight at all. Am beginning to think that the Yankees are threatening us at that point so as to draw all our forces there and then attack us at some other place…in the West perhaps.

MONDAY, JUNE 10, 1861

Ten New Orleans soldiers to breakfast. Felt like visiting today. Made a good many calls around. Talked all the time about the war. Mrs. Goode and the Davises had hurried notes from Manassas…that all our regiments were suddenly ordered and had gone to Fairfax Courthouse. Sister has been very much distressed ever since as she thinks they must be fighting there. But I think the Yankees will soon hear there is a fresh arrival of troops at that point and will keep themselves carefully aloof.

THURSDAY, JUNE 13, 1861

A national feast day observed throughout the Confederacy. Services at our church. The train came just before the second bell rang with soldiers. We had fifteen for breakfast. They said they were Marylanders and Virginians from Memphis. Mrs. Donald came over before church and saw the soldiers who ate here. In the afternoon Lulie (Dr. Bowyer's sister, Mrs. Meredith, later Douglas) came. We were so glad to see her.

Heard of a great victory the Southerners had gained at Bethel, a church in the country near Hampton. Only one man on our side killed and five hundred of the Yankees killed or wounded.

FRIDAY, JUNE 14, 1861

We did not expect any soldiers this morning, but a long train of them came. Mama had breakfast sent to the depot for them. Doctor carried it and brought us such heartrending accounts of the numbers of poor men who had to go off without getting a mouthful to eat. We commenced devising some means by which more soldiers can be fed at our depot. I thought if the country people could send in some supplies to help out the town people it would be a good plan. So I put on my bonnet and went to talk to Mrs. Campbell about it. She thought with me that the town people had nearly exhausted their supplies and it was time the country people were relieving them. Then I went to see Mrs. Davis. She thought too the country folk should be immediately stirred up and said she would send a servant to go round the country with a paper setting forth the necessity of the country people coming forward and sending in provisions to help the village feed the Southern soldiers.

Went to Mr. Johnson's and got him to write a petition from the ladies of the town to the good people of the country in behalf of the Southern soldiers who come through the village of Liberty very hungry on their way to the seat of war.

Then I went to Mrs. Goode's, borrowed a horse and sent the boy off on his mission. Quite tired at night after the day's performances.

SATURDAY, JUNE 15, 1861

Worked my flowers all morning. Heard from Manassas; mistake about the regiment being ordered to Fairfax. Full particulars today of the battle at Bethel, a proud victory. Our men fought so nobly and covered themselves all over with glory.

Before dinner the news came that the country people were already responding to our call, and that two barrels of flour, a bag of meal and a quantity of meat had been brought to Mr. Campbell's[7] factory. After dinner Mr. Campbell came by. We went to the factory and sent for several ladies: Mrs. Wharton, Mrs. Leftwich, Mrs. Johnson. I acted as clerk. Sent for servants and buckets and bags and distributed the provisions round to various ladies in town to have cooked for the soldiers. We had no idea of succeeding so soon in getting country aid. The Liberty people have acted nobly in feeding so many thousand soldiers, and even some very poor people here who could not afford it have been sending their scanty supplies to the depot...bread, coffee and meat for the soldiers.

---

[7]William Campbell owned the tobacco warehouse where the ladies stored food and supplies. This was originally built as the Baptist Meeting House, and later a school operated by Prof. Dunton.

SUNDAY, JUNE 16, 1861

About nine o'clock the train came in. Eight Texans came over and took breakfast with us. They had been traveling three weeks but did not appear much fatigued. Said their company had been paying their own expenses.

No preaching but at the Baptist church. Heard Ellen and Alice read their lessons. Did not read much today and did not go to church. Read the newspaper in the evening. How little it seems like the Sabbath to be reading the newspapers, but we are so excited and anxious about our friends who are fighting at different points it is impossible to keep from reading the newspapers to see where they are fighting and what they are doing.

MONDAY, JUNE 17, 1861

Sue Hobson and Helen Nelson came to see Lulie. Everybody very busy fixing up boxes to send to Mr. Berry tonight at Manassas. Papa writes he was very near to having an attack of scurvy, the men generally with it from lack of vegetable matter. They write us to send pickle to prevent scurvy. What an awful idea that our people should have such a dreadful disease so near home where we have so many vegetables. Everybody in town contributing pickle to send off by Mr. Berry tonight.

In the afternoon I went to Mr. Campbell's factory with Mrs. Johnson and Mrs. Campbell. Found four barrels of flour, several bags of meal, butter and lard just sent in by the country people. I wrote receipts for the day and the names of people to whom provisions were sent to be cooked.

Very busy after supper fixing box to send Papa by Mr. Johnson. Heard that Harpers Ferry had been evacuated. Suppose that is not a very important point since our foundry has been moved to Richmond and the troops there are wanted to defend other points in the interior. Two of Dr. Bowyer's company came up today and I had a letter from Papa. Even a Northern paper admitted the Virginians achieved a brilliant victory at Bethel Monday.

TUESDAY, JUNE 18, 1861

Went to the factory and helped give out provisions. The country people very liberal so far. Four hundred and sixty soldiers to supper, had plenty. Some of the country people had sent in biscuits and bread, which were sent down to the depot.

WEDNESDAY, JUNE 19, 1861

Five hundred soldiers to breakfast; twelve of the New Orleans soldiers came here (Avenel).

THURSDAY, JUNE 20, 1861

Busy at the factory again. Am afraid the country people have sent all they intend to help us feed the soldiers.

FRIDAY, JUNE 21, 1861

A note from Uncle Tom Mitchell, saying he will give five dollars worth of lard to help feed the soldiers as they pass our depot. A note from William Mosby to say his papa and Lizzie would be up here Saturday evening.

SATURDAY, JUNE 22, 1861

Busy fixing bonnet today. About ten o'clock this morning a train came with soldiers. Jordan (the Negro butler) brought sixteen out here. I helped Mama pour out the coffee. These men were from New Orleans. They seemed delighted with the breakfast and Mama's hospitality. They were all very nice looking and gentlemanly. Mr. Mosby did not come.

Mrs. Johnson and Mrs. Campbell at the factory in the evening. Gave out the last of the country provisions for the soldiers except two barrels of flour. Mr. Johnson came home from Manassas, says our regiment, Colonel Preston's, is ordered nearer Alexandria. I fear we will hear of a great fight there in a day or two. Oh, if those miserable Yankees would only go home and behave themselves without all this bloodshed. What a horrible thing is war! And yet we are obliged to defend ourselves and our country, and as wicked as it seems I can't help hoping every Yankee who invades our soil will meet a speedy death and that no one will remain to go back to tell the tale to the North. Went to Mr. Davis's and Mr. Johnson's after supper.

SUNDAY, JUNE 23, 1861

Mr. Wharton preached. His text was "Seek ye the Lord." He said we must not ascribe the victory of our men at Bethel to their courage and strength but to God because the enemy had in every instance fled before our armies and we must not think it owing to their cowardice, but that God had stricken their hearts with a great panic. So he thought the Lord was on our side and we must not trust in our own strength but seek Him.

Nannie and Maggie Davis came down after supper. Mr. Tom Davis had written an account of the little fight at Vienna in which he participated, but only six or seven Yankees killed. They were driven from the train in which they were coming from Alexandria. Our men secured the train and all their baggage. Mr. Davis sent a drawing of the battlefield and a button and a piece blanket belonging to one of the Yankees who was killed. It is not certain how many were killed as they were seized with such a panic that they did not fire upon our men at all. Ah me, why will they insist upon coming down here for our men to kill! What times, what times are we fallen upon.

MONDAY, JUNE 24, 1861

Five Mississippians to breakfast at Avenel this morning. They were from Natchez and dressed in rather fancy costume for the present troublous times, blue jackets and pants with yellow cord looped about fantastically, and yellow cords and tassels on their hats.

Mr. Donald came in to see us this morning, talked a great deal. Mrs. Burks came by to see about getting up a society for sending things to the hospital near Manassas at Culpeper Courthouse. Went out to Mr. Terry's in the evening and took tea there.

TUESDAY, JUNE 25, 1861

Every day pretty much alike. Read the newspapers a great deal. Think about the war all the time. Wonder if they are fighting and where. Go round to the neighbors as soon as the train comes to hear if they have gotten any letters or news. Get ready something for the soldiers to eat at a minute's notice when the telegraph tells us they are coming and are very hungry. Thus it is each day is passed in excitement and anxiety, for who can tell what may happen? All we can do is to pray without ceasing that our Heavenly Father may give us strength for all that He may see fit to bring upon us and if it please Him in His mercy and goodness to put a final and speedy termination to this sad and unnecessary war by turning the hearts of our enemies that they may see the justice of our cause and leave us and our beloved south land to peace and prosperity.

WEDNESDAY, JUNE 26, 1861

A letter from Papa. Colonel Preston's regiment a few miles from the enemy and expecting an attack daily. But the Yankees seem to have no idea of attacking, and as General Beauregard advances they retire and draw in their scouts to Alexandria.

Heard of Mrs. Nelm's death. How sudden it was. She was one of the most healthy persons in the town eight days ago. How this should impress upon me the uncertainly of life. In the midst of our life we are in death. And how continually should we be praying without ceasing that we may be prepared for the summons. O my Father, help me to so love Thee here that the summons to come and dwell with Thee forever may be to me the most joyful that ever reached my ear. Walked out to Mr. Terry's gate in the evening.

THURSDAY, JUNE 27, 1861

Went to the church to hear Mr. Nelm's funeral sermon. Mr. Wharton's remarks were addressed with great impressiveness. They made us all realize the importance of ever watching and praying so as to be ready for death.

Went to the factory in the afternoon. Found more contributions from the country. Sold Mr. Campbell and Mr. Davis the meal and some chickens, which had been sent. Received twenty-five dollars and ninety-five cents. Paid out five dollars for the coffee bought at Mr. Hoffman's.

FRIDAY, JUNE 28, 1861

Did not feel well enough this morning to go with Mama and Sister out to Mr. Donald's. Read *History of the Mexican War*. Never took much interest in it before but our present troubles make me understand and feel more interest in war, and a great many of the military characters who figured in the Mexican War are now conducting the military affairs of my own time and country. Beauregard, Davis, and almost all the men who were brilliant officers in the Mexican campaign are now in our service. Took a walk in the afternoon. After tea went with Sister to Mr. Johnson's to see about sending bottles of medicine to Dr. Bowyer.

SATURDAY, JUNE 29, 1861

Fresh arrivals at the factory, flour, meat, and butter. Had to go over to see about them. The rain prevented our going to the meeting of the ladies at the courthouse for sending things to the hospital at Culpeper Courthouse. Aunt Mildred and Josephine came in and brought a mattress, sheets, and pillows to be sent to the hospital. Mary Burwell came up from Lynchburg in the evening train.

SUNDAY, JUNE 30, 1861

The rain prevented a great many people from coming to church, very few there. Lymon[8], Mr. Wharton's son preached a very fine sermon, his text, the First Commandment. Verily, we are all idolaters for we all love the world and the things of the world so much. After dinner heard Ellen and Alice's lesson. I pray that what I teach them may be hereafter remembered by them and help to turn their hearts to God.

MONDAY, JULY 1, 1861

The train brought four hundred soldiers to breakfast. Seventeen Arkansans up here for breakfast. A rough looking set, can do any amount of fighting. One man, though, quite young looking, said he had two sons in Captain Crockett's company…Colonel Fagan's regiment. We said what a pity he was not in the same regiment with his sons, but he said, "No, if they fall, I would rather be far off, I could not stand seeing either of them fall, so it is better we fight in different places." That was a very sad reflection.

A letter from Cousin Tom Mitchell received, says he forwarded my letters to Mr. Everett and Dr. Douglas on the 11th of June from Danville, Kentucky. I wonder if they will ever reach Boston and Quebec. I earnestly pray that Mr. Everett may receive his and that he may be induced to turn his heart from advocating war to influence his people to advocate peace.

TUESDAY, JULY 2, 1861

Read, worked flowers, practiced. Mary Burwell went home today. Went to see Cousin Betty Quarles today, in the afternoon.

---

[8]Lymon, the son of Rev. John Wharton, later became a professor at William & Mary College.

WEDNESDAY, JULY 3, 1861

Went with Mama and Sister in the morning to see old Mrs. Wingfield. Found Mrs. Sale and Mrs. Bell out there. Expressed my opinion of the Brinkley and Harvey Mitchell performance, remaining in Lincoln's service and sending their wives and children to Virginia. This so highly enraged Mrs. Robert Allen[9] that she almost fought me. I think if she had had a stick or any weapon at hand she would have demolished me in a short time. I think it was dangerous for anybody to have been so mad. I never saw a woman in so sublime a rage, and I hope never to see such a sight again. I am sorry I went out there and very sorry I alluded to Mrs. Mitchell and Mr. Brinkley. Why cannot I bridle my tongue? Verily, the tongue is a source of much evil when we give vent to our uncharitable thoughts and do not bridle it. I was so distressed all that day that I had expressed my thoughts in regard to the Mitchells. It did no good but much harm, for Mrs. Allen had evidently been cherishing much anger towards me and her angry voice, angry words, and manner towards Mama, Sister, and myself were very insulting. Still I hope we may forgive her and try to have as few collisions with her temper as possible. I will avoid her as much as I can in the future. Her nature is unforgiving and I have no hope her angry feelings towards me will undergo a change. Ah me, what a poor wicked world is this! And what poor, vile, wicked hearts we have! I do not think they can ever be entirely changed, then again I feel differently and feel a sure faith that we can be made clean.

Went to the factory in the evening to help send out provisions for the soldiers. A letter from Papa and Dr. Bowyer. They are twenty-one miles this side Alexandria. The Yankees are fortifying themselves in Alexandria. They have lost so many of their pickets sending them out in the vicinity of our camps that they are keeping them very close within their own lines now.

---

[9]Mrs. Robert Allen was formerly Mary Wingfield.

SATURDAY, JULY 6, 1861

No mail. Heard that General Johnston to decoy the Yankees into Martinsburg, there to surround and fight them. There are so many rumors I have long since determined not to believe anything but the official reports of the engagements unless some friend in whom I have confidence writes us some account. Cousin Robert Mitchell stayed all night with us. He had prayers. We sat up quite late, as we all love to hear Cousin Robert talk.

SUNDAY, JULY 7, 1861

None of us went to church. Fan read a sermon. I heard Ellen and Alice's lesson and wrote them a hymn, new.

Letters from Papa and Dr. Bowyer in the evening. Jimmie Breckenridge wrote Fan that a party of South Carolinians near Fairfax Courthouse had mistaken our Botetourt cavalry for Yankees and fired into them, killing one man who sat on his horse carelessly next to Jimmie and was an old schoolmate of his. One other man was wounded. What a pity! We have lost more men through carelessness of this sort than by the enemy.

MONDAY, JULY 8, 1861

Got no letters today. Went to Mr. Davis's after supper to hear their war news. Mr. Davis saw a man directly from Colonel Preston's regiment who said they were all well. Told us up there that Lou Brinkley had gone back to Washington, a very courageous proceeding. She takes her baby and no nurse and no certainty that she will be allowed to pass through our lines to the enemy. The fact of her being General Johnston's niece may, however, help her through.

TUESDAY, JULY 9, 1861

About twelve o'clock some one announced a carriage at the gate. Went out and discovered Mr. Tayloe's carriage from Roanoke, with Ginnie and Rosa Tayloe and Annie Gwathmey on their way to Mr. Munford's. Said they could not possibly stop, but we pulled them out of the carriage and made them stay till after dinner. Then it rained all night. He enjoyed this little visit very much and the girls appeared very happy to stay.

A Mr. Powell came up from the hotel to see his old pupils, the Tayloes, and spent the evening with us. He was dressed up very extensively, a very rare circumstance nowadays when all our men are as they should be, and as the times demand, in coarse soldiers' garb. This Mr. P., proprietor of a female seminary in Richmond, is a regular junior Turveydrop (Dombay & Son).

The girls sat up until about twelve, talking and laughing immensely. They are such pleasant girls and little Ginnie Tayloe is lovely.

WEDNESDAY, JULY 10, 1861

The girls took leave of us soon after breakfast. This was a regular old-fashioned impromptu Virginia visit. How like the days before the railroad when I was a child a carriage full of cousins and friends would appear suddenly at the door just at dark from an adjoining county, sometimes several carriages and outriders. As the cavalcade came up, there would be great wondering who they could be, then a general recognition as the faces of the drivers and the travelers appeared and a great outburst of 'how do you dos' and 'we are so glad to see yous.' Whereupon followed a great getting of supper, fixing of beds, and taking the baggage upstairs.

About ten o'clock Sister, Rosa, and I had our carriage and went up to Uncle Tom's (Mitchell). Found the girls from Cousin Robert's were there to spend the day, which made quite a large company. Willie and Sue Mitchell there too. Don't think they like our not having attended to their mother, Mrs. Harvey Mitchell, General Johnston's daughter, Jane. Had a very pleasant day. Aunt Mildred and Josephine Barnett such very pleasant people.

A violent storm in the evening, hail larger than a partridge egg. We started home just after the storm. Just after our supper, Cousin William Langhorne drove up in his long carriage, with two of his sisters (Mrs. Hunts) children. This little expedition is just going driving about the country and stopping with their relations whenever and wherever they find it agreeable. It is quite touching to see the children, a girl and a boy going about with their blind uncle just to please him, and he seems to enjoy carrying them around so much. They stayed with us a day and two nights.

SATURDAY, JULY 13, 1861

Heard of old Mrs. Wingfield's death. Went out to the funeral at nine o'clock in the morning. Not many persons there. Mr. Wharton made some impressive remarks calculated to enforce upon the living the necessity and importance of being prepared for that which is to happen to us all alike.

Cousin Jane Mitchell was there. Mama, Sister, and I spoke to her but she evidently disliked to speak to us. When we got home found a telegraph dispatch from William Mosby saying he and Lizzie would be up. Went down to the depot to meet them. We were so glad to see Lizzie up here.

SUNDAY, JULY 14, 1861

This was Communion Day at our church. Mr. Lymon Wharton preached. Mrs. Bell was sick so I had to play the organ. William Mosby was sick and did not go to church.

MONDAY, JULY 15, 1861

William went home. Lizzie very agreeable. She stayed a week and seemed to enjoy her visit very much. We rode out every evening and tried to entertain her the best we could in these war times. Little Lewis is so sweet; we miss him very much since he went away. Jimmie Preston stopped with us two days.

FRIDAY, JULY 19, 1861

William Mosby came up for Lizzie. Brought us news of the battle at Bull Run. We were very anxious about our regiment, could not find out if they were in the fight or not. William said he saw Dr. Bowyer's servant in Lynchburg who had run off as soon as the fighting commenced and did not stop until he reached Lynchburg. He was frightened out of his wits. Mr. Davis received a telegram at ten o'clock at night saying there was no one hurt in Colonel Preston's regiment. This was a great relief.

SATURDAY, JULY 20, 1861

Rumors all day that they are still fighting at Bull Run. The whole village in excitement and fearing that at any moment will bring the news of the death of some of the gallant young men from here. I pray they may be spared and return to their homes and families.

Eight hundred soldiers stopped here for breakfast this morning. Everybody sent breakfast to the depot and we hear there was enough for them. Mr. Johnson, Mr. Campbell, Mr. Davis, and Dr. Sale went down to Manassas today.

SUNDAY, JULY 21, 1861

Letters from Papa and Mr. Bowyer, a very few lines in each and in lead pencil, to say they were not in the fight on Thursday, but were two miles off. They expect, however, an attack where they are. Our men were victorious. Five hundred of the enemy killed and only twenty of ours. How thankful ought we to be. I pray that God in His mercy will strengthen the hearts and arms of our people and with His strong arm defend them and finally bring them back to us safe. Our trust is in Him.

MONDAY, JULY 22, 1861

What a day of excitement this has been! A telegram this morning stated that yesterday there was a terrible battle at

Manassas. Another dispatch in the evening said we had gained a glorious victory but had lost many gallant men. A terrible slaughter on both sides, so much confusion it was impossible to tell how many had been killed of our men or the enemy. What an awful suspense after hearing this news before getting a telegram from Mr. Johnson telling us none of Colonel Preston's regiment was killed. Oh! This was a horrible day for us! Although we had won the victory each heart stood still that at the thought perhaps our dear ones had been killed. When the news came that our regiment was safe and only a few in it wounded, we returned our thanks to God, who in His mercy has spared us such an affliction. But our hearts bled for the thousands who will hear that their brothers, fathers, and friends have fallen in this dreadful battle to secure our victory. No letters from Papa or Dr. Bowyer. Our excitement is so great. The battle lasted ten hours, from morning to night. I do not expect Papa and Dr. Bowyer can write for a day or two.

We sat in Sister's room and she read us a chapter and a prayer, and we offered ourselves and our lives to do God's will and service the rest of our days, and promised to show forth our thanks for this merciful deliverance, not only with our lips but with our lives, praying that God will help us. It rained hard all day, and the rain refreshed many a dying soldier, and I expect, saved many a life on the battlefield. We could not sleep much after such excitement.

TUESDAY, JULY 23, 1861

Another telegram from Mr. Johnson saying that Colonel R. T. Preston's regiment is safe, none killed and only a few wounded. What an awful thought that such a terrible battle has been fought in our land.

After we have achieved a brilliant victory we are sad for nearly two thousand of our brave men have fallen. How I dread to read a list of the names of the killed! What a horrible calamity is ours! I even feel sorry for the ten thousand Yankees who were killed, though they don't deserve it.

No letters, no mail from Manassas. I hardly expect a letter from any of them for the living must be very busy burying the dead and caring for the wounded.

I worked in the yard all day to keep from thinking of the dreadful scenes on the battlefield this day and Sunday. How little we thought while we were so quiet here Sunday that our people were engaged all that day in this terrible conflict, and how can we realize anything so awful. In the afternoon I went to the courthouse where the ladies met and packed a bag with linen, lint, and clothes, pillows and everything to send to Manassas to the wounded.

A number of rumors came to the village; some said from three to several thousand of our men killed and from seven thousand to fifteen thousand of the enemy. It is impossible to know the truth. I went over to Mr. Johnson's after supper to talk with Mr. Hooper who had just come from Richmond. He thinks that after such a defeat the Yankees will not attack us again.

WEDNESDAY, JULY 24, 1861

A paper from Richmond says our men have taken General Patterson prisoner. We are so anxious for a letter from some of our people giving us the particulars of the battle. In the afternoon Mr. Davis came up from Manassas. He stopped at the door as he passed through our yard, but he looked so dreadful and was so hoarse we did not like to ask him many questions. The dreadful scenes he has witnessed and the awful excitement he has been through are enough to have deprived him of his reason. All day Sunday he was on a hill looking on that terrible battle in which he had three sons engaged, and he could not find out till the next day whether or not they were alive. What an awful day and although we achieved such a brilliant victory our hearts are filled with sorrow when we think of last Sunday and picture the horrors of the scene on the battlefield. We got a hurried note from Papa, which he wrote with a lead pencil on the battleground. Mr. Davis was too worn out to tell us much.

I went in to see Mrs. Goode. She had a letter from Mr. Goode. He was in the fiercest part of the battle and made many narrow escapes during the day. Our regiment, Colonel Robert Preston's, was also in the thickest of the fight. Papa enclosed me a song, which was found in the pocket of a poor Southerner who was killed. The song was my "Dissolution Wagon" a little altered.

THURSDAY, JULY 25, 1861

Everybody still excited and anxious to hear more news from the great battle at Manassas. I could think of nothing else and grew impatient as the hour for the arrival of the train with the mail. We got a hurried note from Papa again, written in lead pencil, could hardly read it. He wrote that Colonel Robert Preston's regiment was placed to protect a battery and ordered not to fire unless the enemy came to take away the guns.

Mr. William Campbell and Dr. Sale came home from Manassas Junction this evening. Neither of them had seen Papa or Dr. Bowyer. They witnessed the battle from a hill two miles off. We went to see Mr. Campbell after supper, while Dr. Sale came to see us before supper. So we heard all they had to tell. Mr. Campbell gave us the most interesting account and told us everything, which had come particularly under his observation and all that he had heard. He says he hopes he shall never spend such a day as last Sunday. His anxiety while witnessing the battle for his friends and family who were engaged and his anxiety for the fate of the Southern cause kept him in a state of excited anxiety, which never could be described. He gave us many accounts and little incidences, which we had not heard before. He says the Yankees brought large supplies of ice and in fact every variety of luxury with which they intended to regale themselves after they had fought the "rebels" back and gotten the victory. It is also said General Scott, with a pleasure party of ladies and members of Congress from Washington were at Centerville six miles from the Junction where the battle was fought, preparing to have a great feast after their victory. Being confident they would gain the victory, their table was set and they were just about to seat themselves at six P.M. when looking up the road they beheld their grand army flying before our victorious cavalry. These pleasure seekers hastily left their costly viands and joined in the rout, thus leaving our army in possession of everything. This brilliant Northern army that came out of Washington confident of success and of seeing our men retreating ingloriously as they advanced were themselves repulsed and at the end of the ten hours had received a terrible shock, thousands of their number slaughtered, five hundred to one thousand taken prisoner, the rest seized with a terrible panic and flying back to Washington with fifteen hundred Southern horsemen chasing them down and cutting them to pieces.

How surely it does seem that God has heard the prayers of our people and that to His strong arm may we attribute this great victory of our small and nearly undrilled army over such a superior and well-equipped foe.

FRIDAY, JULY 26, 1861

Mrs. Goode spent the day with us. Mr. and Mrs. Campbell and Mrs. Whitlock also came. We talked together about the war. Mr. Campbell told us that Mr. Pendleton, one of our Episcopal ministers, gave his commands in the battle: "Ready, aim, Lord have mercy on their sinful souls...Fire."

A note from Papa, a letter from Lizzie Mosby. William (Mosby) just come from Manassas says Papa took one prisoner; found him lying on the battlefield Monday, pretending to be dead.

SATURDAY, JULY 27, 1861

No letters today from Manassas. We spend nearly all our time reading the newspapers giving different accounts of the battle, and wondering if the Yankees will attack us again, or let the present victory declare our independence and restore peace. We pray they may get up a peace party after this defeat and thus put a stop to this dreadful war.

SUNDAY, JULY 28, 1861

This day was appointed by our Congress as a day of thanksgiving for our victory at Manassas. Mr. Wharton preached an excellent sermon. A large congregation.

MONDAY, JULY 29, 1861

Stayed all night with Mrs. Goode. Sat up till very late; slept very little; thought all the time about the war. Mr. Goode wrote Mrs. G. he thought there would be another great battle before long.

TUESDAY, JULY 30, 1861

I went to Mr. Campbell's factory soon after breakfast. Mrs. Johnson and I gave out provisions for the soldiers. There was at the same time a meeting at our church to elect a vestry. I did not attend.

Mr. Berry came up from Manassas today. He gave us many particulars and says our men have had very hard service for two weeks past. General Beauregard keeps them moving so frequently from one point to defend another that they are without their tents and baggage nearly all the time.

WEDNESDAY, JULY 31, 1861

Felt sick and dispirited all day. Rode out to Mr. Allen's in the evening with Mama and Mrs. Goode. Very warm ride. Mrs. James Allen read us some letters she had just received from Colonel Allen. His regiment suffered severely in the battle of Sunday at Manassas. They were under General Johnston's command. Colonel Allen wrote that the day after the battle he rode over the field looking for and trying to recognize the men of his regiment who had fallen, and that he prayed to God he may never again witness such a heart-sickening sight.

After supper Sister and I went up to Mr. Davis's to see and hear Mr. Berry. He thinks our generals will march upon Washington, and perhaps to Philadelphia. I hope not. It would be so hard upon our men. We stayed up at Mr. Davis's until nine o'clock.

THURSDAY, AUGUST 1, 1861

In the morning sewed on cotton shirts for the hospital, and read newspapers. Felt very sad and helpless about the war. From the papers I fear we will have war, war, war, nothing but the exciting scenes and horrible incidents of war for a long time. I can't see how we can stand much longer the awful suspense and dreadful anxiety we are (now) experiencing. I pray that God will strengthen our hearts and help us daily to put our whole trust and confidence in Him.

In the afternoon Cousin Fanny Royall came up from Lynchburg. Miss Croly came from Mrs. Allen's and stayed till bedtime. She (then) went to the hotel to be ready for the morning train to Richmond. We felt so sorry for her and wished we had attended to her more while she taught at Mrs. Allen's. What a lonely lot is hers, and how very few bright spots in her existence she has to look back upon and how few to look forward to. Cousin Magdalen Christian also called in the afternoon.

CHAPTER V

An Outbreak of Typhoid

FRIDAY, AUGUST 2, 1861

Very quiet day. Sewed on shirts for the hospital. Talked with Cousin Fanny (Royall) most of the day. After tea the Davises came down with Mr. Berry and stayed until bedtime. Talked about the war and the battle (Manassas) all the time.

SATURDAY, AUGUST 3, 1861

Very hot day. Spent our time as usual reading the newspapers, talking about the war and sewing. In the afternoon Sister received a telegram from Dr. Bowyer telling her to come immediately to Richmond. We were alarmed at first; thought he must be sick or wounded but another dispatch relieved us by informing us that there was nothing the matter; he was only on business to Richmond so could not come home. He wanted to see Sister. We all helped her pack and she was soon ready to set off.

SUNDAY, AUGUST 4, 1861

Sister set off for Richmond on the daylight train. Doctor went with her, and Mr. William Jordan took charge of them. We were very uneasy about her all day as the weather was so warm we were afraid the fatigue would lay her up.

Rosa, Cousin Fanny Royall and I went to the Presbyterian Church. Heard Mr. Sloat[1]. Don't like him much, for besides being a Yankee, he has a very disagreeable impediment in his speech, which makes me nervous.

---

[1] Professor A. Sloat was the Assistant Principal at Piedmont Institute.

MONDAY, AUGUST 5, 1861

This evening went with Cousin Fanny up to Cousin* Robert Mitchell's to see Cousin* Jane [wife of Harvey Mitchell and daughter of General Joseph E. Johnston]. I did not expect Cousin Jane to speak to me and sure enough she did not. I felt a little badly at first but soon got over it as Cousin* Lucy[2] and Cousin* Robert were very kind and polite. I am very sorry that it is so that I cannot be as formerly with Cousin* Harvey's family, but having lost all respect for him and being compelled to express the same, of course, his wife and children resent it. I am sorry he forfeited the esteem of his Virginia friends by remaining with the Lincoln Government. I am very sorry that Coz and all his family here can never again be with us but I cannot help it; these are very revolutionary times. Whoever thought that Coz would pass us by without speaking! I am truly sorry for it and feel no ill will to any of them, and I hope nothing worse may occur during the present revolution.

TUESDAY, AUGUST 6, 1861

Cousin Nancy and Cousin Frederick Johnston came in the morning train. Poor Cousin Nancy, she cannot live many weeks longer. She knows this and yet is so cheerful and seems to enjoy everything around her so much. I gave my room to Cousin Nancy and slept in the library.

Doctor came home, delighted with his trip to Richmond but says there is no place like home. He was especially delighted to get back to his own home where he could get plenty of fresh water and air. He gave us all the news. He stayed at Mr. Toombs[3] with Robert.

---

*In those days most folks were called cousin without regard to relationship.
[2] Cousin Lucy was Lucy Phillips, first wife of Robert Mitchell.
[3] Rosa Burwell Todd writes in her story "Virginia Hospitality in the 50s and 60s," published in *Taylor Trotwood Magazine* that General and Mrs. Toombs were guests at Avenel in July while traveling to their

WEDNESDAY, AUGUST 7, 1861

Cousin Frederick went off early in the morning to Craney Island to see Charlie who is in the artillery service there.

In the evening we were very much surprised at Sister's coming up with her Captain Bowyer. Both were delighted to get home, especially Dr. B., and we were delighted to see him too. He had a new uniform and looked better than we had ever seen him. His clothes in his trunk were in a sad plight, so everybody set to work fixing him up to go back again to camp. We sat up quite late, Dr. Bowyer telling us all about the battle at Manassas and everything.

THURSDAY, AUGUST 8, 1861

Talked a great deal, read the newspapers a great deal. Heard Sister's account of her trip to Richmond, who she saw, how hot it was, what agreeable people she met, how delightful it is now to travel and meet nothing but southerners.

FRIDAY, AUGUST 9, 1861

Old Mr. Bowyer came down. Dr. Bowyer had to tell him over again everything about the battle. Rained again this evening so I could not walk.

SATURDAY, AUGUST 10, 1861

Very warm. Spent the day trying to keep cool. Mama rode out to Mr. Donald's with Cousin Nancy and Cousin Fanny in the evening. Mr. and Mrs. Johnson came in after tea. We sat up quite late.

SUNDAY, AUGUST 11, 1861

Mr. Wharton preached. So warm only sang one hymn. The sermon on the universality of sin, and the frequency of

---

home in Georgia from Washington City. The visit to his old classmate at Avenel was not considered unusual. He was too prominent to be unknown even in Liberty.

professing Christians sinning against God…Mr. Bowyer went home in the afternoon.

Old Mr. Dickenson, just from the Kanawha Valley, came to give us the news. He says he left the whole valley in possession of the Yankees, and it will be impossible for our generals to take it again.

MONDAY, AUGUST 12, 1861

Expected Mr. Donald to spend the day with us, but one of other servants died and several others were taken with typhoid fever, so they could not come.

Letters from Papa and some relics picked up on the battlefield: also a map of the field, which brother Tom explained to us. This being Brother Tom's last night at home we sat up quite late.

TUESDAY, AUGUST 13, 1861

Brother Tom left very early to return to Manassas. Sewed and talked to Cousin Nancy. Worked flowers some. Read newspapers, slept, walked out, ate supper. Talked some more with Cousin Nancy and Cousin Fanny, then went to bed.

WEDNESDAY, AUGUST 14, 1861

Another very quiet day. The company came to spend the day with Cousin Robert Mitchell. A letter from Alice begging me to go up, but it is too uncertain these war times to leave home, and the cars are so crowded with soldiers it is not agreeable and sometimes it is impossible to get a seat.

THURSDAY, AUGUST 15, 1861

Sewed very industriously and talked with Cousin Nancy and Cousin Fanny.

A dispatch from Cousin Fredrick (Johnston) saying he cannot stop here, and Cousin Fanny and Cousin Nancy must meet him at the depot. Mama and I went with them to the depot. Saw Cousin Fredrick there for a few moments. He told us our forces on the Potomac had just captured seven hundred of the enemy and killed many more. Such was the rumor in Richmond; don't expect it is true.

Met our Robert, now belonging to Mr. Toombs, on his way to Wytheville to get a horse for himself to accompany his master in the war. All delighted to see Robert, and he overjoyed at getting to his old home again. His happiness seemed intense at seeing us all and the prospect of spending a whole night and day here.

I am so sorry Mr. Toombs is a general; his mind is too valuable in our councils of state and I do not think we can afford to lose his advice now. I wish he had remained in the Cabinet.

SATURDAY, AUGUST 17, 1861

Rained all day. Talked with Robert. He told us all the news from Richmond. Says he likes Mr. Toombs very much. Also that Mrs. President Davis is very anxious to get Robert to wait on her.

Letters from Papa. An account of the Battle of Manassas. Practiced on the piano and wrote some letters. Knit a little which finished the day.

SUNDAY, AUGUST 18, 1861

Rained again, no going out of the house. Read. Taught Alice and Ellen. In the afternoon Sister read a sermon. I commenced reading *The Pillar of Fire*.

MONDAY, AUGUST 19, 1861

Helped sew on calico shirts for Robert. Set out flowers Mrs. Leftwich sent. Read and practiced, but could not walk out of the lot.

TUESDAY, AUGUST 20, 1861

Usual routine, reading, sewing, practicing, walking on the bark walk in the afternoon. Impatient for the mail. No letters. Read newspapers of a battle in Missouri. We gained the victory. General Lyon was killed; McCullock reported to have been killed but contradicted.

WEDNESDAY, AUGUST 21, 1861

Exactly a month today since our great battle and victory at Manassas.

Worked very hard in the yard. Felt very tired. Read and slept a little while after dinner, then walked with Sister in the orchard and went with her after tea to Mr. Davis's. All knitting socks up there for the soldiers. Talked all the time about the war. Wonder how long we can continue in this state of anxiety and distress.

SUNDAY, AUGUST 25, 1861

Went to church. Mr. Wharton's text "Sin is the transgression of the Law." Heard that Mrs. Bell had scalded her hand and that I would have to play the organ. Glad to find it was a mistake, for I cannot keep my thoughts fixed on the services when I play, and I really cannot enjoy the services for thinking about how and what I am to play. I stayed in the gallery until the congregation had gone out, and only spoke to Fanny Allen as I came out.

In the afternoon Nannie Davis, Sister, and I walked in the orchard.

MONDAY, AUGUST 26, 1861

A visit from Mr. Radford directly after breakfast, and Mr. and Mrs. Leyburn to spend the day. Took a long walk in the evening. Met little Becky Bramlett who walked with me. She seems to have a great affection for me ever since she was in my class at Sunday school. Sister read the newspapers out at night. Felt quite hopeful about the war.

A letter from Dr. Bowyer. Can't find out whether his company is changed to Artillery or not... Major Allen resigned. Finished reading *The Pillar of Fire*. Very well written: beautiful descriptions of the gorgeous land of Egypt in the days of the Pharaohs. The author exhibited great power and skill in introducing Moses as the hero of a novel without making him do or say anything which did not correspond with our preconceived ideas of his dignity and sacred character. Throughout the book he clothes Moses with a certain dignity and makes his character in every respect to accord with that in the Sacred Book, at the same time weaving around him a romance of which he is the hero, and surrounding him with pictures so gorgeous as to appear to us in these days unreal. But through all these splendid surroundings and dazzling realities of Egyptian life, Moses and the whole nation was supposed to be the son of Pharaoh's daughter. The sublime and calm dignity of his character never ceases to elicit our admiration. To keep up this sacredness and sublimity of character without writing anything to take away from or add to our idea of Moses derived from the Bible, at the same time placing him in the immediate atmosphere of an unchristian, unholy Egyptian (life) was a nice and difficult task. Thus we have Moses and Miriam woven up into a sort of romance without feeling that they lose their character and dignity as impressed upon them in the Bible. I am sorry the author died about three months ago.

TUESDAY, AUGUST 27, 1861

Rainy day. Read *Appelles*, a sort of novel Eliza Leyburn lent me. Appelles, the hero, is the Grecian painter. Also Alexander the Great with whom Appelles was a chief favorite and of whom Alexander once said, "I can create nobles and lords but never an Appelles." The book is not very well written, I think.

Walked in the evening on the bark road. Too wet to go outside the yard.

WEDNESDAY, AUGUST 28, 1861

Another rainy day. I went out in the yard directly after breakfast to set out a few flowers. Got very wet. Stayed in the house all day. Practiced songs an hour. Read *Conquest of Mexico* by an old Spaniard, Bernal del Diaz, who in his youth accompanied Cortes in his expedition. He writes very familiarly of Cortes and "all of us." It is not very beautifully written but very interesting for being so truthful and circumstantial. Read newspapers at night. Brother Tom's company converted into artillery.

SUNDAY, SEPTEMBER 1, 1861

Went to the Presbyterian Church. Heard Mr. James T. Leftwich preach. Very fine sermon prettily delivered. Sat by Sis Wingfield. She appeared glad to see me, which quite surprised me.

Felt sick when I came home. Lay down after dinner, read a little in *Kitto's Bible Readings*. Walked before sunset. Met Mrs. Davis at the gate. She thinks our troops are marching upon Alexandria and Washington. Heard of Dr. Page's death of typhoid fever near Manassas.

MONDAY, SEPTEMBER 2, 1861

Read, practiced, worked in the flowerbeds. Had letters from Mr. Mosby, messages too, by Jordan. Everybody sick down there. Mr. Mosby and Leslie sick, and four soldiers in the gardener's house.

TUESDAY, SEPTEMBER 3, 1861

Burial service at our church at nine o'clock, poor Dr. Page's funeral. Dr. Wharton preached a very solemn sermon admonishing us all to be ready for the summons of death. I pray that we may be.

After the sermon I called to see Mrs. James Leftwich. Sister went in the carriages to the cemetery. When we got home we found old Mrs. Allen and Julia Allen here to spend the day. They are both charming ladies and we enjoyed their visit very much.

Did not walk outside the yard in the afternoon. Read newspapers after supper, and went to bed very early.

WEDNESDAY, SEPTEMBER 4, 1861
Read, practiced, slept awhile after dinner. Mrs. Pate called. Walked out late in the evening. The Davises walked on our bark walk.

THURSDAY, SEPTEMBER 5, 1861
A quiet day as usual. Rained almost all day. Could not walk. No news from camp. Rain very bad for our poor soldiers. Fixed hoop skirt. Finished the *Old Spanish Soldier's History of the conquest of Mexico*. Enjoyed reading it very much. Wrote letters and received a letter from Papa. Our regiment very near Alexandria. Camp at Fairfax Courthouse left and regiment marched to Munson's Hill to protect our fortifications there, and stayed three days. Papa said all enjoyed themselves very much for they got plenty of milk, peaches, and fruit. Saw Washington City and the enemy around there. No encounter, however, with the enemy except with some picket guards: returned to the camp Wednesday morning. I am dreading to hear of the next battle, which must be before very long, I expect, as our forces are so near to Washington.

SATURDAY, SEPTEMBER 7, 1861
Worked in the yard after breakfast. Wrote letter to Papa. Read and walked in the afternoon. Nannie and Maggie Davis joined us and walked on our walk.
After supper we all went to the church to see Martha (a servant) married. Mr. Wharton performed the ceremony. I played the organ as the bride came in and went out. The bride, groom, bridesmaids and groomsmen were all dressed very handsomely, 'the ladies' all in white laces and flowers, the 'gentlemen' all in black and white gloves. Great preparations had been going forward here all day for the wedding. When we came from the church, I went out to the kitchen to see the

table, which was filled with iced cakes, flowers blanc mange (dessert), candles, grapes and so forth and it really looked beautifully.

SUNDAY, SEPTEMBER 8, 1861

Went to church. A wet, rainy day. Very few persons out. Mrs. Bell did not come so I had to play. Only played voluntary before the sermon and one hymn. Mr. Wharton's text was Peter's denial of our Savior, and he went on to tell us how very like Peter we all are and how little any of us know what we may be tempted to do, how we should not trust in our own strength, what great need there is of watching and prayer. Fan and Rosa and I went to church again at night. Mr. Wharton preached an elegant sermon in which he impressed upon us the error, which is common nowadays, for people to look entirely to the minister and not to the members for the spread of the Gospel and the increase of the church. He said there was no verse in the Bible that required of the minister to lead a holier life than the professing Christians of the congregation. And indeed this is very true, for the world should see and expect to see as much piety in the communicants as in the minister.

MONDAY, SEPTEMBER 9, 1861

After breakfast I rode the pony out to Mr. Donald's. Doctor went with me and carried some bread. We found Mrs. Donald in great distress. Besides losing a number of servants who worked on the farm, she has to mourn the death of Martha, her favorite servant and friend. She cried all the time I stayed, and I wept too to think the cheerful face and voice and welcome smile of our old friend, Martha, could meet me no more. From my childhood she has been a kind, familiar friend, ever ready to welcome Mrs. Donald's guests. Her pleasing face and evident delight at seeing her mistress's friends, her untiring attention to us while we stayed, her great desire that we should enjoy our visit, and her cheerful smiles whenever we went, and when we came away, insisting we should come again, all to make our visit there so charming. And through life I shall remember her with sincere affection, nor can any of us who have enjoyed the hospitality of Mr. Donald's house (Otterburn) ever cease to remember Martha's kind welcome and untiring attention. Her white cap and apron on at the door was always ready to receive us. Then how busy she would be making ready some refreshments to hand herself. All this has been all my life such a familiar picture that in future visits to Mrs. Donald's, I shall find it hard to realize that I shall no more see this good friend and faithful servant. I felt very sad all day after seeing Mrs. Donald. I am very much afraid she will have this dreadful fever.

TUESDAY, SEPTEMBER 10, 1861

Worked in the yard. Commenced reading *Life in Spain*. The Miss Crenshaws called and made quite a long visit before dinner. Took a walk in the evening. Called at Mrs. Goode's.

WEDNESDAY, SEPTEMBER 11, 1861

Read and worked in the flowers before dinner. Went visiting after dinner. Wrote letter to Robert for Maria. Lay down after dinner but for two mosquitoes I could not go to sleep. Fixed sleeves in the calico dress. Walked out in the late afternoon. Met a great many people, some strangers from the hotel. Practiced some Italian songs after supper. Read newspaper; not much news except General Floyd has had a victory in Western Virginia, the battle of Cross Lanes. I am very glad for I like General Floyd so much.

FRIDAY, SEPTEMBER 13, 1861

Directly after breakfast rode out to Mr. Donald's on the pony, Doctor with me. Carried Mrs. Donald some bread. Mr. and Mrs. Donald very low spirited. Seven new cases of fever among their Negroes.

MONDAY, SEPTEMBER 16, 1861

Worked in the yard directly after breakfast. Commenced reading a novel, *The Woman in White*. Never read many novels and so never acquired that fondness for them, which some people have. The habit of novel reading grows upon one. The more we encourage and cultivate a love for fiction the more our fondness for it increases, of course. I am glad I have never indulged the habit of reading novels for I am sure it would have injured me and I would have been too fond of it.

After dinner Uncle Robert Mitchell called and at the same time Mr. Tayloe's carriage drove up to the door. The girls, Nannie Tayloe and Cary Gwathmey, had come from Roanoke. How glad we were to see them. What laughing and talking till eleven o'clock. I felt in a particularly happy mood... amused the girls very much after we came upstairs.

Rumors of a battle near Munson's Hill, where our regiment is. No letters. Miss Goode and Miss Ada called just before tea.

TUESDAY, SEPTEMBER 17, 1861

The girls left us soon after breakfast for Mrs. Munford's. Letter from Papa. Mistake about the battle. Walked in the afternoon.

THURSDAY, SEPTEMBER 19, 1861

Went to work in the flowers and was interrupted by Mr. and Mrs. Sale coming out. They stayed till nearly dinner. Directly after dinner Mama, Sister, and I went to Mr. Donald's. I rode the pony. Delightful to ride.

FRIDAY, September 20, 1861

Concluded to make a muslin scrap quilt for Dr. Bowyer and some soldiers. Went in the garret before breakfast to hunt up scraps. Very busy all day sorting and fixing them. Did not read any in *The Woman in White*.

SATURDAY, SEPTEMBER 21, 1861

Sewed very hard all day on the muslin quilt for Dr. Bowyer. Took a short walk in the evening.

SUNDAY, SEPTEMBER 22, 1861

Went to church. Heard of Mrs. Bell's tenth daughter. Had to play the organ.

MONDAY, OCTOBER 7, 1861

Have not written in journal for two weeks. Nothing of importance transpired in that time. Weather had been very cold; we had fires; then very hot, so that I have been visiting in a thin white dress. A very interesting visit from old Uncle Mat (colored), the last link between the past and the present. He told us a great deal about Grandfather Burwell[4] and Mr. Jefferson and those old times we love to hear about.

Fan has decided to be married in February. Great sitting up at night, great planning and talking, who shall be invited etc. etc. It must be a small and quiet wedding to suit the war times. Very few gentlemen can come from the camps because of the difficulty of getting furloughs...the men who did not go to fight for their country are not worth inviting to anybody's wedding.

Finished reading *The Woman in White*. Fan and Rosa think one of the female characters, Marian Holcome, very like me. I liked the book very well.

Sis Wingfield came home with us from church Sunday. She had not been to see us for a long time, and we enjoyed her visit very much.

Sister has had her trunks packed for a week, expecting to pay Dr. Bowyer a visit, but he telegraphed her not to come yet.

---

[4]William Armistead Burwell, the father of William Burwell of Avenel, was an intimate friend as well as private secretary to Mr. Jefferson when the latter was president.

General Beauregard ordered that all civilians should immediately leave Manassas as it was supposed the Yankees were advancing and there would be a fight near Fairfax Courthouse. No fight yet.

How sad we are to hear of the death of our good friend Mr. Chalmers[5] so good, so gentle, so earnest, so lovable. He was pure in heart and a bright Christian. We will miss him sadly: such truth and earnestness, such simplicity and goodness were his in this evil world. Alas, that so few like him are left. His memory will be sweetly cherished in our hearts while we are here, and we will hope to meet him in that brighter land where he has surely gone.

WEDNESDAY, OCTOBER 9, 1861

All day at the courthouse helping to sew for the soldiers. Did not sew very much, but sewing buttons on overcoats was such heavy work it tired me. Sister had a telegram from Dr. Bowyer to come on to Manassas.

Very tired after sitting up n the high bench all day at the courthouse, so went to bed early. Mr. Berry came down after supper to make arrangements with Sister for going to Manassas.

THURSDAY, OCTOBER 10, 1861

Went to the courthouse again. Had a split bottom chair carried for me to sit in. Sewed hard.

---

[5]One James Chalmers of Lynchburg entered service as a sergeant in Co. B., of Wise Troop, 2nd Virginia Cavalry. He was born in Halifax County on September 21, 1829, and attended UNC and UVA. He was an LLD, an attorney, and enlisted in Lynchburg on May 13, 1861, at which time he was a tobacconist. He was wounded in action in his stomach and suffered a broken arm, which required amputation on September 29, 1861. He died with the rank of Lt. of wounds on October 1, 1861, and is buried in the Presbyterian Cemetery in Lynchburg. (Driver/Howard, 1995, 205)(Christian, 1900, 201)

Walked out in the afternoon. Fan went with me, but afraid of cows and turned back.

Sister and Mr. Berry set off early for Manassas. I hope there may be no battle about therebefore she gets back.

FRIDAY, OCTOBER 11, 1861

Read and sewed on black silk dressing gown. Walked in the afternoon. Borrowed two of Washington Irving's books from Mrs. Goode. Read the newspapers at night to Mama. Cut out a very pretty and appropriate tribute to Mr. Chalmers.

SATURDAY, OCTOBER 12, 1861

Practiced voluntaries for Sunday. Telegram from Sister announcing her safe arrival. Read Irving's *Tour on the Prairies*, not interested init at all. Was continually reminded of Walter Pike [General Pike's son] while reading it. Walked in the afternoon. Took Alice with me. Little Mrs. Leftwich called very late in the evening.

SUNDAY, OCTOBER 13, 1861

Mr. Kinkle[6] came up today; preached and administered Holy Communion. He preached again at night. I felt as if it was peculiarly applicable to me.

MONDAY, OCTOBER 14, 1861

Did not feel well today. Read *Bracebridge Hall*. Had read it before but was more interested in it this time. The style is so easy and natural.

Letter from Sister. She is delighted: found a comfortable house very near the camp, very nice old lady and gentleman, where she got board. Supped in the tent the night before on top of a flour barrel, which served as a table. Cast on a pair of yarn socks for soldier; knit till quite late.

---

[6]The Reverend W. H. Kinkle was the rector at St. Paul's Episcopal Church in Lynchburg for twenty years. He died in Lynchburg on March 2, 1866. (Christian, 1900,253)

Earlier, worked flowers, practiced and read. Went to see Mrs. Dr. James Bowyer and baby in the afternoon at Mr. Sale's. Baby very sprightly and interesting.

WEDNESDAY, OCTOBER 16, 1861
Rosa and I went soon after breakfast to the courthouse to help sew for the soldiers. Worked innumerable buttonholes in overcoats. Cass, Nannie, and Sis Wingfield sat with Rosa and me. We passed quite a merry day. When we came home to dinner, we found Jimmie Breckenridge here with Fan. Quite refreshing to see how much both of them are in love. Only objection I have to it in the world is that they both have red hair. Met Step Cobbs as I came home in the evening and engaged to knit her baby a comfort. Another letter from Sister. She had heard hard, heavy firing from Alexandria at Manassas. Going over to the Battlefield next morning.

FRIDAY, OCTOBER 18, 1861
Read and sewed in the morning. After dinner Step Cobbs and baby paid us a visit. I knit very industriously on the little comfort for the baby.
After supper Uncle Robert Mitchell came down from the Davises and stayed all night. We sat up very late as we all love Uncle Robert very much and delight in hearing him talk.

SATURDAY, OCTOBER 19, 1861
So disappointed this morning to see the rain. Step and I had arranged to ride up to Uncle Robert's on our ponies and spend the day. Finished the little blue scarf and practiced a little on the piano.

SUNDAY, OCTOBER 20, 1861
Mr. Johnson came up from Manassas. Sent us word he left Sister in Lynchburg at Mr. Mosby's. In the evening I went to meet her at the train but shedid not come. Did not go to church today but read a sermon to Mama while Fan

and Rosa were gone to the Presbyterian Church. Taught Ellen and Alice.

MONDAY, OCTOBER 21, 1861
   Very busy all day. After dinner Dr. James Bowyer came in. Sister returned home on the four o'clock evening train. It rained so I could not go in thecarriage to the depot to meet her. She was very full of news from the camp; said she slept every night in the tent and did not take cold. How uneasy we would have been had we known she was sleeping in the tent. We sat up very late hearing Sister's account of her travels.

TUESDAY, OCTOBER 22, 1861
   I was very busy all day. Still raining. Ah me, I am always busy and all about such little things that I hardly know how to write about them in my journal, and besides, paper is too scarce in these war times for such small things as I hemmed a ruffle, made a ribbon bow, fixed curtains for my dressing room, learnt a new song, read Irving's *Abbotsford* and *Newstead Abbey*. Nearly cried over Byron's sad, unrequited love, wished so much he could have married Miss Chaworth. Yet there are cases like his I might cry over everyday; still they are not written about as his are. Could not walk in the evening.
   This was a busy day of little things, again too unimportant even to chronicle in a journal, and yet are not our lives made up of little things scarce remembered a week hence!
   Expect to have to go up to the courthouse tomorrow and return to the uninteresting manufacture of buttonholes on soldier's overcoats.

SATURDAY, OCTOBER 26, 1861
   Did not return to the courthouse until yesterday, Friday, and sewed very hard all day. Came home to dinner and returned to the courthouse in the evening. Cass Wingfield

and I undertook a pair of pants and finished them before sunset.

Very busy all day today arranging the books in the library and fixing up in there generally. Have fixed up those old books so often, so many long years I feel quite endeared to them. The old ugly backed Latin books that I didn't know anything in the world about have a profound appearance to me and because they belonged to my great grandfather's library I have an attachment sincere for them. So with some old English books in our library which I have never read: dry old essays and some old histories that I have hardly ever peeped into, yet from long handling them, I have grown very fond of them and would not part with them on any account.

SUNDAY, OCTOBER 27, 1861

Heard of another glorious, brilliant victory of our troops under General Evans at Leesburg.

Mr. Wharton preached (at our church). Mrs. Bell came to church again and relieved me of duties at the organ. Heard Ellen and Alice's lessons after dinner. Did not feel very well but went to church again at night.

MONDAY, OCTOBER 28, 1861

Commenced to sew directly after breakfast, but the doorbell interrupted me so often I had to put up my sewing and get out my soldier's sock as knitting is the best work in the parlor. Persons calling all day. And an Alabama boy soldier, Donotho, took dinner with us.

In the evening Colonel James Allen, his wife, and cousin Magdalen Christian came to stay all night. Sat up very late talking. I do love and admire Cousin Magdalen so much. What a pity she has such a miserable husband who cannot appreciate her. Uncle William Steptoe took supper here and stayed until bedtime. What a remarkable old man, nearly eighty and like a boy in his feelings.

TUESDAY, OCTOBER 29, 1861

Company all day. Have noticed we have spells of company. Sometimes the doorbell is ringing all day for several days and then again no one comes for a week or so. This is a peculiar fact. The servants say that when company is coming before breakfast Monday, there will be company all the week, and I can believe it is sure enough. Mrs. Donald came in after dinner. Cousin Magdalen and Mrs. Allen went home this evening.

We had a visit from Mr. Winkler[7], too, today. How a vision of him carries me back to my school days. I almost feel like playing the scales again for him.

Promised Cousin Magdalen and Mrs. Allen to go out to Mt. Prospect with Coly tomorrow evening, Wednesday. How I do hate to go from home! But I think people ought to make themselves go sometimes.

TUESDAY, NOVEMBER 12, 1861

Two whole weeks since I wrote a word in my journal. Went to Mrs. Allen's, stayed three days, enjoyed it very much, everybody so pleasant and kind. What a lovely lady Mrs. Allen is! Was made quite sick from eating chestnuts out there.

One evening Fan and I rode over to see Mrs. Cabell Moseley[8]. Very rough road, just under the Peaks of Otter, rocks everywhere, nothing but rocks. Very romantic scenery. Very pleasant visit; such a bright and happy family notwithstanding the poverty around. Oh, it's beautiful to see such real happiness, such refinement and education amid such poor surroundings, the house looking crazy enough to come down with the next storm, no paint even on it. Nothing about the house

---

[7]Mr. Winkler had been a music tutor at Avenel.
[8]The George Cabell Moseley home, Ingleside, is located near Fancy Farm, just off Route 43, north. George C. Moseley married Mary Daniel Whitlock who was a frequent visitor at Fancy Farm. They were married on December 17, 1835, and had twelve children. For more information about this family, please see the Chapter on Hunter's Raid.

that we consider tolerably comfortable, and yet such a contented and happy family within. It is indeed a good chapter on contentment to go up there, and I hope I may go up there again sometime, though it would be an exceedingly uncomfortable place to stay at. Returned home on the pony Saturday evening. Encountered Mr. Kelso[9] again. He rode in with Mr. Donald and me. A heavy storm had swollen the creek (Big Otter) so we had to come home through Mr. Nichol's[10] place.

---

[9] Mr. Kelso purchased the Andrew Donald farm and lived there at Fancy Farm. Robert N. Kelso married Susan Pollard, a first cousin to Mary Daniel Whitlock. This couple lived at Fancy Farm and had two sons and two daughters. Thomas Kelso was in the Confederate army and died in 1867. Robert who was in the 2nd Virginia Cavalry was wounded and died in 1862, loved and mourned by all who knew him. In 1875 in Botetourt County Robert N. Kelso married Jane D. Harvey.

[10] Mr. Abel Nichols owned Three Otters, on the Peaks Road. Mr. Nichols came from Bridgeport, Connecticut, to Liberty in 1822. He established a dry goods business here and in 1837 built his home which he called Three Otters. He married Clarissa Baldwin Linus, also of Connecticut, in 1824. She was a devout and active member of St. John's Episcopal Church. In the early years, Episcopalians worshipped at the courthouse. When their first church was built Mr. Nichols had the brick made at Three Otters. He also built a brick building in town which was later used for the offices of the *Bulletin-Democrat*. He was instrumental in getting the James River and Kanawha Canal built between Richmond and Lynchburg and after its completion his store merchandise came from New York to Lynchburg by water. The Nichols family was known for its generous hospitality and Mr. Nichols set the standard with large hunt parties to the Peaks of Otter followed by barbecues and dancing in the spacious double parlors at Three Otters. Mr. Nichols was too old to join the young men who left for battle during the Civil War but played a vital part in contracting for Army provisions. When he learned that General Hunter was headed toward Liberty and would pass near his plantation, he packed up the large stores of provisions in his custody for the Confederate Army as well as his own cattle, sheep, and hogs and headed for the dense hiding places of the Dismal Swamp. He camped several months there until the danger was passed. His son, George, received a medal for bravery at the Battle of First Manassas.

Heard the victory at Leesburg confirmed. We rejoiced over it, the most brilliant victory yet. Heard the Yankees had sent a tremendous fleet down to whip us on the southern coast and take our harbors and forts. Hope the storm had 'used' them up.

MONDAY, NOVEMBER 18, 1861

Rode to Mr. Leyburn's and back after dinner, I on the pony, Mama and Rosa in the carriage. Delightful ride. Wish I could ride all the time. Today Fan and I very busy fixing to go to Roanoke, going tomorrow. Mr. John Ed Patterson stayed all night with us last night. So refreshing to see him; so like old times. He is the finest trimmed soldier I have seen; looks elegant and seems to have enjoyed the service more than anybody I have seen. He talked a great deal, and told us many new things about the Battle of Manassas, and was very agreeable. Sam Davis, too, came down and spent the evening with us. He is at home for the first time since the war commenced six months ago.

Our returned soldiers were very near suffocating not having been in a room for so long, so we had to open the windows and doors to give them air; whereupon we took very bad colds, but that made no difference. We must not think of ourselves when our soldiers are here.

Mr. and Mrs. Leyburn happened to come just after supper. I suppose they must have felt cold in the parlor while we were suiting the temperature to our soldiers, but we did not think to consult them at all. Heard that our bridges on the railroad in east Tennessee had been burned. Dreadful news. Hope it is untrue. Twelve hundred soldiers are just passing our depot now. I must go down to see about it.

CHAPTER VI

Death of Maria

TUESDAY, NOVEMBER 19, 1861

We went up to Salem, Alice with us. Had a very pleasant ride and got to Cousin Fredrick Johnston's about 12 o'clock. Found the Tayloes there to meet us. We all went together to shop at the stores. Met Mr. Thornton Tayloe on the street. Bought gloves and gaiters. Nannie and Rosa Tayloe took leave of us at the stores. Alice, soon after she had finished her shopping, told us good-bye, and then we were left in Salem to take a fair and liberal start for home, which we did at three o'clock the following morning.

We had found the girls at Cousin Frederick's[1] dressed in deep mourning for their mother who had been dead for two weeks. Poor girls, how sorry I am for them. How impossible for the world ever to seem the same bright place to them without their mother. What a great and valuable woman she was too, and so pious. I never expect to see another woman like Cousin Nancy. She combined more noble qualities with more kindness and simplicity than I ever saw.

SATURDAY, NOVEMBER 23, 1861

Paper is getting so scarce in our Southern Confederacy I have to convert my scrapbook into a journal. I hope the war will be at an end and the blockade opened before I write through this book. Will also have to adopt a more laconic style for my diary. Can't afford paper for so many words.

---

[1] Frederick Johnston's family home was in Salem where Longwood Park is now next to the Salem Museum. Johnston became the court clerk for Roanoke City. It is thought that his father, Charles Johnston, was the founder of Roanoke College.

Fan and I returned from Roanoke last Wednesday morning at sunrise. Had a charming little visit of a week. Went and came without an escort. Southerners have a good time now travelling without any Yankees. Everybody gets perfectly acquainted with everybody in a few minutes. Fan and I got in the cars here without a single acquaintance but before we got off at the Lick[2] some old southern gentleman, having found out our names and knowing Papa, had introduced us around so we became quite intimately acquainted with the passengers and they were very sorry to part with us.

Found Nannie Tayloe[3] and her cousin Thornton Tayloe from Alabama at the Lick depot to meet us. Got in the carriage and were soon at Mr. Tayloe's for supper. Made the girls laugh very much by describing how the old gentlemen had gotten acquainted with us in the train. At first Fan and I, having no escort, determined to be very "recluse," so we put down our veils and hardly spoke to each other. Presently a gentleman sitting behind us suddenly thrust a little book in between our shoulders and said, "Ladies, here is a trophy from the battle at Leesburg last week. My friend Moore got it out of a Yankee's pocket." This was a very unexpected piece of information and attention and we laughed very much under our veils. The gentleman soon attacked us again, don't know why he took up with the impression that we were fond of seeing curiosities, but he left his seat and returned with a watch which he handed us to look at, telling us that the paper in the top of the case was from the wall of the room in which General Washington died. We looked at it and thanked him. Just then we met the western train. Both trains stopped and the passengers who discovered acquaintances in the western train put their heads out and had a great conversa-

---

[2] Roanoke was known by the name of "Lick" or " Big Lick" at this time.

[3] The Tayloe home was called Buena Vista and located where the Roanoke Regional Preservation Office is now.

tion. Western train had on board forty-five Yankee prisoners, which General Floyd had just captured in western Virginia. Great excitement when this news was given us. Then we found out the name of the gentleman behind us who had given himself up to entertaining us all the way. He was introduced out of the window to some of the train passengers as Captain Rousseau of Texas and the gentleman next to him was Colonel Barker, aide to General I.C. Breckenridge. When the cars went on again these gentlemen still pursued us with attentions and very ingeniously found out our names. Captain Rousseau said he knew a great many Burwells, said it seemed to be his fate to meet Miss Burwells in Virginia. And Colonel Barker proved to have an old friend of Papa's in Washington. So he expressed great pleasure in meeting us. Captain Rousseau was a very funny looking man and a very funny dressed man…very tight pants, very drawn up coat with a black bottle sticking out of the pocket, very high pair of boots which came half way up his thighs, and a very funny walking man. The black bottle had been passed around among sundry lieutenants and captains, though it had not produced a great deal of hilarity up to the time of our leaving the train. Still, the black bottle was very suggestive and I was sorry to see officers of the highest rank in our army on such terms of intimate companionship with a black bottle. It was still sadder to see these elderly gentlemen, who ought to have been setting a better example, inviting, and in case they refused, insisting on the young officers coming up and taking a drink. I can hardly expect our cause to be favored by God when I reflect on the great wickedness of our people. Colonel Barker, as we were getting off the train, asked us to pray for him. Don't know whether he was impressed by the contents of the black bottle or not, but I think I did remember him in my prayers that night.

 Friday was fast day. We were still at Mr. Tayloe's. Went to the Lick to church. Mr. White, Presbyterian, preached a very excited sermon on the times, calling upon the Southern people to fast and pray and everywhere to be lifting up our hearts to God to give us victory over our enemies and restore us to peace, he also predicted a very long and bloody war. I pray it may not be so.

Had a delightful visit at Mr. Tayloe's. Mr. Tayloe not at home, but in Richmond at the Convention. The girls, Nannie, Rosa, and Ginnie are lovely. Liked Cousin Willie Tayloe's wife very much. Her little girl is the sweetest little child. Little Mary Gwathmey, too, is a lovely little thing. The children were very devoted to me and entertained me greatly. I passed the time hemming handkerchiefs, playing the piano, telling stories to the children, talking with the girls and walking out. We enjoyed our visit so much and the girls seemed very sorry we could not stay longer. Told them about Fan's wedding, they said they would certainly come over.

Saturday morning Emma Carr came over for us to go to her house. Arrived at Mrs. Watts just before dinner. Nobody there, for a wonder, but Mr. Nat Burwell, Jr. and a Mrs. Morris. Major William Watts home from the war, Manassas, quite sick, looks very badly and has a bad cough. Don't think he ought to go back but he says he will. My sweet friend, Alice, is looking beautifully in her caps since her hair was shaved, and is more fascinating than ever, I think. She is just as much fallen in love with now as when she was Miss Watts. Little George is very sweet too. Mrs. Watts is looking better than I had expected to see her, but she never leaves her room and the sitting room, which is next to it.

Alice has prayers every night and Mrs. Watts begged us to sing her some hymns, Emma and Fan would get in a giggle, and I, assisted by Anne Gwathmey, would either have to give up singing altogether or go through the whole hymn by myself.

Emma's baby, two months old, is a nice little thing, beautiful brown hair, very long. Sorry it is named Maria.

Went to church again Sunday. Carried Mr. Thornton Tayloe some refreshments, as he seemed to be restless at church Thursday. Wanted to keep him quiet. Sat just behind the Tayloes and Rosa passed the two cakes and a bit of candy to her cousin Thornton, which appeared to amuse him highly.

Sunday evening Anne Gwathmey and I took a long walk. Sat on the fence on top of the Round Hill a long time, talking and admiring the scenery.

Monday morning I went to walk directly after breakfast. Met Mr. Thornton Tayloe coming to see us. Alice was busy housekeeping and could not come in the parlor for some time after he got here. I think he is in love with Alice so when she did come in I determined to play a great deal so as to give him an opportunity to talk. Consequently, I sat down to the piano and gave myself a good long hour's practice. Played almost everything I knew, Alice had to beg me to stop!

Mr. Tayloe stayed until three o'clock dinner, and while we were at dinner some ladies called and remained until it was nearly dark. I was very sorry we had company all day, for I wanted to stay more with Mrs. Watts and this was our last day at Oaklands[4].

WEDNESDAY, NOVEMBER 27, 1861

Not written in journal for several days. Saturday evening, November 23[rd,] had company: Cousin William Langhorne arrived about dark in his long carriage from over the mountains. William Mosby came up from Lynchburg with Mr. Henderson to stay till Monday. Mr. Henderson, perfect picture of a widower, very sprightly, a quaint old sprightliness, very fond of being teased about the girls, and of talking about love. Ah me! What a class of people are widowers. How they immediately seem to lose all their former dignity and love to feel like they were back in their youthful days.

Very sorry there was no preaching anywhere in the village on the Sabbath. How I hated to stay in the parlor all day with nothing to do but talk idle gossip. Sister read a sermon

---

[4] The William Watts home was called Oaklands and located in what is now north Roanoke City.

in Mama's room, but I had to stay in the parlor with Mr. Henderson. Took a walk with him in the afternoon. Very cold. He forgot to put on his overcoat, did not discover it till we were coming back after walking a mile. Declared he was not cold. Oh! Widowers! From very drawn up old men before their wives die, they suddenly spring up afterwards into very young and sprightly men! All signs of rheumatism instantly vanished and altogether the change, which appears, is alarming to one who is acquainted with the cause. Mr. Henderson became more and more lively and left with a ring on his finger! Mr. Mosby very agreeable.

Tuesday night, Mrs. Leyburn and Mrs. McNeese came, stayed all night and left us today, Wednesday.

Delighted with Mrs. McNeese who is so agreeable. She has been once or twice to visit her relative in Ireland and interested us very much with her accounts of manners and customs there. Mr. Leyburn and Eliza arrived just before supper last night.

Mr. Leyburn went on to Manassas this morning with two large carpetbags of tracts to distribute among the soldiers. We sent letters and packages to Papa and Brother Tom by him. What a hard time they must have at the camps this cold weather. Today I had a sore throat, could not go out. Sewed all day. Mrs. Berry and Ellen Davis came in and sat all evening.

THURSDAY, NOVEMBER 28, 1861

A most beautiful day, quite a summer day. Stayed in the yard all day working in my flowers. A shower came up in the evening so could not walk. Fanny Allen came and stayed all night. I love Fanny very much...she is such a sweet person. A letter from Alice who is a complete character. Every department of her character is equally balanced and she is a wonderful woman, an unparalleled woman. I have always loved her and find more about her to love every time I see her.

FRIDAY, NOVEMBER 29, 1861

Sewed in the morning and walked in the evening. Fanny Allen went to Mr. Wingfield's after dinner.

Read Papa's story, the chapter in the last *Messenger*, which he sent home from Camp. A very good little poem by him in the same *Messenger*, "The Red Suave." Wish I could get the other numbers of the *Messenger* with the first chapters of "Empire and Exile." The chapter I read I liked better than I expected as I think Papa's forte is political, not story writing.

After supper read the newspapers aloud. Not much news. Poor Mr. Mason with Mr. Slidell[5] has been taken to Boston to

---

[5] James Mason of Virginia and John Slidell of Louisiana, elderly statesmen, had slipped out of the country in October as Jefferson Davis's commissioners to the governments of England and France, traveling with the dignity of their own eminent positions and with letters of instruction from the Confederate Secretary of State. Their mission was to make clear that the Confederate States are not to be viewed as revolted or rebellious subjects or provinces seeking to overthrow lawful authority. The South was making no revolution but trying to avoid aggressive northern sectionalists. The south had set up a competent and responsible government for which they wished to be recognized. Mason and Slidell reached Havana on a blockade-runner on November 7, 1861, and took passage on a British Mail Steamer, *Trent*, to England. Capt. Charles Wilkes, a self-willed, opinionated, contentious northern Navy officer was cruising off the coast of Cuba when he heard about Mason and Slidell. On November 8, he sailed ahead to lie in wait for the *Trent*. He compelled the vessel to stop by firing a shot across the bow and sent armed men aboard to make the arrests. After he acted, he was told by his superiors to deliver the prisoners to a Boston prison, which he did. The British reaction was indignation over this act of violence, an affront to the British flag, and international law for which they demanded reparation and redress. Since the embarrassed northern government could not afford to have the British join the South in war against them, they quickly agreed to King Albert's suggestion of full reparation of the unfortunate passengers, an apology to them and to the British and a release of Mason and Slidell. Wilkes, who had not acted under instruction, would be dealt with by the northern government. (Catton, 1963,109-116)

be imprisoned. I do feel so sorry about him, hope he will be kindly treated and somebody will give him some tea. He is a great lover of tea. No prospect of an attack again at Manassas, Papa writes.

SUNDAY, DECEMBER 1, 1861

Went to Presbyterian Church, and heard Mr. Sloat. Text was "The Night Is the Day at Hand," a very impressive sermon. Church very full of smoke, had to shut my eyes and found that I listened more attentively to the sermon as my eyes were not wandering over the bonnets, etc. and so my thoughts did not wander much.

Fanny Allen came home with me from church. Took a walk after dinner. After supper we talked and sang some hymns. Heard Alice and Ellen recite their catechism.

MONDAY, DECEMBER 2, 1861

Sewed and knit all day. Took a walk in the evening. Very cold. Fanny went to Mr. Sale's. Knit after supper.

TUESDAY, DECEMBER 3, 1861

Sewed before breakfast. Fanny came in after breakfast, took leave of us and went home. Great deal of hog killing going on. Mama busy in the kitchen all day. Wound yarn for jackets after supper. Went to bed very early.

WEDNESDAY, DECEMBER 4, 1861

Sewed buttons on Robert's shirts for Maria and wrote him a letter for her. Read first part of *Swiss Family Robinson* so as to be able to write out the story for little Allen Watts. Walked in the afternoon and after supper stoned plums for Christmas cake and mince pies.

THURSDAY, DECEMBER 5, 1861

A lovely day. Stayed in the yard a great part of the morning. Knit pair of worsted cuffs for Mama. Took a walk in the evening and found Mr. Henderson here when I got back. Quite surprised to see him up here again so soon, but think old widowers think they have no time to lose. He stayed very late and pressed his suit with impassioned ardor of a boy of sixteen. Really seemed in love.

The times so hard I did not think it would be right to make him come again when I have no idea of encouraging him. So I discarded him at once. He is an amiable nab and I love and admire his many good qualities. Says he thinks I could soon learn to love him enough to marry him, but I can't agree with him. Poor widowers, they have a hard and lonely time and I cannot chime in with the general abuse, which the world generally heaps upon them for wanting to marry again. It is true human nature they should desire to have their home circle brightened once more, and it is a high compliment to our sex inasmuch as it shows their high appreciation of us. A compliment, too, to the first wife, for had she not been found a very agreeable appendage there would exist no desire to have her place filled.

FRIDAY, DECEMBER 6, 1861

Another summer's day. So I was out in the yard again. Had the pony saddled right after dinner and rode quite heroically about by myself till sunset. Nannie Davis promised to go with me but had company and could not. The evening was so lovely I felt I could not give up my ride so proceeded on by myself. Went a little way in several different directions not far out of sight of houses. The sun was so bright and the landscape so peaceful and beautiful I could not feel afraid of anything. How I did enjoy that evening on the pony! The prospect so charming, air so delicious, the sunshine so enchanting, it was quite dreamland as I paced along and enjoyed the scene.

SATURDAY, DECEMBER 7, 1861

Another glorious day, which I enjoyed to the fullest extent. In the yard all morning and on the pony all evening. Emma Graves rode with me. The air and sun were so delicious we rode to Mr. Donald's creek (Little Otter).

SUNDAY, DECEMBER 8, 1861

Went to our church (St. John's Episcopal) for the first time in a whole month. Enjoyed going through our service once more very much. Letters from the camp at Centerville. Papa enclosed various facetious sketches of Mr. Leyburn's visit... how he was taken to the guardhouse because he was without the countersign, etc. Poor Mr. Leyburn, he is too good a man to be laughed at, but Papa's pictures are funny. Walked out in the afternoon.

MONDAY, DECEMBER 9, & TUESDAY, DECEMBER 10, 1861

The weather is still marvelously beautiful and too warm for fire. Stayed out nearly all day, took a ride again in the afternoon. Went with Emma Graves but did not go out of sight of houses, only trusted ourselves a certain distance in each direction by which means gave ourselves a very good ride. Quite tired at night but sewed and sang till bedtime.

Arose early on Tuesday and sewed on under shirt till breakfast. Directly after breakfast went with Fan to see Nannie Davis who is sick in bed. Mrs. Donald and Mr. Donald came to dine with us. Enjoyed their visit so much as we always do they are so kind and agreeable, knit and sewed alternately during the day.

Cousin Bettie Quarles and Marion Steptoe called in the afternoon. Such a lovely evening and I had to sit still in the house! How I hated not to go out and enjoy the beautiful afternoon. Just as we were ready to go to bed, Cousin Armistead Burwell arrived but I did not go downstairs to see him.

TUESDAY, DECEMBER 31, 1861

Last day of the year 1861. Have not had a moment to write in my diary since December 10th. Have devoted almost the whole time waiting on Sister. Her baby was born 13th December. A darling little girl[6]. Great excitement in the family, the first baby since Rosa was a baby. Our first niece and Mama's first grandchild. What a dreadful day the day she was born! How anxious we were about Sister, who was very ill. How I prayed and wept! Oh, I hope I shall never pass such another day! How thankful I am to God that He heard my prayer and spared her life. How little did I deserve He should answer my prayer such a vile sinner do I feel myself.

The weather has been charming and I have been out on horseback almost every afternoon. Ellen Davis, Emma Graves, and I without any escort. How I do enjoy these rides, especially after staying in Sister's sick room all the mornings. The sun is brighter when I get out.

Christmas Day passed in bed until late in the afternoon. Had sat up holding the baby all night and had been up the night before too. So I felt quite sick. Very sorry I could not go to church.

In the evening, two of our breakfast soldiers came to pay us a visit. One of them brought Mama a silver cup he picked up on the battlefield at Manassas, with a soldier's name engraved on it. They were both very honest, brave soldiers and seemed very much pleased with our kindness and attention to them. Not the first people by any means, but very gentlemanly and well behaved. Talked a great deal about the battles they had been in, one had been in the battle of Manassas and was slightly wounded, the other a boy of about eighteen, a printer from St. Louis, John Gay, had been out in western Virginia with Generals Wise and Floyd, and had endured innumerable hardships.

---

[6] This child, named Lillian Bowyer, was subsequently married to James Lawrence Campbell of Bedford.

Mr. and Mrs. Leyburn and Mrs. McNeese came in the evening and stayed all night. Mrs. McN. went in the morning train to Petersburg.

We have great distress about Maria (a servant). Poor Maria, the doctor thinks she has a cancer in her stomach and he cannot do anything more for her, but she does not know it and talks about getting well. How sad it is. I cannot realize she will not wait in my room again. So kind and faithful, so attentive to my wants. How sad that one whom I fell so interested in should not be a Christian. I must pray more for her that her heart may be changed and she may receive into the fold of Christ so that death may be clothed in beauty and she may rejoice rather than be terrified when the summons comes for her to go and be at rest.

Oh! My Father, hear my prayer, renew her heart, pour into it Thy Holy Spirit. Open her mind to receive instruction and help me to teach her.

After staying with Maria and nursing Sister, there is no time left for anything else, these short days. I try to ride or walk a short time every afternoon. Rosa and I rode yesterday to Uncle Tom Mitchell's to see Aunt Mildred. Told her about Fan's wedding. Very hard to fix for Fan's wedding, Maria sick, Sister sick. I am so busy all day I am very tired at night. Rode out with Emma Graves and Ellen Davis in the afternoon.

NEW YEAR'S DAY, JANUARY 1, 1862

Arose at seven; dressed, sewed ribbon around neck of black silk dress. Went to Sister's room. Had breakfast at nine. Went to see Maria. Was sent for to hurry back to the house to see the young ladies from Mr. Donald's. Helped Rosa and Fan entertain them for two hours. Practiced a little for the first time in four weeks. After that, stayed with Sister and nursed the baby. Dinner at three. Sister's room again after dinner. Mrs. Pace to see Sister. Had to entertain her till nearly dark. Then walked out very rapidly as far as Mr. Dickenson's.

Went to see Maria again. Told her I prayed for her. She appeared very glad to hear it, but when I asked her if she did not think she ought to pray herself, she said she could not think of anything but her pains. So I told her that showed we should never put off praying till we get sick.

After supper returned to nurse Sister and the baby. Great difficulty getting the baby to sleep but succeeded about 10 o'clock. The doctor had to come again tonight to see Sister. At eleven o'clock I retired very tired though I had not had my ride on horseback as usual on account of high winds today.

THURSDAY, JANUARY 2, & FRIDAY, JANUARY 3, 1862

Devoted the morning hours to stoning the plums for wedding cake. Went morning and evening to see poor Maria. She requires very little waiting on. Nursed the baby a great deal for Sister who is not well enough to get up. Visit from Willie Mitchell. It is so amiable of him to come to see us after we had treated his mother and sister so badly.

Wednesday and Thursday still stoning plums. I walked in the afternoons. Go to see Maria, nurse the baby, and wait on Sister.

SUNDAY, JANUARY 5, 1862

Sick all day. Very sick in the night, woke with sick stomach and headache at 2 o'clock, though I had gone to bed entirely well.

MONDAY, JANUARY 6, 1862

Quite well again. Arose at seven o'clock. Fixed up old hood for a servant before breakfast. Went to see Maria after breakfast. Took a prayer book with me and read a Psalm to her; she did not appear at all interested in it. Still, I will not give up hope that her heart may be changed and she may die a Christian while I can pray for her. Marked all of Fan's new clothes.

SATURDAY, JANUARY 11, 1862

A beautiful day. Gathering a bunch of violets and heartsease in the yard. The winter has been so mild the flowers have hardly stopped blooming, rosebuds all over the bushes. In the afternoon rode on the pony to Mr. Donald's. Fan and Rosa went in the carriage. I invited Mrs. Donald and the girls to spend the day with us Tuesday.

SUNDAY, JANUARY 12, 1862

Went to church morning and night. Mr. Lymon Wharton preached. Wished old Mr. Wharton had preached. Took a walk in the afternoon. Heard Ellen and Alice's lesson. Went to see poor Maria. She seems to expect yet to get well and has an old root woman waiting on her. But Dr. Sale thinks she will not get well and I do not think so either, and yet I cannot bring myself to tell her so.

MONDAY, JANUARY 13, 1862

Wrote a letter to Mrs. Gilliam for Doctor to take to Richmond. Also a note to Rev. Mr. Woodbridge, telling him about Doctor and requesting his kind attention and consideration in Doctor's behalf. I am so very sorry Doctor has to leave home for employment. He is so faithful and good; I don't know what we will do without him.

We were very much surprised this morning to receive a telegram from Papa in Lynchburg telling us he is sick and will be at home this evening.

Company all morning. In the evening Fan and I went in the carriage to meet Papa at the Depot. His appearance shocked us so that we could hardly speak. We were altogether unprepared for such an alteration. He has the camp fever and is so weak and emaciated I should never have known him. Still he is quite cheerful and we hope the comforts of home will soon restore him.

About dark went to Maria's house. She had a very sick spell while I was there. I rubbed and put on mustard plasters. She asked me to look in the old trunk and get some money tied up in an old piece of sock and keep it and if she died, give it to Robert. I would have given anything then to have talked with her about dying and prayed for her but could not for weeping.

TUESDAY, JANUARY 14, 1862

It seems everything is against Fan's wedding fourth of February. Jimmie is uncertain about getting a furlough, Maria is very ill, Papa is sick. Dr. Bowyer writes he is not well and will probably come home sick in a few days. Sister and the baby require a great deal of attention since the baby's nurse is sick.

Such a list of troubles…looks quite discouraging.

WEDNESDAY, JANUARY 15, 1862

This is the day I had set apart to write invitations to Fan's wedding, but everything is involved in such uncertainty we do not know how to proceed. Went to Maria's house and stayed with her nearly all day. Sat with Papa and sewed a little. Papa looks better but is very feeble and unlike himself.

THURSDAY, JANUARY 16, 1862

Went to Maria's house soon after breakfast. Found her composed. After taking a cup of coffee she roused up and talked a little. She said she was praying all the time. I knelt by the bed and prayed aloud for her the prayers for the sick in the Prayer Book. She still seems to have a faint hope of getting better. Nursed the baby almost all day.

A telegram from Captain Bowyer this evening saying he will be at home tomorrow. I hope he is not sick. A letter from Nannie Tayloe. Her cousin, Thornton, had me a chair made. It was very kind of him indeed. Had an invitation to a ball from Mr. Patterson. How absurd to be having a ball these dreadful war times.

FRIDAY, JANUARY 17, 1862

Stayed with Maria all the morning. Read prayer for her. Helped Sister dress the baby and stayed with Papa some. Brother Tom came in the afternoon train, looking quite badly. Our house is quite a hospital.

Passed much of the day waiting on the sick and visiting. Persons coming and going all day to see Papa and Captain Bowyer, old country gentlemen whose sons are in Captain Bowyer's battery come to inquire after their sons.

Stayed with Maria much of the day. She seems anxious to die, poor thing, she suffers so much. I do everything I can for her. She seems to like me to wait on her and says I am to her as her own child would be.

SATURDAY, JANUARY 18, 1862

Just as I was going to Maria's house the doorbell rang and to our astonishment Hamilton Pike[7] was announced. How very glad I was to see him. I never expected to lay eyes on him again. He was greatly altered of course, but very handsome and agreeable with the same kind, gentle, unaffected manner as of yore.

Went to see Maria before dinner She said she had wished for me so much in the night.

Hamilton stayed with us till ten o'clock at night when he took leave of us and went to the Depot Hotel to take the early morning train to Richmond. I was very sorry his visit had to be so hurried, for seeing him, was like hearing a strain of some favorite old song unexpectedly. It revived many, many recollections of the period when I first knew him so long ago, and I contrasted my feelings, tastes, and fancies now with what they were then. What a contrast!! And how many, many

---

[7] Captain Luther Hamilton Pike of Arkansas was the son of the controversial Brigadier General Albert Pike. Hamilton was a Captain of an artillery company in his father's command. His brother was a beau of Rosa Burwell.

changes in my little world! How many loves and friendships since then made and broken! But so it is with life, each month and year find something gone which can never return, some link broken in our old friends' lives, some fancy changed.

SUNDAY, JANUARY 19, 1862

No preaching today at our church. Went to see Maria after breakfast. No train this morning so Ham could not go but came back to see us. Delighted to see him again. Stayed again with us till late at night. Again took leave and went to the hotel. I liked him better this evening than ever before. He is my special favorite. So sorry to tell him good-bye. Never expect to see him again.

MONDAY, JANUARY 20, 1862

No train yet, so Ham came back to see us. We were more pleased than ever to see him as his stay with us has endeared him more to us and we became more attached to him as he remained longer. It was very amiable of him to be entertained entirely with and to give himself up entirely to entertaining so many ladies all by himself.

Uncle Robert Mitchell and Fred came to see us today. Ham as usual took another melancholy leave of us after supper.

TUESDAY, JANUARY 21, 1862

The train took our dear brother Ham off from us this morning. We were really very sorry to give him up and miss him a great deal. It is very sad to feel that we may not expect ever to meet again one whom we all feel so well acquainted with and for whom we have so sincere an attachment. But it is so in the world. We meet many whose smiles of friendship cheer us on our journey a little way, then we meet them no more. Still the memory of those may sometimes cheer, and we rush on and on into the future, making new friends when the old ones fail us, and keeping our pathway bright with the smiles of pleasant friends; thus along life's journey we may find a bright present by looking back upon the old enjoyments and grasping the new.

WEDNESDAY, JANUARY 22, 1862

Stayed all day with Maria again. Prayed for her and read to her. She is still in a dying condition.

When I came back to the house found a letter from Mr. Mosby and one from Walter Pike (brother of Hamilton). Walter writes he envies Ham his visit to us.

THURSDAY, JANUARY 23, 1862

Stayed again with poor Maria today. Prayed again for her and do pray for her the whole time. She has been in great agony the last three days and prays for death. Poor thing, how she suffered, and how distressing to stay with her. There is very little I can do for her, and yet it seems to give her so much pleasure for me to be with her. It is very disagreeable to stay in the room now, but by holding camphor about me and having lime sprinkled, it is possible and I must not shrink from my duty. If I were in the agonies of death, she would have been by me all the time. I pray she may be taken from her great suffering tonight. O God, save her soul I beseech Thee is my constant prayer. How sad to part with a true and faithful servant, and how we reproach ourselves for not having done more for them, poor souls! How we should pray continually for them that God would send the light of His Gospel Salvation into their darkened understandings. I felt sick from staying in Maria's house so many days.

FRIDAY, JANUARY 24, 1862

What a wretched, wretched day I have spent! Oh, I pray that I may never again witness such human agony! All day with that poor dying woman, praying that she might be speedily removed from this miserable world and her great suffering, and that her poor soul might be washed clean in the blood of Jesus and presented pure and acceptable to God in Heaven. What a horrible day!

At the bedside of that poor dying woman, and she begging me to get the doctor to give her something to take her out of the world. Oh! How dreadful it was! I pray there may not be another such scene in store for me, yet God's will be done. Passed the first part of the night in prayer for poor Maria and hoped it might be the will of God to relieve her of her suffering before morning.

SATURDAY, JANUARY 25, 1862

Awoke very early. Maria is still alive. Stayed with her all day again. She did not suffer quite so much and seemed more patient. She required the constant attention of four servants, and how kind they are to her! I could not help thinking while I nursed her how much better was her condition as a slave than it would be had she been a poor white woman, or even a free colored woman. Here she had every attention which money and kindness could command, whereas in the other case she might be without friends or comfort. As a slave every want is provided, every comfort secured, and the first physicians in constant attendance. Verily, an Abolitionist would have his creed shaken could he realize the vast advantages of being a slave of kind owners in such a case as this.

SUNDAY, JANUARY 26, 1862

A sad, sad day. Heard very early in the morning that Maria died at two o'clock in the night, just about the hour that I woke up and was praying for her. I felt as if I couldn't look at her again, but about twelve o'clock I went down and laid some flowers on her breast. How can I ever forget the agony of my heart this day! My ever-faithful friend who always loved me and felt almost a mother's interest in me gone, gone. I can never see her more, but God has promised to hear all who call upon Him in faith and I have prayed that we may meet again in Heaven.

At four o'clock in the evening we attended the funeral. Mr. Wharton read the service and the colored people prayed and sang around the grave. It was almost more than I could bear and at night I was almost sick from distress. Did not sleep any.

MONDAY, JANUARY 27, 1862

Tried to shake off my deep grief as I felt it was making me ill. Went to breakfast and saw old Mr. Bowyer who had come the day before. Went in Papa's room for I had not seen him since Saturday. Mr. Speed[8] came up from Lynchburg and I had to talk to him too. Would have felt so much better in my own room where I could have given way to my grief, but in spite of my sad thoughts I had to be downstairs. Retired at ten o'clock, Mr. Radford and Mr. Bowyer were here, so had to stay in the parlor with them till ten. How little I felt like it!

Eliza slept in my room. Poor thing, how distressed she is, and all the servants are at Maria's death. How faithfully they have waited on her day and night. They are such kindhearted creatures when they are well treated.

---

[8] John Speed was a Lynchburg attorney who died in 1866.

CHAPTER VII

Fan's Wedding

TUESDAY, JANUARY 28, 1862

Mr. Radford and Mr. Bowyer spent the day. Sister concluded, as they were here, to have the baby baptized. So she sent for Mr. Wharton. When he came he found us all in a general discussion as to what her name should be, but no two seemed to agree. Willie Mitchell had just called in and suggested Cora which I thought was very pretty. Each one suggested something different. Some wanted a fancy name and some wanted a family name. The controversy was becoming embarrassing when Mr. Wharton took the Prayer Book to commence and Dr. Bowyer and Sister must name her anything she liked, so she called her Lillian, the very name I suggested at first.

Mr. Wharton took dinner with us and everybody was very agreeable. Soon after dinner the train came and Mr. Bowyer and Mr. Radford left. What an interesting picture these two fat old gentlemen are as they sit side by side in two large rocking chairs and smoke two long pipes. Their attachment to each other, too, is beautiful. I wish they lived nearer us so that I might see them together oftener.

Heard that Hamilton Pike has passed in the evening train on his way home. I am so sorry he did not stop, especially as I had been hard at work all day making him a watch pocket and had just finished it. Don't think he liked us as much as I thought he did, from his not stopping. Don't suppose we will ever meet him again now. His home and his interests are so far removed from ours it is hardly probable that he will remember long.

WEDNESDAY, JANUARY 29, 1862

A regular summer's day. Could not stay in the house. Worked flower beds and went to poor Maria's house.

Lucy and Martha were dividing up her things. It makes me so very sad to go down there now. Practiced some of my favorite songs. Walked on the tan bark road with Fan and Rosa an hour in the evening. Sat in Mama's room with Papa till bedtime. Read newspaper aloud. The Yankees reported to be landing their Burnside Expedition on the coast of North Carolina. Don't doubt the North Carolinians will give them a good fight. Our Confederate army has been defeated in Kentucky at the battle of Fishing Creek.

THURSDAY, JANUARY 30, 1862

Made some collars for Caroline and Eliza. Finished reading Mr. Slaughter's book, *Man and Woman*. It is very well written and calculated to produce much good result. I pray that it may. Commenced reading *The Autocrat of the Breakfast Table*.

Did not feel enough interest to read it through regularly. It is a very ostentatious book in which the author makes a great effort to be of hand, and seems determined to make the public acquainted with every little commonplace thought he ever had. He also seems very anxious to put into a book all the little items he had gleaned from reading and traveling and has labored to present them to his readers in what I suppose he considers an off hand style but which to me is very heavy.

Attended to the greenhouse flowers, practiced song an hour, and sewed. Received a chair, which Mr. Thornton Tayloe sent. It was really so kind of him to send it. Papa received letters from Secretary Benjamin of the War Department saying that he would see that Jimmie Breckenridge gets a furlough. Fan has fixed for the 27th of February, so I suppose we will go to fixing for her wedding again.

SATURDAY, FEBRUARY 1, 1862

All day cushioning and covering the chair which Mr. Tayloe sent me. Played some songs after supper. No mail today.

SUNDAY, FEBRUARY 2, 1862

No preaching at our church, and did not go to Presbyterian Church. Read some stories to Ellen and Alice, and taught them. Walked an hour on the lawn in the afternoon. Sang hymns and read after supper.

MONDAY, FEBRUARY 3, 1862

Today brought deep snow and could not walk. Sewed and read newspaper account of the Burnside disaster of the Yankee fleet sent down on our Carolina coast to make war upon us. How rejoiced we are to hear this news.

THURSDAY, FEBRUARY 6, 1862

Arose at four o'clock and dressed, had breakfast and went to the depot with Brother Tom to take the train to Lynchburg. Brother Tom's furlough was out and he was obliged to go and I obliged to go to Lynchburg to do some shopping for Fan. The rain poured and I walked through the mud to the depot holding an umbrella. Waited some time for the train. No fire in the barroom at the hotel but I had to sit there until the train came.

It continued to rain all day. Arrived at Lynchburg. Took a hack and went straight to Mr. Mosby's. They were quite surprised to see us on such a morning. They had just finished breakfast. Found Mr. Henderson there. How happy I am to get to Mrs. Mosby's. How everything in the house brings up some old recollection. How many happy hours of my childhood have been spent there. How dear the memories, which cluster around the library and the parlor where I have had such bright hours. 'Tis sad to think of all this and bright too. 'Tis sad to look at the old pictures, to sit on the same old chairs and sofas and remember the scenes and friends once so intimately connected with them. I do not allow myself to remember or ponder o'er the past when I am there. Still, I am so happy in the same old love which the family feel for me and this makes me feel somewhat like the time gone by. I love Mr. Mosby more and more every visit, and Aunt Judy too. Even the servants of the family share my affection and yet the place is not in my heart to home.

Found William sick. Lizzie as pretty as ever, with three children and she not yet twenty-one. What a pity she married so young, Cousin Mary sick with one of her old headaches. Spent the day going round talking to them all. Brother Tom quite sick and could not go on to Manassas as he intended. After supper I played on the guitar and sang for Mr. Mosby. He likes my singing and my songs. Slept with Aunt Judy. Leslie went in the evening train to Liberty (Bedford) on business. I sent a letter home by him.

FRIDAY, FEBRUARY 7, 1862

Mr. Mosby and I went in the carriage on the street. Looked for a nice trunk for Fan, and for a wardrobe. No trunk in town. Bought white silk for Fan. Sent it home by Mr. Hewitt. Stopped in at Mr. Mosby's law office and wrote a note to Fan. Mr. Henderson came in and went with me to Mr. Payne's bookstore. Bought a new guitar for Rosa, cards and envelopes for wedding. Dr. Ben Blackford[1] came in while I was there. He was at home on furlough. Asked him to take a seat with Mr. Henderson and me in the carriage as he was going to the same place as we were, Mrs. Otey's. Lizzie and William were waiting there for us. Called at printing office to see about having invitation cards printed, and went back to Mr. Mosby's.

---

[1] Captain Benjamin Blackford of Lynchburg was the surgeon in charge of the hospital complex in Liberty.

After dinner went to see Cousin Fanny Rudd and Mrs. Judge Wilson. Mrs. Rudd, Mrs. Speed, and Mr. Speed came after supper to hear me play.

SATURDAY, FEBRUARY 8, 1862

Brother Tom left Mr. Mosby's for Manassas. How hard it must be for our poor soldiers to go back to camp this bad weather, after the comforts and luxuries of home for two weeks.

Such a dreadful day that I could not go out on the street at all. Enjoyed staying with the family all day. Indeed, I wish I did not know anyone in Lynchburg; it takes so much time from the family at Mr. Mosby's to receive and return so many visits. The Langhornes called and Miss Ella Payne. No time to return any calls this visit.

SUNDAY, FEBRUARY 9, 1862

Went to Mr. Mitchell's[2] church. Mr. I.T. Leftwich preached a very flowery sermon. Would have much preferred going to my own church, but the family all go to the Presbyterian Church and I always loved Mr. Mitchell.

After dinner Mr. Henderson, Florence, and I walked down to see Aunt Mary Holcombe. Going home, Mr. Henderson begged me to extend my walk. Sorry I did as I got my cloak full of white paint by it. He still talks of love a great deal and insists on my marrying him. O widowers, widowers!!

MONDAY, FEBRUARY 10, 1862

A gloomy letter from home. Papa thinks the Yankees are advancing upon us in so many places and in such numbers we will hardly be able to withstand, and that it is not improbable they will get possession of our railroad before long.

---

[2] This is Jacob Mitchell, minister of the 2nd Presbyterian Church in Lynchburg. He died in 1877.

Mr. Toombs, too, has written Papa a gloomy letter, and Fan wrote Mama was thinking seriously of burying her silver. This letter made me feel very little like shopping, but Lizzie and I went to the bonnet store. Everything was dear. I had to pay sixteen dollars for a nice bonnet. Got beautiful straw colored bonnet, some worsted and white flowers for bridal veil. Bought nothing for myself and do not mean to buy anything till the blockade is opened.

Returned Mrs. Rudd's visit before supper. George Langhorne called. Played and sang for Mr. Mosby, Mr. Henderson, and Mr. Speed after supper. Retired at ten quite fatigued with the day's shopping.

TUESDAY, FEBRUARY 11, 1862

The telegraph brought news that General Wise's brigade on Roanoke Island, North Carolina, had all been taken prisoners. This filled us with sorrow. Packed my trunk and took leave of all the dear ones at Mr. Mosby's. Lizzie came to the depot with me, and Mr. Henderson brought me home. The cars were full of drunken soldiers. Mr. Henderson courting very industriously all the way.

Found Papa very sad about our surrender at Roanoke Island. He says our generals ought not to have attempted to defend that barren point but should have brought our troops further in the interior to give the Yankees a good fight in the country.

WEDNESDAY, FEBRUARY 12, &
THURSDAY, FEBRUARY 13, 1862

It was a beautiful day that I sewed, practiced and worked flowers. Thursday I helped Sister sew for the baby. Wrote to Lizzie and walked in the afternoon. I sang for Rosa and Papa. The baby was sick, helped Sister nurse her until half past twelve and then could not sleep for Eliza's coughing.

SATURDAY, FEBRUARY 15, & SUNDAY, FEBRUARY 16, 1862

A miserable day, it was snowing all day. Did not look up from my work. Made two black crepe collars for Eliza Mosby. Stayed with Papa until bedtime. My eyes were quite sore at night.

There was no preaching on Sunday at our church. Too bad to go to the Presbyterian Church, so read and heard Alice and Ellen's lessons, also helped nurse the baby.

Heard good news from the West of the great victory of General Floyd and General Pillow at Fort Donaldson, Tennessee. We rejoiced greatly.

MONDAY, FEBRUARY 17, 1862

Papa went to Lynchburg. Today is a dreadful day. I am so afraid he will be sick again. Kept very busy all day sewing for the baby, cutting up citron and icing cake. The wedding to be the 4th of March. Mr. Berry came in the evening, brought his pipe, and was very sociable.

TUESDAY, FEBRUARY 18, 1862

Passed the morning writing and sewing. After dinner helped Mama ice cake, then went with Rosa up town to get china toys to put in bride's cake.

Heard the sad news that Fort Donaldson was taken Sunday. Our men defended it bravely for five days but the Yankees had fresh reinforcements and became victors at last. The telegraph brought news too that Nashville, Tennessee, had capitulated to the Yankees. In that case they are not so far from our railroad and may get here very soon. This made us very gloomy and we felt little like fixing for a wedding. Perhaps we are only baking cake for the Yankees after all.

We sat in Mama's room till bedtime, making plans in case the enemy should reach us and take our homes. It is too sad to think about and we just put our trust in God and hope and pray for victory. The mail brought a letter from Papa and a note from Lizzie (Mosby).

WEDNESDAY, FEBRUARY 19, 1862

Telegraph from Papa to tell us the news not so bad as at first supposed from the West. General Floyd was not killed, not many of our men were killed, our generals have fallen back to Nashville where they will make a stand and fight. There will be a desperate fight!!

French vessels are reported at Norfolk. Wonder if they will bring news that our independence is recognized by France and England. I hope so. Very busy all day doing a little of everything.

SATURDAY, FEBRUARY 22, 1862

A dreadful day. The day, too, for the inauguration of our first president. But I do not feel as if this was any time for us to be having a celebration of any kind till we are certain we have conquered the Yankees. Papa came from Lynchburg looking better and much pleased with his visit. He brought letters from Mr. Mosby's. I directed and sent out the last invitations for Fan's wedding.

SUNDAY, FEBRUARY 23, 1862

It is terribly muddy. Papa, Rosa, and I went to church. Mr. Wharton preached a fine sermon from the text "I know in whom I have believed and that He is able to keep that which I have committed unto Him against that day." Mr. Wharton also made some very earnest and appropriate remarks about the war. He said our recent defeats, Roanoke Island and Fort Donaldson, were because our men since the great victory at Manassas had ceased to put their trust in God and were trusting in man and their own powers. We ought therefore to pray now. The president has appointed next Friday to be a day of humiliation, prayer, and fasting throughout the southern Confederacy.

MONDAY, FEBRUARY 24, & TUESDAY, FEBRUARY 25, 1862

Busy helping Fan fix her room. It is too windy to walk much. Mr. Davis and Mr. Berry came down and spent the evening with Papa who was quite fatigued from making a speech on the war to the country people at the courthouse.

A beautiful day Tuesday. Attended to greenhouse flowers, sewed, practiced and walked. Made miniature Confederate flags to stick in the wedding cake for ornaments as we can neither get candies nor flowers enough.

Received a note from Mrs. Donald saying she would not be able to come to the wedding. She is in great distress because her favorite nephew, Midshipman Camm, lost an arm in the engagement at Roanoke Island, and two other nephews are lying ill at Nashville.

WEDNESDAY, FEBRUARY 26, 1862

It is dark and rainy today and I could not go out of the house. Learned some songs, read Papa's story, "Exile and Empire," all that has come out. Received letters from 'over the mountain.' Mrs. Breckenridge is not coming, the Johnstons are not coming. Perhaps Alice Morris will come. Expect we will have a very quiet wedding. A telegraphic dispatch from Capt. Bowyer summoning his men who are at home on furlough to come immediately back to Manassas. Wonder why? It is too muddy now everybody says for the Yankees to advance upon Manassas.

SUNDAY, MARCH 2, 1862

Such a bad day I could not go to church. Heard Alice and Ellen say their lesson, read and took a short walk on the tanbark road.

MONDAY, MARCH 3, 1862

Very busy dressing cakes and fixing things to put on the table for the wedding. Had several letters from persons invited regretting their inability to come to the wedding. The dreadful roads, the recent landslide on the railroad and the war will prevent almost everybody from coming. I am very sorry for we have arranged everything so nicely. It is a pity the few persons we have invited cannot come. Still the train tomorrow will bring some of our friends from Botetourt and Roanoke. But the irregularity of the mails makes it probable that the invitations have not gone straight. Even the Breckenridge girls who are in Richmond have not been heard from and I expect they have not received our letters telling them what day the wedding would be. One consolation, however, Jimmie came today. Better no company with the groom than a large company and no groom. He came after tea from the hotel and spent the evening with Fan.

TUESDAY, MARCH 4, 1862

The eventful day of the wedding actually arrived! There is great disappointment… no train down (eastward). Jimmie Preston and Willie Beale, two of the groomsmen, could not get here. Leslie Mosby and Captain Harris came up, the only groomsmen who could come.

The hour, too, at length arrived for the bride to put on her veil and her white silk and tulle dress, and a most beautiful bride she was. The house was very brightly lighted, large fires everywhere, beautiful flowers in vases setting about which looked particularly lovely at this season when there are none blooming in the yard.

The ceremony was performed at nine o'clock[3]. Everybody in the room looked bright and happy, and the doors each side of the room presented a tableau of black faces crowding around to see the bride and the ceremony. And I think the

---

[3] Bedford County Marriage Book 1, Page 66, shows the marriage of Mary Frances Burwell, age 24, to James Breckenridge, age 23 of Botetourt County on March 4, 1862. James was the son of Cary and Emma Breckenridge.

servants enjoyed the ceremony and the whole occasion, the abundance of cake and good things more than the white family. The supper table was beautiful and everybody seemed to enjoy the whole thing immensely, especially Uncle Robert Mitchell who never had room at a party before so as he could sit in a chair and enjoy his supper.

Rosa with Ellen and Nannie Davis were the solitary bridesmaids as Eliza Breckenridge and Rosa Tayloe were disappointed in [not] getting here. The bridesmaids on hand however were very bright and pretty in their white muslin and gay flowers.

Altogether the evening passed very brightly and we came to the conclusion that a small company was more agreeable than a large one. Still, I could not help regretting that everybody we invited could not have gotten here to see how pretty Fan looked, how lovely a bride she was and what a bright little evening we had. The company left at two o'clock. I did not get to bed before three.

WEDNESDAY, MARCH 5, 1862

This is Ash Wednesday, but no service at our church because of Mrs. Graves' funeral.

Leslie Mosby and Captain Harris came out after breakfast and took leave of us. I did not feel well and went to my room and lay down. Uncle Tom Mitchell and Uncle Robert and Miss Maupin left after breakfast. The train brought down Jimmie Preston and Willie Beale who were both in a high state of wrath at the irregularity of the trains, which prevented their getting to the wedding. Jimmie Preston said he had been waiting at the Christiansburg station four days. He was so disappointed. Jimmie's sister, Jinny Means, came too. She is so lovely and beautiful! I enjoyed seeing her so much.

THURSDAY, MARCH 6, 1862

Fan and her Jimmie, Jinny Means and Jimmie Preston all went off in the train directly after breakfast. We were left quite sad and alone. It snowed and the day was quite gloomy, besides Mama, Sister, Rosa and I talked over the wedding. Sent out hundreds of plates of cakes around the neighborhood. Read the newspapers about our defeat at Fort Donaldson, surrender of Nashville, and the good news of our gallant little ship, the *Nashville*, coming from England and escaping from the Yankee *Man of War* which was chasing her and landing at Beaufort, North Carolina, with a large supply of ammunition and other things for our Confederacy.

FRIDAY, MARCH 7, 1862

Went to the stores directly after breakfast to buy some things for Cousin Mary Mosby and Cousin Fanny Rodes. Made pin cushions and walked an hour on the tanbark in the afternoon. Had a very kind, pleasant letter from Charlie Griffin. He is stationed at Craney Island and thinks there will be a fight there before long.

SATURDAY, MARCH 8, 1862

Wrote to Fan and Alice Morris. Read newspapers and walked in the afternoon. After supper William Matthews, a Tennesseean, came to see us. He is on his way home and had a very bad cough. He is in great distress about his father and sisters as the Yankees have possession of all the country around, and his home is not very far from Nashville. I hope his father and sisters are not interrupted. William is a very handsome young man, a brave soldier and a pious Christian. A most remarkable young man to have been a whole year in camp with reckless associates and yet never drank a drop of spirits, read the Bible, and lived the life of a Christian.

SUNDAY, MARCH 9, 1862

Went to church and heard Mr. Wharton whose subject was our trust in God. This is certainly a time when our whole trust should be in Him and our prayers for His help should be unceasing. William Matthews took leave of us after dinner and went off in the train to Tennessee. I trust he may find his father and his sisters undisturbed by the Yankees. After I heard Alice and Ellen's lesson, Major Roemer came. It is strange that he who left his own country, Hungary, a few years ago to find a peaceful haven here should now be in the very vortex of war again and commanding a regiment of strangers in a foreign country. He is a brave and intelligent man.

Rumor of a victory in Missouri by Price and McCullough. I hope it is true. The report is that we have killed a thousand and captured seven thousand of the enemy, but I am afraid this news is too good to be true.

MONDAY, MARCH 10, 1862

Got ready to go to church to attend the funeral service of Colonel Edmond Goode[4] but it rained just before the bell rang and I did not go. The afternoon was beautiful and I walked more than an hour. Wrote to Mrs. Gilliam and also to Doctor.

TUESDAY, MARCH 11, 1862

Went on the street soon after breakfast to make some purchases at the stores. The village is very full of militia just ordered out to take their part in the war. They were a poor, discontented looking set, and I could not help feeling sorry for them. The meanest men among us are the merchants who make the poor soldiers, who are going to fight for them, pay double prices for the clothing they are obliged to have. These merchants are our worst enemies and should be dealt with accordingly. It was a sad picture today to see the poor half-clothed soldiers on one side of the counter and the comfort-

---

[4] Col. Edmond Goode was the oldest brother of John Goode. He graduated from VMI in 1846 and was adjutant to the 28th Virginia Regiment. He saw action at the Battle of Manassas. In 1861 he was appointed Col. of the 58th Virginia Regiment. He remained in camp in the mountains west of Staunton during the winter and contracted the disease from which he died in March of 1862. (Goode, 1906, 14)

able well-clad merchants on the other side, demanding such incredible prices for the commonest clothing, which the poor soldiers wanted. The poor soldiers, too, going off to defend the merchant and his goods. What hearts some men must have.

Went to Mrs. Evans' bonnet store. Found her sister, the tailor's wife, weeping bitterly because the militia had been ordered out and her husband was obliged to do so. She said she did not care if we did get whipped so the war could end. In fact she was not only distressed but also appeared very mad about the war. Poor people, I am so sorry for them, it must be so hard on them, and then they have very little property at stake in the issue.

The evening train brought glorious news of a great victory at Norfolk in Hampton Roads, our first naval engagement. Only one large vessel and two small ones whipped out the whole Yankee fleet. Most remarkable!! Our vessel, the *Virginia*, on a new model came on her trial trip and made this brilliant war on the Yankee ships which were standing triumphantly around and soon succeeded in sinking two of the largest Yankee vessels, burning one and crippling others. Wonderful! We had great rejoicing over this news. There was great loss of life of Yankees on board the vessel which sank. Our men very gallantly sent boats to rescue some of the miserable, perishing Yankees as the ship was going down. The Yankees ran up a white flag, but while our men were under the flag helping the Yankees into boats, the Yankees at Newport News disregarded the flag and fired into their own men who were escaping the sinking vessel with the assistance of our brave officers. This fire from Newport News killed some of their own men and two of ours.

The papers state that Captain Jimmie Tayloe was severely wounded. He was one of our gallant men sent over in the boats to rescue some of the sinking Yankees. They ought all to have been left to sink to the bottom of the sea!

WEDNESDAY, MARCH 12, 1862

In the morning I went to Mr. Hoffman's store to buy a green veil. Copied for Papa a memorial to the Legislature and Senate of Virginia, petitioning that honorable body to establish some manufactories among us so that our poor people may have some honest employment and so we may be independent of Yankees, French, and all other nations when the war is over. Our utter dependence upon the Yankees is alarming. We are deprived of all the comforts and necessities of civilized life now that we no longer trade with them. It is high time Virginia was making up and producing her own fabrics. I hope the Memorial may do some good.

After dinner I went to see Mrs. Bramblett. Poor woman, her husband is a painter and can get no painting to do during the war. She showed me a very nice dress she had spun and woven for herself. The old spinning wheels and looms are in great demand now having been thrown aside many years as the Yankees manufactured and sent back the southern cotton in cloth cheaper than the indolent Southerners could make it for themselves. So the whole manufacturing world belonged to them and we have been content to fold our hands and let them make everything possible to send to us for the money rather than put ourselves to the trouble of introducing manufactories among ourselves. Well, we are an indolent people, no two ways about that when we know there is somebody working for us and making everything we want. What has been the use, then, of individual labor! Still, we can work when the pinch comes. But I like indolent people, not very indolent people, but people slightly inclined to indolence! They are the most social, easy to get along with people, good humored, forgiving, hospitable people in the world and it is always pleasant to be with such.

Went to see Cousin Betty Quarles, and when I got home I found the papers had come. Oh, so sad, poor Jimmie Tayloe's death was announced. He died of his wounds received under the Yankee flag of truce while he was helping to save the lives of some of the miserable Yankees from the sinking ship. How much better to have sunk every Yankee in the world than to have lost the life of such a man. Oh, it is too sad!! So young, so brave, so handsome, so generous, so warm hearted and affectionate! His poor sisters, how my heart bleeds for them! He, their pet and darling, sent to an untimely grave by a Yankee bullet. How sad! He had just been through the fight at Roanoke Island and had a narrow escape, his hat and clothes shot through, but he escaped uninjured, and he fought gallantly through the last battle, but to think he was not shot till after the engagement while performing a mission of mercy. I wept about him and dreamed it was a mistake but woke again this morning to the sad reality. None of us know what heartbreaking sorrows are in store for us before this dreadful war is ended. More of our time should be spent in prayer and communion with God, but we are such miserable sinners that our thoughts instead of being on serious things are always dwelling upon the subjects of frivolity and naiveté.

THURSDAY, MARCH 13, 1862

Went in the yard to plant some flowers, but my thoughts were with the girls, poor Jimmie's sisters, all day. What a sad day for them! I can but weep to think of them and of their gallant brother, their darling brother who is no more. This world is so full of sorrow, and this is one of the keenest afflictions which could befall us...a fresh young heart taken suddenly from our midst in the full enjoyment of all which surrounded it, never more to see the sunny smile which has always brightened our home circle, this is the deepest grief of which our poor hearts are susceptible. Rained in the evening and I could not walk.

FRIDAY, MARCH 14, SATURDAY, MARCH 15, & SUNDAY, MARCH 16, 1862

Friday I spent the day darning stockings and talking with Rosa about romances. Told over the old Bagby romance with

Sister. Walked on the lawn in the afternoon. After supper read newspapers. Read aloud General Floyd's report of the fight at Fort Donaldson, Tennessee. General Floyd is a brave man and a patriot whatever else they may say about him, and I do like him very much. He is handsome and agreeable. Wrote a letter to my new brother, Jimmie.

Saturday I intended to have gone to the courthouse to hear Papa's address to the volunteer companies, which are to go off today, but could not on account of the rain. I mended flannels and wrote to Nannie Tayloe. Poor Nannie, I do feel so sorry for her!

On Sunday I was at home all day and read. Heard class of Ellen and Alice, and walked in the afternoon. Papa talked a great deal after supper, as usual. It is very instructive to hear him talk. All the information I have derived from his conversation, rather lectures, for he does all the talking, which cannot come under the head of conversation.

MONDAY, MARCH 17, 1862

Attended to the flowers, and stayed some in Mama's room. Papa on the street all day talking with the militia and encouraging them about the war. The newspapers brought news of a great battle being fought between the Missouri and Arkansas line. General Price, McCullough, and McIntosh formed a junction and are supposed to be driving the Yankee army of thirty thousand before them south where they will be penned in and have to surrender. Our generals sent a courier to General Pike[5] telling him to meet them, but I don't

---

[5] A brigade including two regiments of Cherokee Indians and one of Creeks, were under the command of Brigadier General Albert Pike west of the Mississippi. These were among the army of 20,000 General Van Dorn had gathered to drive the Yankees out of Missouri. The battle was lost due to a poorly trained army. Pike's Indians attacked first and when they came under artillery fire were terrified and took to the woods. General Pike was an Arkansas lawyer with a knack for persuading the red man to embrace the doctrine of States Rights.

think from Walter's last letter his father was near enough to help them with his Indians.

When Papa came home he brought Dr. Chalmers with him. Rosa and I took a walk and then [went] in the parlor to help entertain Papa's company. He had other company, too, for us to entertain... a young man from Bowyer's Battery. I was very glad to get acquainted with Dr. Chalmers for the sake of our friendship for his poor brother. Had heard the Lynchburg girls talk a great deal about Dr. Chalmers. He is held in much admiration by them and very justly for he seems to be a very well educated, pleasant gentleman. He talks very well and is very handsome. Just the person I had imagined him to be! Rosa and I succeeded so well in making ourselves agreeable to Papa's company that when it was proposed to go to bed, Jordan, the butler, made his appearance to show them upstairs, they openly refused to retire. So we had to sit with them till nearly twelve o'clock. I had talked a great deal of nonsense during the evening. It is such a pity that I can always talk so much nonsense and am so very frivolous, but it is my nature and seems so hard to overcome. Still I pray that I may although I am continually repenting of some frivolous conversation.

TUESDAY, MARCH 18, 1862

Arose late and got to breakfast after the others had finished. Walked with Dr. Chalmers around the yard and got him a pretty bunch of flowers which he pressed as a souvenir. Seems to be quite fond of flowers and sentiment. Had Papa's other young man back to dinner. The train did not come, so Dr. Chalmers had to stay another night. It was very agreeable. Rosa and I sang for him a great quantity and he appeared to be quite reconciled to stay and got up quite a flirtation with Rosa in the end.

WEDNESDAY, MARCH 19, 1862

Papa left home this morning for Richmond and from there he expects to go to the camp. Planted some flowers before it began to rain. Could not walk today, so read and sewed on Aunt Clary's [servant] caps. Helped nurse the baby who was sick.

Newspapers announce the death of two generals, McCullough and McIntosh, but Price and Van Dorn are carrying on the fight. It is also stated that a great many of our officers were killed in the engagement. I am so anxious to hear the particulars as Ham Pike was McCullough's' aide, and I expect Ned Dillon (a cousin from Indian Rock) was in the fight too. What dreadful times are these! Every mail brings the tidings of the illness or death of some valued friend or dear member of our household band.

THURSDAY, MARCH 20 and FRIDAY, MARCH 21, 1862

Another rainy day, so I entertained myself with reading, practicing, and sewing. A letter came from Fan who expects to come home next week. Read aloud the story of "The Ivory Mine" in Chamber's *Miscellany*. Had supper handed in Ma's room, and went to bed at ten.

On Friday, I went out in the yard after breakfast. Later, took my sewing in Sister's room. Helped nurse the baby, walked and sang her to sleep. Annis Berry came in and sat till dinnertime. Sang over some songs. After dinner Eliza Bowyer made a visit which kept me from walking till quite late. Read newspapers to Mama.

Winchester has been evacuated by our troops and all that country given up to the enemy. The Yankees have burnt Mr. Mason's fine house and other houses and are committing other outrages on our people. This is a dark hour of our revolution, still I am hopeful. Our army of the Potomac has fallen back to the line of the Rappahannock. Brother Tom writes that the Division of the Army to which his battery is attached is ordered to Gordonsville to be the reserve corps, and to be ready to go to the first place attacked by the enemy. *The Whig* tonight contained a beautiful notice of poor Jimmie Tayloe. Whenever I think of him, I weep, for his death will always be a fresh sorrow.

SATURDAY, MARCH 29, 1862

No time to write in journal for the past week ... very busy having a bad cold. Fanny Allen and Jane Harvey came home with me from the Methodist church last Sunday, and stayed several days. I love them both so much and enjoyed so to have them here, and missed them sadly when they went away. Today I have been confined to my room with my cold. Spent the day darning stockings. I wrote a note to Fanny Allen.

Read in newspaper proceedings of the Ladies Meeting, styling themselves Ladies National Defense Society. The object being to get the money subscribed for building a gunboat for the defense of our shores. The Mobile Ladies are also building one of these ironclad vessels, and the Richmond, Lynchburg, and Williamsburg Ladies are organizing societies for the same purpose. If the ladies of the other towns and villages throughout the state will do the same we may succeed in getting the requisite $100,000 or $150,000.

SUNDAY, MARCH 30, 1862

Too sick to go out of my room all day. At night Mama and Sister insisted on sending for the doctor to look at my throat. I knew it was only common sore throat, but they would send for the doctor about eleven o'clock. He sat a half hour and talked but found nothing to do for me.

MONDAY, MARCH 31, 1862

Felt better and stayed in Mama's room. Papa expected me to go to the camp but no train.

TUESDAY, APRIL 1, 1862

Fan and Jimmie came home in the morning train, looking very well and intensely happy. Have never seen a young couple so overwhelmingly in love. It is beautiful. Papa took leave of us and went off in the evening train. After supper old Dr. Bowyer and Dr. James Bowyer came from Dr. Sale's and sat till bedtime.

WEDNESDAY, APRIL 2, & THURSDAY, APRIL 3, 1862

Mr. Bowyer dined with us on Wednesday, a damp, rainy day. I could not go out today. Jimmie went to Lynchburg in the evening train, and we were left by ourselves. I sat up till very late talking in Mama's room.

Had company all day on Thursday. Mr. and Mrs. Donald spent the day, and a good many ladies called on the bride. Mr. and Mrs. Donald are in distress about their two young nephews who have recently died of typhoid or camp fever. Oh! This dreadful war.

FRIDAY, APRIL 4, 1862

Jimmie came back this morning. A rumor of a fight near Winchester in which our troops under Stonewall Jackson have been victorious. The rumor remains to be confirmed.

William Matthews came in this evening on his way back to Tennessee again. He is a model soldier, and if all our soldiers were like him, full of prayer and trust in God, I should not doubt the success of our cause.

SATURDAY, APRIL 5, 1862

Our bride and groom, like all other brides and grooms, are very poor company for anybody but themselves. They stay in their room all the time, so we do not see much of them except at meals.

Sis, Nannie, and Cass Wingfield came to see Fan. The first time any of the family has been here for a long time. We are very glad to see them again.

SUNDAY, APRIL 6, 1862

I did not go to church. I did not think it is right for me to feel as I do about Mr. Sloat's preaching. But I do not like to hear him. He is a thorough Yankee and I have no admiration for his character. He is not kind to his hired servants, and he is just a real Yankee, which is saying everything against one. Still it is not right to encourage such a prejudice when we are obliged to hear such a man preach now and then.

Read and helped nurse the baby. Heard my little class and walked in the evening. I have felt very much depressed about the war, although I have no idea we will ever give up. Yet I fear the enemy will get the advantage of us before long and in all probability will occupy Richmond. What will we do up here then? They will have our whole line of railroad, but we must trust in God. His arm alone can save us and we must pray without ceasing, that He will strengthen the hearts and arms of our men and give us the victory over our enemies.

Sis Wingfield sent me some beautiful lines copied from some newspaper, written by Mrs. Jordan on the death of Jimmie Tayloe and his young friend and companion, Lieutenant Hutter, both killed in the naval engagement of the *Virginia*. It was a brilliant victory, but oh! I can never think of it without sorrow for poor, dear Jimmie.

CHAPTER VIII

Ladies' Hospital Association

MONDAY, APRIL 7, 1862

Dark, rainy, day! I sewed all day and made under sleeves. James Breckenridge went off to camp today.

I am so sorry for Fan. It was very sad to us all to see Jimmie go away. Still, we must pray that he may be spared through the battles and come back to us with his same bright face. Sister tried to cheer Fan, but it was a very dismal character of cheering for she is all the time distressed about Dr. Bowyer.

TUESDAY, APRIL 8, 1862

Another rainy day so I was in the house all day. Letters from Mr. Mosby's Lizzie, Cousin Mary, and Mr. Mosby, himself. Mr. Mosby sent me a new patriotic song written by Mrs. Jordan, a very good song, and I will try to arrange an air for it.

FRIDAY, APRIL 11, SATURDAY, APRIL 12, & SUNDAY, APRIL 13, 1862

On Friday, I went with Mama to call on Mrs. Pate who is sick. Worked in the yard and Nannie Davis came in the evening. So I could not walk.

On Saturday, Rosa and I went to see Emma Graves. Wrote several letters, read and sang for Mama after supper.

On Sunday, went to church. Mr. Wharton's sermon was on charity and kindness to one another. Met at church an old "springs" acquaintance, a Mr. Bowyer. Did not particularly care about remembering my acquaintance with him, but he waited at the door and came home with me. Mr. Wharton's sermon had the effect of making me more kind than I would have been, I expect. After all it is very selfish of us to be more pleasant to those whom we think interesting than to those who fail to entertain or interest us.

Saw at church a nice young man, a boy, who seemed to be such a good Episcopalian that I took a fancy to him. He was very handsome but looked very delicate. Mr. Bowyer told me his name was Caldwell and that his family is at our hotel having taken refuge here from the Yankees who are expected in their county of Greenbrier.

WEDNESDAY, APRIL 16, 1862

Preaching at our churches, it is Passion Week (Holy Week). Expected to hear of a great battle at Yorktown. Papa writes hopefully and thinks we will be victorious.

FRIDAY, APRIL 18, 1862

It is Good Friday and I went to church in the morning. Read and practiced some hymns in the afternoon. No news yet from Yorktown. Tried to walk but it rained, and I felt weak from fasting.

SATURDAY, APRIL 19, 1862

A letter from Mr. Mosby. He writes if we are victorious at Yorktown, a speedy peace will ensue, if not, the war is just begun and neither we nor our children will ever see the end. We have been in quite an excitement this week about Captain Bowyer's battery. By some deceit, cunning, and bribery, Dick Johnson had himself elected Captain, but we hear that Colonel Taylor says no man but Captain Bowyer shall command the battery in his brigade. So we don't know what the issue will be.

Assembled in Mama's room after supper and talked about what we will do if the Yankees are victorious at Yorktown. I think it will be best to destroy or conceal all valuables, and remain at home as I don't think anything can be worse than having no roof.

Had a headache but tried to work it off with my hoe. Just as we were fixing to go to call on Mrs. Caldwell, Sister received a dispatch from Dr. Bowyer telling her to take the afternoon train to Richmond where he would be a day or two on business. We all turned in and helped to fix her and the baby. Got them ready by the time the train came. Rosa and I went with them to the depot. When the train had gone, we went in the parlor and called on Mrs. Caldwell. Found her a very pleasant lady. Got acquainted with her nephew.

SUNDAY, APRIL 20, 1862

Easter Day and a shocking one! Could not go to church and had just prepared to spend the Sabbath in reading and teaching the servants when all my plans were interrupted by Mr. John Harvey come to spend the day. Had to sit up in Mama's room the whole day with him. He made himself very agreeable, but I felt very stupid. Very sorry for Mr. Harvey, his life seems to have been one long series of misfortunes.

MONDAY, APRIL 21, 1862

Another long weary day with Mr. Harvey in Mama's room. Tried to sew a little. Too wet to walk in the afternoon. Went to look after flowers in the greenhouse.

TUESDAY, APRIL 22, 1862

A letter from Papa advising us to prepare ourselves if worst came to worst and our army should be defeated at Yorktown and Richmond should be occupied by the Yankees. In that case marauding parties will be sent up on our railroad and our houses plundered, perhaps destroyed. We should try to preserve our silver and valuables. Took a walk in the afternoon on the lawn.

WEDNESDAY, APRIL 23, 1862

Sister came home quite unexpectedly this morning. She brings very discouraging news from Richmond. Congress has adjourned and the members gone home which I do not consider a brave proceeding by any means and one which is calculated to spread panic through the country. I do think Richmond will be taken. And what are we to do? Ah me, everything looks dark and hopeless today but we must trust in God.

THURSDAY, APRIL 24, & FRIDAY, APRIL 25, 1862

Too cold to work flowers. No fight yet below Richmond. This suspense is horrible. Next week we may have to leave our beautiful home and fly from the Yankees. But God's will be done; we must give ourselves unto His hands.

In the evening, young Mr. Caldwell called. Rosa entertained him. I walked down in the orchard. As soon as the weather is pleasant I want to plant some flowers around poor Maria's grave. How hard even now to realize that she is nevermore to be with us here, and how sadly do I miss her each day. After supper Rosa and I sang with the guitar for Mama.

SATURDAY, APRIL 26, 1862

Cut some beautiful flowers and sent them to Mrs. Caldwell. She said they made her feel better. Couldn't go out on account of the dampness, no sun all day. So much afraid Mr. Mosby cannot come tomorrow. I will be so disappointed if he does not.

Practiced some of my favorite songs. Wrote to Papa and had a letter from him today. He says Richmond is in better spirits. Heard they were going to establish some hospitals here and that five hundred sick soldiers are expected today.

Rain, rain, rain! They say we have so much rain because there is so much firing of cannon and fighting on the coast, and that it was so in the Crimean War and in our old Revolution. Uncle Robert Mitchell came and stayed all night with us. He is my beau-deal f a nice old gentleman, so true, so pleasant, so warm-hearted and affectionate.

I heard that Dr. John Jordan had been shot on the Peninsula; his remains are being brought up on the train. What a sad time is this! Any moment may bring us news that some dear friend or member of our home circle has been shot by the Yankees.

SUNDAY, APRIL 27, 1862

The sun shone out very brightly this morning, and Mr. Mosby was actually incited to come up at last. We were delighted to see him so unexpectedly before breakfast.

Went to church. Mr. Wharton preached a sermon on acquiescence to the will of God, and praying us to consider our present trials small. A great many refugees at church driven from their homes in eastern Virginia by the Yankees. I do feel for them!

Dr. Blackford, one of the surgeons, came home with us, also Mr. Speed, who is attending court here. So we had quite a dinner party. I do hate to have company on Sunday, but it so happens that we do have a great deal and I always feel as if I had passed the day so unprofitably, having indulged in so much idle and vain conversation.

MONDAY, APRIL 28, 1862

We have heard that New Orleans is occupied by the enemy. What a blow to our cause. Still we must not despair. Our army has not surrendered at New Orleans, only fallen back eighty miles from the city so if the Yankees attempt a further invasion we can give them a good whipping.

Mr. Mosby stayed with us all day. How happy I am to have him up here once more, and how sincerely I love and admire him.

Mrs. Caldwell and young Mr. Caldwell called in the afternoon. Uncle William Steptoe came out from the courthouse and stayed till the evening train came. After supper Dr. Blackford came over and brought three young surgeons to spend the evening, a Dr. Eves, a Dr. Todd, and a Dr. Letcher.

They made themselves quite pleasant. Dr. Eves played on the piano and sang for us. We thought of introducing Fan as a young lady but Sister persuaded us not to do so. It would have been very funny.

TUESDAY, APRIL 29, 1862

Felt quite stupid from having been up so late last night. Worked the flowerbeds before dinner. Took a nap, read Dickens, and walked a little after dinner.

WEDNESDAY, APRIL 30, 1862

A close rainy day except for an hour or two directly after breakfast when I was attending my flowers. Practiced, read Dickens, and nursed the baby. After supper I sang with Rosa for Mama till bedtime. Learned "My Maryland" from Dr. Eves. It is a very plaintive song and has a beautiful chorus.

THURSDAY, MAY 1, 1862

Like almost every other May Day that I can remember, this is a sad, dark, cold day. How many early May Day disappointments did my young heart bear? Many a white muslin was prepared for me in my school days to wear the first of May, but alas, how very few May Days admitted of white muslin array, always doomed to disappointment. May Day seemed always the coldest day of spring just because we had so long anticipated a bright warm day and prepared so many nice white muslins for our festivities. Such a clatter there had been too for a month about who should be Queen, how many Maids of Honor, and who should be elected. Then a great row and jabbering and an election, the prettiest girls all selected for the Queen's train. Then arose the mighty question wherewithal are the refreshments to be procured. Then the mandate: each girl must bring fifty cents or a dollar. Next morning would bring each girl with an identical fifty cents or a dollar tied in the end of her pocket-handkerchief or deposited in some safe or mysterious place. Thereupon followed immediately that most momentous and gigantic question "What am I going to wear?" This question involved much thought by night and by day, much imploring of Mama to purchase new ribbons and muslin, much resistance on the part of Mama at first with a final giving way to unceasing entreaties, and in the end a liberal outfit of bows, laces, and muslins. Then arises that profound question, will Madam, the Proprietress, allow gentlemen to be invited? Madam becomes immediately positive on this subject. No young gentlemen to be invited, no persons save the immediate families and relatives of the young ladies. By this means the invitations are of course extended to every single young man in town, for, of course each one of them is brother, cousin, or uncle to one of the girls and is thereby included in the immediate family or relative invitation. Thus a most intense excitement prevails all round in the school and out of the school. Every day a new question is loudly discussed, ... shall we have dancing?

Most of the girls incline to have dancing, but their various mamass are against it. So, after vociferous discussion, whether there shall be dancing the whole thing ends in a great deal of dancing, if the party finally comes off. A final excitement comes on about who shall write the speeches for the Queen and the First Maid of Honor. The nicest young lawyer is pitched upon for that distinguished part which he performs with more grace and beauty and sends in by the girl who happens to be his nearest relative in the school. Thus passes the whole month of April in intense excitement and busy preparations. And sometimes the girls have been known to sit up half the night before to see whether it would rain.

At last the day arrives, the eventful day for which there have been so many plans and about which so many, many dreams, daydreams and night dreams, and alas, alas, alas, the day is dark and cloudy. The rain, the cold rain falls upon many a bright hope. The real disappointments in after life are never more chilling than that early May Day disappointment.

Oh! I could write chapters on May Days! I remember them although so many years have intervened, so many years of grown up pleasures and stern sorrows. Yet each May Day of my childhood is vividly impressed and right before me now.

The first I remember so well, in a white dress trimmed with scotch-broom flowers. Grandma sewed them on, up and down and in wreaths around. Then they all came up before me one after the other. The happy young faces around me too I see at this moment, some in bright pink bows, some in blue with hair braided, some in curls, all happy and laughing, a gay and careless band. Oh! Where are they all now, those bright faces that are bright before me now as I look back? Alas, alas evanescent as the flowers then around them, their brightness soon faded. Some were early laid among the dead. Some whose brightness faded 'mid the cares of life hardly remember the fleet winged joys of those fair days. All, all are scattered and the dear delights of those early May Days lost forever, lost. 'Tis sad to remember them now. What a curious world that the memory that once made us so happy should bring so much that is sad.

FRIDAY, MAY 2, 1862

Felt very sad about the war and more like giving up our cause as lost than ever before. It seems so utterly hopeless for us to attempt to hold Richmond, and when the Yankees get possession of that city it would seem that our cause was about gone. Ah me, what a sad thought! Yet it will certainly be so. I feel that the enemy will occupy Richmond in a short time, and then what is to become of us and our poor Confederacy? Still, we must keep on praying that God in His mercy may avert such a calamity and if it be His will that we shall not get the victory over our enemies, we must pray Him to prepare our hearts and guide us in the way we should go.

MONDAY, MAY 5, 1862

Very busy all the morning setting out verbenas in the yard. It rained all the evening so I could not go out. I kept up my spirits by reading Dickens.

TUESDAY, MAY 6, 1862

Arose at half past five. Heard Ellen's lesson as usual while combing my hair. Did not finish reading before breakfast. Had note from Lizzie Mosby. William intended to come up today. So sorry he did not. Wrote to Alice Morris and read the newspaper which said our troops are vacating Norfolk. How sad, sad this is! We must trust in God who alone can give us the victory. Our president has appointed next Friday week as a day of fasting and prayer throughout the South.

SUNDAY, MAY 11, 1862

Went to church and Mr. Wharton preached a very fine sermon. In attendance was a large congregation including many refugees. In the afternoon Rosa and I went again to our church to see a servant man of Dr. Sale's baptized. Mr. Wharton made such plain and improving remarks which all the colored people could easily understand, and they seemed to be very much interested.

Dr. Eves came home with Rosa and sat some time. He thinks the ladies visit the hospital too much. He says there were no less than fifty there today. Our poor sex, they will go everywhere! A few might do some good, but so many must be very troublesome to the sick as well as to the surgeons.

We heard that William Wright was mortally wounded at the Williamsburg battle, which was fought Friday. His father has gone off to see about him, but Williamsburg is in the possession of the enemy and he will not be able to go through. Our surgeons have gone in under a flag of truce.

MONDAY, MAY 12, 1862

A grand meeting of the ladies at the courthouse for the purpose of organizing a sort of society for attending the hospital. I was elected secretary, Mrs. Sale, president, and Mrs. Leftwich, vice president.

Like all other ladies' meetings, which always appeared to be ridiculous, we got very little done. The town divided into wards and a hospital was assigned to each ward. Dr. Blackford was there and conducted himself with admirable propriety among so many ladies. He made very few suggestions and agreed with the ladies about everything! However, he told me privately that he did not agree with them and that all their excitement about cooking for the sick soldiers was entirely unnecessary as he could easily command a cook for that purpose, and have everything prepared at one place. However, the ladies must have some excitement and they flatter themselves that they do an immense amount of good when they do none. Dr. Blackford came home with me from this remarkable meeting and stayed till dinner. After dinner I went to Mrs. Goode's. She made my lace into a fashionable collar.

I made several visits on the subject of the Ladies' Hospital Association and concluded the ladies had undertaken rather too much to pledge themselves to furnish the sick at the hospital with food daily when it is in the power of the surgeons and the government who could do it with so much more regularity and certainty. But, of course, I have nothing to say about it, and everybody would think me especially heathenish to express such an opinion.

TUESDAY, MAY 13, & WEDNESDAY, MAY 14, 1862

On Tuesday I went to Mrs. Sale's and wrote circulars for the Ladies' Hospital Association to be sent in the country. Mama furnished meals for all the sick at Reese's hospital today. Was busy all day.

On Wednesday it rained nearly all day. Set out some flowers between the showers. Read newspapers and felt much excited about the war, and the humiliating fall of New Orleans but pray it will be a very short time occupied by the enemy. The evacuation of Norfolk is sad too. And the necessary burning of our gallant ship of war, *The Merrimac*, all looks disheartening. But it was necessary our troops should be concentrated and now we are all ready for a big fight eighteen miles from Richmond. The Yankees are advancing and now is to be the desperate struggle. Oh, how I dread to hear from it! I pray we may be victorious, but what a long list of killed and wounded must follow.

CHAPTER IX

"So Much Excitement"

WEDNESDAY, JUNE 11, 1862

Almost a month since I wrote in my journal, a month of anxiety and excitement about the war. Good deal of company and much time devoted to procuring from the country and giving buttermilk and cornbread to the convalescent soldiers who throng our yard. Poor things, they are far from their homes and are ignorant and poor. We do all we can for them. Mama spends a good part of her time making and filling haversacks for those who are well enough to return to their regiments.

The great battle at Richmond has not come off yet, but the Yankees have been so far repulsed although we have lost some gallant young men, among them Lawrence Meem and Charlie Terry, Lizzie Mosby's brother. Poor Lizzie, what a sad time it has been for her. Mr. Mosby has been to see us and so has William.

Mr. Henderson also came up last week, with his old gallantry. The train was delayed a day and night last week and our friends stayed with us. Those passengers who stayed with us were Mollie Gwathmey, old Colonel Tayloe her uncle, Gilmer Breckenridge and Mr. Radford. Poor Gilmer was on his way to his brother John who was wounded. The telegraph said "not dangerously," but when Gilmer reached Lynchburg he met the remains of poor John being carried home. What an awful time this is!!

Mollie Gwathmey, too, was on her way to Richmond to see her brother, George Tayloe, who was also wounded at the battle near Richmond.

The surgeons have been out to eat strawberries during the season, and Ellen Davis and I have been out riding every evening on our ponies. And thus has one whole month nearly passed by.

Now we are in great excitement about the news of the battles in the Valley of Virginia. Jackson and Jewell's commands have been achieving brilliant victories over the enemy. Our brothers-in-law are in Ewell's division and we are anxious to hear the particulars of the last engagement. Oh, I pray that the lives of our dear ones have been spared.

The day before yesterday, Walter Pike[1] came. We were all so delighted to see him again, but he had so altered we would never have recognized in him our old mischievous, noisy Walter. Very tall, handsome, quiet, and dignified, strange words these to be applied to our old Walter. Who would have believed even he could be dignified and quiet. Yet, so it is!

FRIDAY, JUNE 13, 1862

Friday morning we were very much surprised by the arrival of Col. Preston, Jinny Means, and little Preston. Papa came home very unexpectedly. It is delightful to hear him and Col. Preston talking over their adventures and experiences of the Campaign. They have stood the hardships and fatigues remarkably well. I should have thought the exposure would have laid them both up.

SATURDAY, JUNE 14, 1862

Today, Dr. Eves came to take leave of us. He had passed many eventful evenings with us, but now had received orders to take charge of a hospital in Danville. We were very sorry to take leave of him as we were getting to feel like old friends.

---

[1] Walter Pike and Hamilton Pike were sons of General Alfred Pike. These boys appeared to be frequent visitors at Avenel.

SUNDAY, JUNE 15, 1862

Did not go to hear the Yankee preacher at the Presbyterian Church. Col. Preston said he could not go to hear a Yankee.

TUESDAY, JUNE 17, 1862

Took a walk directly after breakfast with Jinny Means to call on Mrs. Goode. Long walk with Rosa in the afternoon. Sang for Jinny Means after supper. Two common soldiers came to get some supper. One was very tidy looking and struck us as being like Jimmie Breckenridge.

Alas, it seems I have very little time to write in my journal nowadays. There is so much excitement, so much company, so much sitting up at night, so much sleeping to be done in the mornings, so much dressing and undressing and staying in the parlor that there is very little time for anything else.

WEDNESDAY, JUNE 18, 1862

Arose very early and went with Jinny Means to the depot. She went up to see Lulie[2]. We missed her and little Preston very much. Took a walk in the rain in the afternoon. Heard Bowyer's Battery had distinguished itself in the last engagement under Jackson. Captain Bowyer and his men fought desperately and captured a Yankee battery twice, whereupon General Jackson complimented Captain Bowyer and said those guns should not be considered Confederate property but belong to the men who had won them and be carried home by them as private trophies.

THURSDAY, JUNE 19, 1862

Worked in the yard after breakfast until 12 o'clock. Went to see Doctor who is sick and read some chapters and hymns

---

[2]Lulie was Dr. Bowyer's sister who married three times, Dr. Samuel Meredith, Mr. Douglas, and Mr. Holiday, perhaps not in this order.

to him. Got ready to go to Uncle Robert Mitchell's. Sister, Rosa, and the baby went in the carriage and I on the pony. Had a delightful ride and a charming visit. Uncle Robert, Aunt Lucy, the girls, and Fred, all very agreeable. I got home about sunset. Played songs for Mama and Papa after supper and retired at eleven o'clock.

FRIDAY, JUNE 20, 1862

Worked flowers for an hour after breakfast, and then read to Doctor. I copied a song for Papa, "Old Salabartz" to be published. Wrote to Robert and fixed velvet basque[3] to ride in. Went to choir meeting in the afternoon. Mrs. Belle's children sick so she could not come, so there was no singing.

Mrs. Sale sent me word to come to her house to a meeting of the Ladies' Hospital Association. I went and found that the ladies talked as usual and did nothing. I sent for Dr. Blackford to talk to him about getting clothes for sick soldiers. Dr. Blackford came home with me and stayed all afternoon.

SATURDAY, JUNE 21, 1862

We were agreeably surprised by the arrival of Captain Bowyer before breakfast. He says the Yankee's guns he took are splendid. He looks well and in fine spirits. After breakfast I took a walk in the grove and then went to see Doctor and read to him. After dinner we had a visitor, a Mr. William Bowyer, who kept me in the house all afternoon. A wholly uninteresting creature!! Mama was quite sick in bed all day.

After supper, Colonel Mallory and son and an old Mr. Fisher came to tea. I, being housekeeper pro tem, had a great excitement fixing up another supper for them. I bestowed particular attention upon the tea, whereupon all the company chose coffee, which was hurriedly gotten up. If the coffee had been good and the tea unbearable, everybody would have chosen tea! Ah, me, such is life.

---

[3] A basque is a woman's blouse with a tight fitting waist.

After tea Nannie Davis and Dr. Christian[4] came over and spent the evening. Made themselves very agreeable. Like Dr. Christian very much. Hope Nannie will marry him. Retired about twelve o'clock.

SUNDAY, JUNE 22, 1862

Did not get up very early. Just before the second church bell rang, Mrs. Bell sent me word she could not come to church and I must play the organ. Wish she had sent me word sooner that I might have practiced something. As it was, I had to make up everything as I went along, and to add to my embarrassment, Dr. Blackford brought his German friend, Mr. Kroutner, a beautiful performer, to church and told us after preaching he would bring Mr. Kroutner out after dinner and we would have some sacred music. So after dinner they came, Dr. Christian with them. Mr. Kroutner took his seat at the piano after they had been here half an hour. As we expected to play some sacred music, to our surprise he struck up "Thalberg's Home," and continued to play several pieces, which I did not care to hear on Sunday. He said he didn't know any hymns or sacred pieces.

Old Mr. Bowyer came in the evening train. Hardly had time to hear Ellen and Alice.

MONDAY, JUNE 23, 1862

Directly after breakfast went to read to Doctor. Company all the morning, company in the porch, company in the passages, company in the parlor, company everywhere. Mr. —— called to see me. A very frisky widower. Don't know him very well.

---

[4]Until 1861 Dr. Marcellus Christian was a surgeon in the U.S. Navy. When the war broke out he offered his services to the state. After the war he settled in Lynchburg, continued his medical profession and soon won the esteem of all as a just, honorable and generous man. Dr. Christian died of pneumonia in 1879. He married Nannie Davis in 1867. She died in 1873, only six years after their marriage. (Christian, 1900, 327)

TUESDAY, JUNE 24, 1862

Company all the morning. In the afternoon I escorted Mrs. Smith and family out to see the fine prospect from Otey's Mountain Road. I rode the pony and took the carriage for the Smiths. They seemed highly pleased with the ride and the view and I was very glad I had the means of gratifying them so much.

Mr. Tom Davis and Mr. John Davis came to spend the evening, but I was feeling so sick I could not talk. So they went away at eleven o'clock. I was suddenly very sick at the stomach. I could not account for it. Went to bed in great haste and had to say my prayers very hastily.

WEDNESDAY, JUNE 25, 1862

Felt very badly all day. Sewed and practiced a little. In the afternoon took a ride on the pony with Ellen and Mr. Tom Davis, a charming ride, which refreshed me very much. Got home about dark.

Found a house full of company, Louisianans, to supper. Brother Tom's friends, and Brother Tom himself, whom I had taken leave of just before riding, are back with us again. He had met three officers unexpectedly at the depot and they persuaded him to stay a day or two longer as they said that Taylor's Brigade, to which they belonged, had suffered so much from fatigue and loss in the last battles under Jackson in the Valley, it would be impossible for them to go into another fight until the men had time to rest. These officers appeared very fond of music, so we gave them a large dose, played and sang tremendously, and they expressed themselves highly delighted.

Captain Clark[5], from New Orleans, is an exceedingly nice, pleasant gentleman. And very smart, but I have had to cultivate the acquaintance of so many new gentlemen

---

[5] Information from the Diary of Lucy Breckenridge of Grove Hill, Botetourt County, says Lettie later became engaged to Captain Clark.

since the war began that I hardly think much about them or know what I do think of them. Knowing them such a short time makes it not very interesting to study their characters particularly.

THURSDAY, JUNE 26, 1862

After breakfast, Rosa and I took a dreadful walk to Cousin Betty Quarles'. I had promised Mrs. Smith to inquire if Cousin Betty would take some refuge boarders. Quite sick after I came home, lay down almost all day. Took some medicine and felt better about sunset. Dressed and went in the parlor to help entertain a crowd of gentlemen who came to spend the evening. These included Dr. Todd, Dr. Moses, Dr. Robinson, Captain Clark and an Alabama soldier. Dr. Todd played the violin for us and surprised everybody by performing beautifully. About eleven o'clock we all concluded to go over and serenade the Davises. Sister and Rosa went with their guitars and Dr. Todd[6] with his violin.

FRIDAY, JUNE 27, 1862

Did not feel very well so did not get up till late. After breakfast Captain Clark and Dr. Robinson came out to take leave of us. They heard this morning that Taylor's Brigade was in the fight at Richmond, yesterday and today. So they with Brother Tom are in great distress at being absent from the field, and are going off this evening hoping to reach there in time for the fighting. But I doubt if they will. It is very sad to know they are going right into a fight.

---

[6] It is evident that Dr. Todd was a frequent visitor at Avenel and although Lettie does not allude to it in her journal, a romance between Rosa and Dr. Todd was beginning to blossom. They were married on February 15, 1865, in Liberty. (Bedford County Marriage Book 1, Page 67, shows the marriage of Rosa, age 19, to Dr. Charles H. Todd of New Orleans, Louisiana.) He was born in Shelby County, Kentucky, and this couple lived out their lives after the war in Kentucky.

SUNDAY, JUNE 29, 1862

Had to play the organ again today. Mr. Wharton preached a sermon on scandal and talking about our neighbors.

I thought all day about the battle at Richmond. We returned thanks to God at church for His merciful goodness in giving us the victory so far, and earnestly prayed that He might continue to give strength and courage to the hearts and arms of our men till our enemies shall be scattered and driven from our shores. I had a prayer in my heart all day for our dear brothers and friends whom we knew to be engaged in the fierce battle today. How I pray they may be spared and return to us once more. Oh! What a terrible time is this!

MONDAY, JUNE 30, 1862

A telegram giving us news of continued victory. Yesterday a desperate battle was fought. Jackson's forces were engaged. Could hear nothing about the killed and wounded. What agony many hearts are enduring throughout the South. Every moment expecting news of some dear one having fallen in the battle.

Heard that Colonel James Allen was killed, shot through the head, in Friday's fight below Richmond, and brought into the city and interred on Sunday. What a shock to his poor family and to his wife. So sad, so sad.

TUESDAY, JULY 1, 1862

Jane Harvey came in for Mag. She still hoped to hear that the news of Colonel Allen's death had been a mistake. Alas, it was not.

After dinner I rode out as far as the Donald's creek (Little Otter) on the pony. Edward Mallory, a refugee boy, rode with me.

After supper Drs. Todd and Letcher came over and stayed till after twelve. Dr. Todd played for us again on the violin. Dr. Letcher was very agreeable.

Still no news from Brother Tom. Sister is miserable. A message from Mr. William Gilmer saying the Breckenridges, James and Cary, were safe after Friday and Sunday's engagements.

Mr. Harvey came in the evening just from Richmond, but could give us no more news than we had from the telegraph and newspapers.

WEDNESDAY, JULY 2, 1862

Sewed on dress again today and finished it. Read, walked and did not feel very well, so anxious about the battle. After supper Dr. Blackford and Dr. Moses came to spend the evening. They brought us the latest telegraph news that our army is still victorious. We rejoice greatly, but still the list of our killed and wounded has not reached us yet. And there is sorrow merged with joy, for who knows what the next telegram may bring? Still, we hope and pray and pray and hope.

FRIDAY, JULY 4, 1862

Went to inquire after Mrs. Goode in the morning. Called to return Emma Graves' music. She lent me more, but I did not feel like playing till we hear whether or not our brothers have survived the fighting which seems to continue every day. They have been fighting a week, our forces getting the advantage each day and renewing the attack every morning. Jackson's Division is farthest from Richmond, and it is impossible for us to hear from them or for them to communicate with the city. They are in such close pursuit of and contact with the enemy. This suspense is dreadful. Each day we hope to hear, but day after day passes without any news from Ewell's Division or Taylor's Brigade. Still we hope and pray.

SATURDAY, JULY 5, 1862

No news from Brother Tom. If he had been killed, I think the news would have been brought to Richmond, so we hope he is yet safe.

Walked out in the grove directly after breakfast, with Sister, the baby, Alice, and Caroline.[7] Got some sourwood blooms. Had verbenas moved in the sun. Made silk tobacco bag for Captain Clark. Prayed all the time I was making it that he had not been and would not be killed in the battles, though we have not a word from him either since he took leave of us to join his command on the battlefield. Walked in the orchard in the evening. Felt sick and retired early.

SUNDAY, JULY 6, 1862

No news yet from Taylor's Brigade. We are very anxious to hear something from it, but it seems impossible. No hard fight has been reported since Tuesday. Our army still has the advantage, but the Yankees have not surrendered. I pray we may continue to be victorious and that our dear ones may be spared and restored to us.

Did not go to church. Do not like to hear a Yankee Presbyterian preach and never go to hear him. Read and prayed during the day. Read sermon to Mama. Heard Ellen and Alice's lessons. A short walk in the afternoon.

MONDAY, JULY 7, 1862

Telegraph says Yankees are being reinforced as well as our army, and a terrible fight is expected today fifteen miles below Richmond.[8] Another day of anguish and prayer for the safety of our brothers and friends, and the success of our cause.

Helped Papa fix his sea-grass hammock, which Mr. Mason gave him.

---

[7] Alice and Caroline are servants.
[8] This was probably the Battle of Gaines Mill, now part of the Richmond National Battlefield Park, southeast of Richmond near State Route 156. Lee suffered 9,000 casualties and the Northern Army lost 6,800 men. This was the first major victory of Lee's career. (*Civil War Battlefield Guide*, 1990, 65)

TUESDAY, JULY 8, 1862

Very warm today, could not walk. Rode out to Mr. Donald's with Papa late in the afternoon. After tea, Mr. Tom and Mr. John Davis came down and stayed till twelve o'clock. Slept in the library, as it was so hot in my own room.

WEDNESDAY, JULY 9, 1862

William Mosby came up to breakfast and spent the day with us. He is very sprightly and such good company; we all love him very much and always enjoy his visits.

Dr. Letcher sent me some New Orleans papers, General Butler, the horrid wretch, has taken the papers of New Orleans in his own hands and only allows publications favorable to his own cause, that of the Yankees of course. To think that our chief city is under Yankee rule! 'Tis too humiliating, and very little for the bravery and patriotism of its citizens.

After tea Dr. Todd and Dr. Moses came out and spent the evening. The moon was very bright and we sat in the porch. Sang with guitar accompaniment, strolled about the yard and enjoyed the moonlight and the fresh night air after the hot day.

We are so relieved to hear that brother Tom and James Breckenridge are safe after the terrible fighting at Richmond where we lost so many, many gallant men. The artillery was not much used so Brother Tom was not exposed.

THURSDAY, JULY 10, 1862

Read newspaper account of the battle at Richmond. Walked in the grove, it rained in the evening so did not have to water my flowers. Played game of chess with Papa after supper. Music on the piano with Papa on the violin. Read chapter to Mama and went to bed.

FRIDAY, JULY 11, 1862

Rained all morning so could not go out. Returned Dr. Letcher's New Orleans papers. Sent Dr. Moses a sheet of gilt-edged notepaper on which he could write to his sweetheart. Read Dickens. Had a great many soldiers in the back porch to dinner, not at our table. Darned stockings.

Letter from Mrs. Gilliam. She writes from Richmond that a gentleman had just told her that Captain Bowyer was in the battles as aide to General Ewell, as his artillery was not engaged.

Judge Wingfield came to give Mama some money. He is just from Richmond and says he thinks there will not be any more fighting there for some time as both armies seem to be exhausted and must recruit. He gave us, too, a sad picture of the wounded who arrive from the battlefield and have no surgeons or nurses to attend them when they arrive at the Richmond depot.

Heard tonight of the death of Mrs. General Watts. How many hearts are saddened by her death. What a splendid woman she was and what a lovely Christian! How I will miss her form at Oaklands, I loved her so much and ever found in her a friend kind and true. I cannot bear to think of Oaklands without her. Oh! The sad, sad changes in life! How terrible they are! But they are intended to turn our hearts and minds from this weary world and remind us our portion is not here.

FRIDAY, AUGUST 15, 1862

More than a month since I have written in my journal. Company, company, company! Have just lived in the parlor this summer, company all the morning generally. A ride on the pony in the afternoons.

Some of the refugee boys or surgeons to escort me. Surgeons usually to spend the evenings. Return from my ride every evening, jerk off riding habit, dress in white muslin in desperate hurry and go in the parlor to entertain surgeons. Sometimes the refugee boys to spend the evenings. I like Mr. Smith's family so much, charmed with Miss Maggie. She has spent two evenings with us to serenade her, Dr. Todd with his violin and Rosa on the guitar.

Rosa, Willie Mitchell, and I went one night to spend the evening at Mr. Smith's. So we are in such a whirl of surgeons, and refugees that I have no time to chronicle the interesting events of the day.

Willie Mitchell, Rosa, and I made an ineffectual attempt to go to the Springs. Packed up and set off early one morning in the train. Arrived at Shawsville depot, three miles from the Springs and were informed by Mr. Booth, the proprietor, there was not a solitary cabin unoccupied. They are completely overrun. So we had to come home in the evening train, travel-worn, jaded, and disappointed.

We have had a visit from a very nice little Baltimorean, Mr. Patton, one of Gussie's (Mrs. Samuel Shoemaker, Sr.) friends. Took him on Wingfield's Mountain. He was in ecstasies about the view from there, but unfortunately, had forgotten his sketchbook, but said he would sketch it from memory.

Let me see, what else have I done in the last month? How soon do we forget the trifles which make up our lives and which, though not noted by us, are heaping themselves up into real forms and will be altogether the sum total of a lifetime. Now I can scarcely remember what I have done in all this long month, and yet the words, thoughts and actions of that month will never die and must be answered for if evil or rewarded if good. Ah! How important then should our every little thought, word, and action become in our own eyes, and how should each word, thought, and action be prayed over.

Have been to see Fanny Allen and Cousin Magdalen Christian one evening. Been several evenings to see Mr. Donald, and spent the day with Mama and Papa at Uncle Tom Mitchell's. Found on return home from these days Cousin Barton and Charles Harvey from New Orleans, with Cousin Barton's wife, Cousin Sally, with whom we are delighted. She is a real nice Southern lady.

Sister went to Richmond with the baby and found Brother Tom had come home by way of Gordonsville. She stayed one night at Mr. Blairs' and came to Mr. Mosby's next day. Met Captain Bowyer in Lynchburg, both returned home, spent one day and went then to Colonel Preston's, where they are now. We miss the baby terribly.

Fan went to see Brother James at Gordonsville, returned home and has been very sick ever since with a form of typhoid fever. Have been sitting up with her three nights and feel very stupid in consequence. I was ready to go to Oaklands to see Alice and Emma (Watts) when Fan was taken sick, so I could not go.

Last Saturday and Monday our forces were engaged with the enemy near Gordonsville. A most fierce and desperate battle both days. We are very much relieved to hear that the cavalry was not engaged and that dear Jimmie is safe. Oh! This dreadful time and these terrible battles! How can we for a moment be cheerful when such awful scenes are enacted around us?

Met Sis Wingfield on the mountain one evening last week. We had not seen each other for a long time. Cannot make up my mind to go to the house.[9] Yet Sis and I are as good friends as ever.

~

The journal ends here. Fan died of typhoid fever in August. Jimmie Breckenridge was killed at Dinwiddie Courthouse in 1865. Jimmie was a young attorney when the war started in 1861. He enlisted in Co. C of the 2nd Virginia Cavalry along with his brothers, John, Gilmer, and Cary. His brother, George, was too young at the time but joined as soon as he became eighteen. His brothers, John and Gilmer, were also killed in the war. Lettie Burwell never married and continued to live at Avenel as its mistress until she died in 1905. She is buried at Longwood Cemetery in Bedford on the plot with other members of her family.

---

[9] Belleview, the Wingfield home on the outskirts of Liberty.

Although Lettie Burwell's journal ends on August 15, 1862, Lucy Breckenridge of Grove Hill, Botetourt County, Virginia, begins her journal on August 11, 1862, and continues through December 25, 1865. The lives of these families were intertwined.

The Diary of Lucy Breckenridge of Grove Hill is recommended reading for all who wish to explore the wartime lives of these families.

From Lucy's journal we learn that on October 28, 1862, Lucy, Eliza, and Emma Breckenridge, sisters, caught the stage, probably at Fincastle or Buchanan to Bonsack where they were met by Kate Bowyer and continued on to Avenel where they arrived in time for dinner. While at Avenel for a two-week visit, they met Captain Frank Clarke of New Orleans recovering from wounds he received at Sharpsburg. Lettie was later engaged to him but they were never married. He became permanently disabled in April of 1863 from wounds received at Fredericksburg. He continued to be in and out of the Breckenridge home through October 1863.

Lettie is described as lovely and unselfish, and Rosa is pretty and interesting. Mr. Willie Michel (the original French spelling of Mitchell) of Washington was described as smart, conceited, and handsome nephew of General James Johnston and an accepted beau of Rosa. This appears to be the eldest son of Robert Mitchell, formerly referred to in Lettie's journal as Willie Mitchell. Dr. Todd, a surgeon attached to the Confederate hospital at Liberty was another beau of Rosa. During the two-week visit there were trips to the Peaks and one to Natural Bridge. There were many young men who came to call...Doctors Moses, Letcher, and Blackford, Hamilton Pike, and Lt. Frederick Richardson, who was on leave at this time. He was later promoted to Captain of Co. F, of the 5th Louisiana Infantry and killed in action at Gettysburg on July 4, 1863. Dr. Blackford gave a "candy stew" for these guests. The following month in December, Lettie, Rosa, Dr. Todd, and Captain Clarke returned the visit by going to Grove

Hill for about two weeks. Dr. Blackford came later for a few days and vaccinated everybody.

CHAPTER X

Confederate Hospitals in Liberty

On May 1, 1862, the Confederate government established a hospital unit in Liberty for the convalescent soldiers, making the town a military post. Seven existing buildings were used with a capacity of 800–1,000 beds for a total rent of $285 monthly. Additional buildings were to be erected. The existing buildings used included the following:

THE TOBACCO FACTORIES OF:

1. William T. Campbell. A three-story brick structure located across Bridge Street from old St. John's Episcopal Church. Letitia Burwell reported in her diary that Campbell's factory was used to store provisions into Liberty from the farms for distribution to town cooks to feed soldiers passing through by train. According to E.B. Stone, this building was also used as a bakery where all the bread was baked for the hospitals.

2. Micajah Davis, located on the south side of the railroad track between Liberty House (hotel) and the bridge; actually very close to the east side of the bridge.

3. John M. Reese's building was located at the railroad crossing on Grove Street near Plunkett Street, near where the old woolen mill now stands. Later this became the site of Alberti Tobacco Company. One level of Alberti faced the railroad track and one level faced Plunkett Street. The building was

burned during Hunter's raid at which time it was being used as a wayside hospital. A wayside hospital was usually located on the railroad to receive incoming patients from the trains. This receiving hospital separated the wounded into groups by the nature of their calamity. From here they were directed to a specific hospital to provide the type of care needed. Designated sites were established for particular problems such as surgery or small pox.

John M. Reese also sold insurance for the Virginia Fire and Marine Insurance Company of Richmond and Charlottesville, as evidenced by the following ad from the *Bedford Democrat* of January 29, 1860.

JOHN M. REESE
LIBERTY, VIRGINIA
Agent for the Lynchburg Hose and Fire Insurance Company, which insures almost every kind of property (?)...and the Lives of Negroes. Risks taken...in Bedford.

He will aid parties in obtaining policies from the Virginia Fire and Marine Insurance Company of Richmond and the Albemarle Company of Charlottesville, both of which are responsible companies.

4. John Crenshaw owned a tobacco factory located on the northwest corner of Washington and Crenshaw Streets, where a tobacco manufactory is shown on Gray's 1876 map. E.B. Stone also states that this is the location of the hospital. Crenshaw's mansion home was Cedar Hill,[1] on the corner

---

[1]William V. Jordan began selling tracts, which made up his home place, Cedar Hill, in 1854 and continued through 1857. (Deed Book 37, Pg. 402 and D. B. 39, Pg. 82.) All of these totaled 21 acres, which he conveyed to Col. John Crenshaw. In 1855 Crenshaw hired a carpenter, Richard Raines, to build a servant's house on the property for $50, add an addition to the tobacco factory for $200, and build a well house for $20 (Chancery Suit, Raines vs. Crenshaw). Crenshaw had six children. A daughter, Lucy, married Alexander Jordan, and in 1866 a

of Crenshaw and West Main Streets, which he purchased in 1855 from William V. Jordan. The house faced West Main Street and the factory was behind the house, probably facing Washington Street. For whatever reason, John Crenshaw objected to the Army taking over his factory for their use as a hospital. He frequently requested its return for his own use.

5. THE FURNITURE FACTORIES OF:

William D. Toler was on the west side of North Bridge Street. An 1860 deed described this property as being on Bridge Street, at a corner near the bridge over the railroad "where Toler has erected a furniture warehouse 16 feet north of the house occupied by James M. Ragland." Mrs. Toler was the former Jane Terry. The following advertisement from the *Bedford Democrat,* November 5, 1858:

LIBERTY FURNITURE WAREHOUSE & MANUFACTORY
BRIDGE STREET, LIBERTY, VIRGINIA
WILLIAM D. TOLER

Grateful for the past encouragement of a generous public, most respectfully solicits a continuance of their patronage, and would hereby inform them that he has employed some of the best workmen in the state, and having greatly extended his facilities for manufacturing furniture, he is now prepared to fill orders of any magnitude, whatever, and to furnish articles in his line, of the most fashionable styles and finished workmanship.

Proprietors of Springs Hotels and all in want of furniture are invited to call at his establishment on Bridge Street where they will find:

---

daughter, Eliza M., married William V. Jordan now returned from the war where he was wounded. A son, John Balda, was a tobacco commission merchant in Lynchburg, who advertised in the *Bedford Democrat* in 1857 as having an auction commission house and would attend sales in any part of the county.

CONFEDERATE HOSPITALS IN LIBERTY 173

Bureaus at prices ranging from $8 to $75
Wardrobes ranging from $2 to $20
Chairs, (pr. set) at prices ranging from $4 to $70
Washstands at prices ranging from 75¢ to $25
Superior Spring beds, Shuck and Hair Mattresses, &
Coffins made to order, and undertaking promptly attended to.

6. THE CARRIAGE FACTORY OF:

I.N. Clark—Clark's Carriage Manufactory employed six men in 1860 to build carriages and buggies. In 1860 their products were valued at $6,500.00. The six employees were paid $33.00 per month. This shop was located on the east side of North Bridge Street, between the bridge and Depot Street. (Daniel, 1985,88).

7. PIEDMONT INSTITUTE:

Located on Piedmont Hill (East Main Street), was formerly a boy's school. According to E.B. Stone there were annexes attached to the main building which probably were erected by the Army for hospital needs. Piedmont became the small pox hospital.

On a vacant lot north of the courthouse, the government erected several large buildings for storing food brought in from the farms to be shipped to the army by railroad. These buildings and a brick railroad station were burned by General Hunter in his raid on Bedford.

Under Dr. Benjamin Blackford[2], surgeon in charge of the conglomerate of military hospitals, there were at various

---

[2] Dr. Benjamin Blackford was born September 8, 1834, and entered the Confederate Army April 23, 1861, and left Colonel Garland's command for Manassas Junction. In May 1861, he was appointed surgeon of the 11th Virginia Infantry when Garland's command was formed into a regiment. He established hospitals at Culpeper and Front Royal where he remained surgeon in charge until March 1862. When Gen. Johnston's army was falling back from Manassas he was on duty at Gordonsville. In May 1862, he was ordered to increase

times assistant surgeons Letcher, Todd, Moses, Sommerville, Leyburn, Selden, Moore, Frierson, Nesbitt, Fields, Harper, Claggett, Eads, and Liberty's own Dr. C.A. Board. Drs. Selden and Moore, though not present initially, became permanent and the wards were divided into two sections under the supervision of these two surgeons respectively.

Of the known doctors in Liberty and Bedford County at the time of the war, many entered the service of the Confederacy in some other capacity. Dr. Thomas M. Bowyer was Captain of the 28th Va. Infantry and later transferred to Artillery Service. Dr. Bowyer survived the war and after some years became the director of Liberty Sanitorium, later Granville Sanitorium. Dr. William P. Thurman and Dr. John Y.M. Jordan were physicians who served in the Bedford Light Artillery.

Dr. David M. Claytor, a Liberty physician, was wounded at Cedar Run in 1862. Dr. Triplett E. Lowry was assistant sur-

Granville Sanitorium is now an apartment building on College Street.

hospital accommodations in Farmville, Danville, Lynchburg, and Liberty and on completion of this transferred his hospital stores and staff to Liberty, Virginia, where he stayed until the end of the war. After the war he resumed practice in Lynchburg. He was elected president of the Medical Society of Virginia and in 1889 was elected superintendent of the Western Lunatic Asylum at Staunton, now known as the Western State Hospital. He died December 13, 1905.

geon at a field hospital in Manassas. He returned to Liberty and served at a local hospital until 1865. Dr. John A. Nelson was assistant surgeon of the 2nd Va. Cavalry and died in service in 1863.

Dr. Charles A. Board served as assistant surgeon in the hospital at Liberty. He was educated at the University of Virginia, completing courses in medicine and dentistry. After the war he continued to practice medicine in Liberty. He served the town twice as mayor, was clerk of the school board for many years and remained active in civic affairs until his death in 1910.

The known matrons at the hospital were Mrs. Sarah Gish and Mrs. Louisa Yancey; the assistant matrons were Mrs. William Fizer (Mary Oney), Mrs. Frederick, Mrs. Samuel Harris, Mrs. John Hoffman, Mrs. Jacob Haynes, Mrs. Armistead and Mrs. Fannie Hurley. Mrs. Lucy Davis was matron or mistress in chief of the laundry department.

Soon after the hospital became a fixed institution the sympathy and zeal of the ladies were directed toward the patients who, they believed, needed delicacies the hospital could not supply. A number of housekeepers pledged themselves to send in rotation a daily dinner to the hospital, composed of wholesome delicacies suitable for the sick. This effort was kept up for some weeks at considerable trouble to the housekeepers, but the surgeons put an end to the benevolent work by requesting them to refrain from sending any edibles at all. The ladies were very indignant, believing it done in a spirit of jealousy, but no doubt the surgeons were activated by superior wisdom!

Bedford history tells us that the women of the town took turns caring for the sick and disabled soldiers and were daily seen wending their way to these hospitals with baskets of dainties prepared by their own hands. Outstanding among these nurses was Mrs. Mary Oney Fizer, wife of William Fizer. Whenever it was learned that a trainload of Southern soldiers would pass through town, "Miss Mary" would help to

Mary Oney Fizer with her baby. Courtesy Bedford Museum.

spread the news and to solicit food for the soldiers. When the train stopped at the station, she would pass through the cars seeking any sick or disabled to whom she might minister. Her portrait, painted by a Northern soldier whom she had nursed back to health, hangs in the Bedford County Museum. Mary Oney Fizer was the daughter of James W. and Mary E. Thomas Oney. She was a regular nurse at Campbell Hospital. Mary never wore a dress but instead wore a wrapper, as it was commonly called. She died in 1901 leaving two children, Charlie and Mary B. Fizer.

From her diary on May 4, 1864, "Our hospitals are filled with wounded...I have heard nothing from my Will since the fight."

And on May 10, "Received a letter from Will this morning. How thankful I am that he is unhurt."

On May 15, she wrote, "Made arrangements to take two of our soldiers home and nurse them. Would that each could have the pleasure of nursing our own loved ones, but this cannot be and I shall endeavor to fill the place of loved ones at home as near as it can be done. They all suffer for no attention...."

On May 20, "I have spent the night in tears sitting over one who is away from home and friends. Listened to his wild ravings of home, mother, and wife until I imagined I could hear the same cry from my own loved ones on distant battlefields. Often through the night have the words, 'Mary, darling, don't grieve' sent a warm stream of life back to my heart chilled." Mary Fizer's honorable discharge, signed by Benjamin Blackford on April 21, 1865, is preserved in the Bedford Museum.

HONORABLE DISCHARGE
Surgeon's Office, Gen'l Hospital; C.S.A.
Liberty, Virginia, April 21st, 1865

Special Order:
By reason of the present aspect of the military situation and because of the limited supply of subsistence here at the Post, the following named matrons are this day discharged from further duty in this hospital.

Benjamin Blackford, Surgeon In Charge
Mrs. Armistead (Piedmont)
Mrs. Gish (Campbell)
Mrs. Fizer (Campbell)

To: Mrs. Mary Fizer, Campbell's Hospital

Among the first memorial associations in the South was the one at Liberty, organized in 1866. These ladies soon conceived the idea of erecting a monument in the Confederate cemetery on Piedmont Hill to the soldiers who died of wounds or disease in Liberty's hospitals. A simple shaft was erected in 1875 bearing the inscription:

OUR CONFEDERATE DEAD
1861-1865

Upon investigation many years later it was found that no legal right had ever been obtained to this cemetery and it was deemed wise to remove the monument and all that could be found of the sacred dust of those who slept here to Longwood Cemetery. A central plot was chosen and in 1920 the remains were removed, placed in a concrete vault, and the monument again erected above them.

The following is a partial roster of the known deaths, which occurred in the Confederate hospitals at Liberty. When Richmond was burned, many military records were lost. While most who died in Liberty's hospitals were buried on Piedmont Hill, the bodies of a few were claimed by relatives and sent home for burial. The following was compiled from old records in the National Archives in Washington, DC, by Raymond W. Watkins of Falls Church, Virginia, in 1981.

Thomas Adams, Co. A or K, 47th Ala., died Febr. 11 or March 11, 1863
E. D. Altizer, Co. K, 54th Va., died prior to July 1863
S. E. Arrington, Co. G, 38th Ga., died Sept. 5, 1862
W. Armstrong, Co. G, 43rd Ala., died April 15, 1864
D. Angle, Co. G, 57th Va., died May 23, 1864
J. M. Barton, Co. G, 24th Ga., died Nov. 14, 1862
Robt. J. Byrd, Co. H, 15th Ala., died Nov. 16, 1862
James F. Barrett, Co. I, 24th Ga., died Febr. 8, 1863
J. Burrough, Co. F, 2nd Va., died May 27, 1862
Sgt. Wm. Byrd, Co. D, 33rd N.C., died Sept. 7, 1862
R. J. Baker, Co. G, 47th Ala., died Sept. 8, 1862
J. M. Bist (?), Co. D, 14th N.C., died Sept. 18, 1862
E. G. Blackwell, Co. B, Cobb's Ga. Legion, died Jan. 1, 1863
Josiah Belfrey, Co. K, 12th S.C., died Jan. 22, 1863
J. A. Binns, Co. A, 12th Ga., died Feb. 8, 1863
F. Barnett, Co. D, 16 GA., died Feb. 8, 1863
S. Blackman, Co. D, 1st S.C., died March 4, 1863
T. J. Butler, Co. A, 44th Ala., died April 11, 1864
Thos. Broadwater, Co. I, 7th S.C., died May 15, 1864
R. Beveridge, Co. I, 62nd Va., died June 26, 1864
John Carter, Co. D, 6th S.C., died Feb. 4, 1863
James Craig, Co. G, 3rd S.C., died prior to July 1863
Wm. Carroll, Co. D, 11th Va., died prior to July 1863
Frank Calnan, Co. E, 14th La., died April 4, 1863
W. T. Cain, Co. F, 16th Miss., died May 20, 1862
J. W. Covington, Co. K, 3rd Va., died May 27, 1862

Willis Carver, Co. E, died Sept. 15, 1862
J. W. Carr, Co. K, 4th Ala., died March 4, 1863
J. Childers, Co. I, 6th S.C., died June 25, 1864
J. W. Day, Co. I, 9th La., died May 11, 1862
Dan'l Duke, Co. E, 15th Ala., died May 22, 1862
W. Dykes, Co. E, 4th Ala. Btn., died Jan. 21, 1864.
Alexander Eagle, Co. G, 6th N.C., died June 6, 1863
J. N. Forbes, Co. A, 21st Ga., died July 29, 1862.
John M. Fink, Co. K, 5th N.C., died Feb. 23, 1863
J. M. Freeman, Co. H, Va. Cavalry, died June 27, 1863
J. S. Freeman, Co. G, 3rd,Tenn., died June 25, 1864
J. M. Guthridge, Co. D, 22nd Va., died May 23, 1862
J. S. Gamble, Co. G, 13th Ala., died May 27, 1862
Corp. Lewis Godfrey, Co. A, 49th Va., died June 19, 1864
L. G. Getty, Co. B, 34th N.C., died Sept. 11, 1862
L. Galloway, Co. A, Tenn Cavalry, (he could be Lewis
    Galloway, Co. A,12th Green's Tenn. Cav.)
T. (?) J. Garner, Co. B, 39th Ga., died prior to July, 1863
John H. Grooms, Co. B, 61st Ga., died Oct. 10, 1862
W.C. Hemphill, Co. G, 24th Ga., died Nov. 13, 1862
W. Hall, Co. D, 33rd N.C., died Feb. 22, 1863
J. S. Holmes, Co. B, 1st La., died Dec. 23, 1862
W. O. Holland, Co. K, 41st Va., died Sept. 1, 1862
R. Howard, Co. I, 1st Md., died Sept. 5, 1862.
A.S. Herndon, Co. I, 6th N.C., died Sept. 17, 1862
W.J.E. Head, 3rd S.C., died Jan.23, 1863
W.W. Hudson, Co. K, 26th Ala., died Feb. 10, 1863
Chas. N. Hunt, Co. E, 44th Ga., died Feb. 3, 1863
J.L. Hanson (Hinson), Co. L, 3rd Ga., died Mar. 4, 1863
Andrew J. Hamrick, Co. H, 28th N.C., died Mar. 17, 1863
J.R. Hilts (?), Co. C, 16th Ga., died June 26, 1863
J.B. Harris, Co. A, 18th Ga., died July 31, 1863
J. H. Holt, Co. F, 2nd S.C. Battn., died June 14, 1863
T.P. Irwin, Co. L, 2nd Miss., died Feb. 6, 1863
Ellis Jacobs, Co. F, 13th Ga., died Oct. 13, 1862
James Jenkins, Co. I, 9th La., died May 11, 1862

J. Jackson, Co. C, 3rd N.C., died Sept. 27, 1862
Wm. Y. Joplin, Co. D, 30th N.C., died Jan. 29, 1863
M. Jacobs, Co. F, 61st Ala., died June 25, 1864
Jesse Johnson, Co. F, 45th Ga., died April 5, 1863
W.A. Key, Co. D, 7th S.C., died prior to July 1863
H. Keisler, Co. E, 23rd S.C., died Sept. 28, 1864
B. Patrick Lands, Phillips Ga. Legion, died May 24, 1862
Wm. A. or O. Lovelace, Co. A., died Sept. 9, 1862
R. J. Land, Co. H, 15th Ala., died Jan. 23, 1863
J. L. Lunsford, Co. C, 30th N.C., died Feb. 16, 1863
J. P. Lines, Co. I, 3rd Ark., died Feb. 19, 1863
J. W. Light, Co. B, 42nd Va., died June 1, 1863
E. B. Ladiner, Co. E, 1st Ala., died Aug. 6, 1863
J. R. Linbarger, Co. D, 41st Ala., died Jan. 14, 1864
W. B. Ligon, Co. C, 9th La., died Feb. 9, 1864
James Liles, Co. G, 20th Ga., died May 6, 1864
Corp. Geo. Wm. Milum, Co. F, 10th Ala., died prior to July 1863
J. M. Morrison, Co. I, 15th Ala., died prior to July 1863
Dan'l Miley, Co. A, 4th Texans, died July 22, 1862
A. F. Moorman, Co. K, 21st Ga., died prior to July 1863
F. A. Moorill, Co. L, 2nd Miss., died March 4, 1863
Edwin Miller, Co. F, 15th N.C., died Oct. 23, 1862
J. A. McDonald, Co. D, 13th Ga., died Sept 19, 1862
G. McGee, Co. E, 4th Texans, died Jan. 12, 1863
J. A. McGowan, Co. B, 8th Fla., died Feb. 2, 1863
A. T. McKee, Co. E, 9th Ala., died March 29, 1863
Sgt. Sam'l. J. McClain, Co. F, 21st Ga., died June,1862
Rbt. McNair, Co. D, 12th Ga., died Aug.5, 1862
H. E. McKee, Co. M, Phillips Ga. Legion, died June 1, 1864
Wm. McCanby, Co. G, 2nd S.C. Rifles, died March 13, 1864
M. Mahoney, Co. C, 19th Miss., died Sept. 16, 1862
F. F. Mason, Co. A, 32nd Va., died Jan 6, 1863
Wm. Mizell, Co. G, 50th Ga., died Mar. 26, 1863
John Moore, Co. G, 41st Ala., died May 1, 1864
J. A. Mannering, Co. G, 53rd N.C., died May 19, 1864

N. A. Miller, Co. B, 28th N.C., died June 24, 1864
E. Wm. Marshall, Co. F, 23rd N.C., died Feb. 12, 1863
J. M. Nichols, Co. E, 6th Ga., died July 18, 1862
W. G. Northern, Co. I, 55th Va., died Feb. 20, 1863
R. T. Norton, Co. H, 55 Va., died June 28, 1863
Alfred E. Norman, Co. K, 21st Ga., died Nov. 20, 1862
F. Odomill, Co. I, La., died Oct. 9, 1864
T. Josiah Pelfrey, Co. K, 12th S.C., died Jan. 22, 1863
N. W. Price, 6th Va. Cav., died May 14, 1862
John Pitchford, Co. H, 44th Va., died May 30, 1862
Sgt. Raymond Pican, Co. H, 15th La., died June 20, 1863
E. F. Posey, Co. C, 59th Ga., died Jan. 30, 1864
F. Peyton, Co. E, 27th Va., died June 27, 1864
T. S. Peters, Co. H, 60th Va., died Oct. 1, 1864
Hezekiah Rooks, Co. K, 16th Ga., died Dec. 11, 1863
H. G. Ransom, Co. G, 15th Ga., died prior to July 1863
Elhannan Redding, Co. C, 26th Ga., died Sept. 1, 1862
D. H. Rice, Co. E, 8th S.C., died Sept. 7, 1862
Geo. Reed, Co. E, 48th Ala., died Feb. 10, 1863
F. S. Redman, Co. A, 6th NC, died June 28, 1864
Chas. Reinhardt, Co. I, 11th NC, died June 29, 1864
J. B. Suggs, Co. H, 8th La., died Sept. 3, 1862
B. F. Stewart, Co. E, 3rd Bn., S.C. Inf., died Sept. 7, 1862
Martin L. Surls, Co. E, 31st Ga., died Sept. 27, 1862
Wilson L. Sikes (Sykes), Co. G, 44th Ga., died Jan. 8, 1863
J. M. Smith, Co. I, 35th Ga., died June 2, 1863
Lt. H. G. Saunders, 4th Va. Hvy Arty., died Aug. 24, 1863
John J. Shilling, Co. G, 9th La., died Dec. 16, 1863
Colvin M. Thomas, Co. I, 9th La., died May 21, 1862
A. W. Turner, Co. H, 48th Ga., died Feb. 23, 1863
W. T. Tucker, Co. G, 8th Va., died Nov. 26, 1864
Wm. G. Tuton, Co. E, 2nd Fla., died prior to July 1863
P. F. Talley, Co. B, 30th NC, died Feb. 23, 1863
David Welch, Co. B, 14th Ga., died Feb. 22, 1863
J. Wordly, Co. I, 48th Va., died Sept. 30, 1862
Wm. B. Wood, Co. K, 7th SC, died Jan. 1, 1863

W. M. Wilson, Co. D, 14th Ga., died July 17, 1863
D. B. F. Wilson, Co. K, 31st Va., died Sept. 3, 1863
W. F. Wallace, Co. D, 41st Ala., died March 30, 1864
P. Williams, Co. I, 48th Miss., died May 15, 1864
G. W. Wallace, Co. F, 10th Tenn. Cav., died May 24, 1864
Rbt. Woods, Co. L, Palmetto Sharp Shooters, SC, died May 12, 1864
Wiley Weere, Co. H, 15th NC, died prior to July 1863
E. B. Waller, Co. H, 3rd Va., died prior to July 1863

While the above list is only a partial one, it is all that is available. A more complete one might have included northern soldiers and prisoners.

A letter from Jasper Goldman of Georgia, a patient at the Liberty Hospital complex reveals his interesting comments about Liberty and the hospital.

July 4, 1862, Liberty, Virginia

Dear Father and Mother,
It is with solemnary that I endeavar to right you a few lines to let you no whar I am and how my health is. Myself and Marion are at a place called Liberty, sum too hundard miles from Richmond. We left the regiment about fore weaks a go. My health is sum what beter. Marion has got the typhoed fevor. He has bin confinde to his bed a weeke. He is right sick but doing as well as could be expected under the surcomstances. I am takeing all the care of him I can. I have not heard from Fate since I left the regiment. Conciquentley I have not heard from home eather. I am very anchus to hear from Fate since the battle to no weather he was kild or not. And I want to hear from you all and right weather you have heard from Fate or not since the battle.
Father I have but vary little nuse to communicate to you. Whar we are us a vary pretty place. It is a purfick montain all around, sum of the hyest I ever saw. The people are vary good to us hear. The lades has bin bringing in sumthing good to eat every since we

have bin hear till the last few days. The Dr. made such a fuss about thear coming and they have nearly stopt. Paw, I want you to right me how crops are back thar. And how wheat and oats turnd out. Wheat is vary good out hear. People has just comenced cutting wheat out hear. Corn is from knee to wast high. Paw, I want you to send me tin dollars. We are hear with out eny money at all. We have not drawed no money in fore months. You will oblige us vary much by sending the money that I right for as soon as you can as we can't git eny from the regiment. Nothing more at presant Your dear son until death, good by.

Jasper Goldman

Direct your letter to Liberty, via Com. F. 22nd Reg. Ga. Vol. In the care Dr. Blackford in charge.

There would not be another letter from the Goldman boys until late August. But during July and August, several things of interest would happen. On July 20, 1862, the first of the Goldman brothers would give his life for the Confederacy. Marion Goldman died from complications of typhoid fever on that date. It had been previously thought that Marion died at Richmond from the measles but the above letter from Jasper indicated he had typhoid fever and he probably died at Liberty, Virginia, where he is presumed to be buried. Jasper recuperated enough to be able to rejoin the 22nd Georgia around the end of July. With the enemy no longer a threat to take Richmond, General Lee decided to take the fight to northern Virginia. So in mid August of 1862, orders were issued for the Confederate troops to start marching north. The next letter from Fayette was dated August 23rd in which he said, "the 22nd Georgia has now marched to 120 miles north from Richmond." One week later, on August 30, 1862, they will be heavily involved in the great battle of Manassas (Bull Run). Late in the same letter, Fayette mentions the death of his twin brother, Marion, when he says, "My dear brother has paid the debt that we all is got to pay." (Goldman, 1999, 24)

The winter of 1863 severely strained the capacity of Lynchburg and Bedford Hospital units. Although Bedford was not a battlefield, it became a valuable refuge for the aftermath of battles. From the partial list of soldiers who died here, we see that in 1862 there were 46 deaths in the hospital here, 60 in 1863, and 27 in 1864. We might hope the number was reduced in 1864 due to improved medical knowledge and treatment. Certainly the smallpox vaccine had an impact.

CHAPTER XI

Medical Correspondence

The hospital in Liberty was established on May 1, 1862. The buildings used for hospitals were all in town, unoccupied and belonged to John B. Crenshaw, William D. Toler, I. N. Clark, Micajah Davis, John M. Reese, William T. Campbell, and Piedmont Institute. Most were glad to have the rental money for an unoccupied building.

The smallpox hospital was located just out of town at Piedmont Institute, isolated so as to limit the spread of disease and to contain the odor so prevalent with smallpox. By January 1863 another building was erected on the hill near the Institute also for the care of smallpox patients. All of the smallpox hospital buildings accommodated 200 patients.

These hospitals were referred to as general hospitals to distinguish them from field (regimental) hospitals. An admission to a general hospital did not restrict troops to a particular unit, whereas each regiment had its own field hospital. A general hospital was not a single building itself, but included multiple buildings, which were sometimes divided into divisions. (Houck, 1986, 17)

The official correspondence in the Confederate Calendar reveals the variety of problems faced by Benjamin Blackford, Surgeon, in charge of the hospital unit in Liberty and gives us a clearer view of the hospital's needs and requirements. It appears that this hospital worked closely with the one in Lynchburg, accepting overflow patients etc. when brought by train from the battlefields. Reference is made to hospital buildings being erected. These were all located adjacent to Piedmont Institute.

Railroad cargo was changed from tobacco hogsheads to wounded soldiers coming to this area from three directions.

The Va. & Tenn. RR brought soldiers to Lynchburg and Liberty from campaigns in the southwest, the Orange & Alexandria brought them to the Lynchburg area from the valley campaigns in the north, and Southside RR from Richmond. The sick and wounded suffered much exposure on the trains and many were too sick to be moved, but care in these hospitals was considered superior to being treated on the battlefield or in tent hospitals.

Correspondence Regarding Hospital Establishment

May 27, 1862, from Surg. Gen. S. P. Moore[1], Richmond, Va. to Surg. Benjamin Blackford, Liberty Hospital:
The hospital accommodations at Liberty will not be required to exceed 800 to 1,000 beds.

May 27, 1862, from Surg. Benj. Blackford, Liberty Hospital, to Surg. Gen. S. P. Moore, Richmond, Va.:
Request the return of steward ordered to report at Lynchburg, have about 500 sick at present, need the steward's services.

June 6, 1862, from Benj. Blackford, Surg., Liberty Hospital, to Gen'l. S. Cooper, A&I, CSA:
I have received appointment as Surgeon in the Provisional Army—accept—I was born in Virginia—resided in Lynchburg—am 28 years of age.

June 16, 1862, from Benj. Blackford, Surg. Liberty Hospital, to Dr. S. P. Moore, Surg. Gen'l. Richmond, Va.:
Request the appointment of another medical officer here—have accommodations for 700 patients—only 4 assistant surgeons.

---

[1] Samuel Preston Moore of South Carolina was formerly a surgeon in "The old army." Moore ranked as a Brigadier General in Confederate Service.

July 7, 1862, from Benj. Blackford, Surg., Liberty Hospital to Dr. S. P. Moore, Surg. Gen'l., Richmond, Va.:
Request the appointment of another medical officer here—have nearly 800 sick in the hospitals—only 5 assistant surgeons.

October 25, 1862, from S. P. Moore, Surg. Genl., Richmond, Va., to Benj. Blackford, Surg. Liberty Hospital:
In reply to yours as to erecting hospital buildings—the work must be commenced without delay.

March 3, 1863, from Benj. Blackford, Surg., Liberty Hospital, to Surg. S.P. Moore, Richmond, Va.:
This hospital was established on May 1, 1862. Following are buildings as hospitals with specified rent: Crenshaw's, Campbell's, Davis's, Reese's, Piedmont, Tolers, and Clark's Factories, smallpox Hospitals—total rent $285 per month, capacity 725. Am now erecting hospital buildings.

Oct. 16, 1863, from Surg. Benj. Blackford, Liberty Hospital to W.A. Carrington, Med. Dir., Richmond, Va.:
Have received letter as to terms on which hospitals are held and whether they are convenient, etc.—now occupy four large tobacco factories, two cabinet shops, one large brick building, once used as an Institute—buildings comparatively new before the war—large, well ventilated and easily heated—last winter when hospital was full, one stove made every part of the ward warm and comfortable—wards in factories and shops are large and commodious—there are in the Piedmont Institute two large and four or five small wards—the latter used for offices—rented May 1862, when the hospital was established—most if not all were unoccupied when rented, no application to relinquish them. One large hospital building has been completed and occupied—the second is about completed—these will accommodate about 130—are on the hill with the Piedmont—together they will form one division of the hospital, 200 patients—during prevalence of smallpox, erected a smallpox hospital, accommodating 30 or 40—these are all the C.S. buildings

at the post — As to relinquishing any of them, I think owners will not want them — very little tobacco being raised — difficult to get labor — is much cheaper to rent at the present figure than to build — respectfully urge against relinquishing any of the buildings — This is the largest hospital on the Virginia & Tenn. RR — in case of active campaign in the southwest, hospital would be filled — if army retreats from Abingdon, the hospital at Emory will be abandoned, which would leave the hospital at Montgomery Springs and this one the only ones on the Va. & Tenn. R — the country is remarkably healthy — men convalesce more quickly here than at most hospitals in the state — country well supplied with provisions — cheaper than in Lynchburg or Richmond.

Jan. 13, 1864, from T.R. Baker, Lynchburg, for Surg. R.K. Taylor, Med. Purveyor, CSA, to Surg. Benj. Blackford, Liberty Hospital:

Your requisition for blankets or comforts received — have only on hand a dozen blankets and no comforts — return the requisition — might get them in Richmond.[2]

Sept. 24, 1864, Surg. Benjamin Blackford, Liberty Hospital to E.S. Gaillard, Med. Insp., Richmond, Va.:

I enclose a statement of number of patients between specified dates. Capacity of hospital, allowing 800 cubic feet per man, is 350 — as this is largely a convalescent hospital, I have not observed this rule strictly — many do not occupy their beds during the day — hospitals are well ventilated, elevation is very high — Surg. Gen'l. allowed discretion — I allow about 600 cubic feet per man[3] *— when I have many sick and wounded allow 800 feet.*

---

[2] The stores and medical supplies were chiefly stored in Richmond, Va.

[3] 600 cubic feet of air per patient is a good allowance under the circumstances, though modern hygiene in stationary hospitals allows not less than 1200 feet.

Nov. 5, 1864, Circular No. 41, from Liberty, Va. Gen. Hospital, sig: Benj. Blackford:
The hospital librarian will not allow books or newspapers to be taken from the Library between 9:00 A.M. and 3:00 P.M. —after that hour the secular papers will be distributed to the different wards— order does not apply to religious papers.

Febr. 4, 1865, from Surg. Benj. Blackford, Liberty Hospital to Surg. W. A. Carrington, Med. Dir. Richmond, Va.:
I received letter regarding observance of Par. II, Cir. No.7, SGO, June 1864—have endeavored to carry it out in making assignment according to capacity of officers—skin diseases are assigned to separate wards—cases of hospital Gangrene, Erysipelas[4] etc are treated in tents kept for the purpose—to economize fuel, I concentrate convalescents in large wards and close others when I can do so—wards are being whitewashed and renovated for the Spring campaign.

Correspondence Regarding Smallpox

Blackford, age 28, was assigned to the hospital unit here in May 1862, at a time when smallpox was a grave medical problem. At this point in time soldiers and children were vaccinated not only for their own protection but to make scabs available for vaccine. Children were vaccinated routinely and their scabs used as a continuous source of vaccine. These precautions hopefully would control a possible epidemic. The worst year for smallpox epidemics was 1863. Smallpox hospitals (or pest houses) were used to isolate infected soldiers from other patients. A smallpox burying ground was inevitably nearby. Another precaution to prevent the spread of smallpox was to deny leave of absence on medical certificate to men recently exposed to smallpox. The following corre-

---

[4] These cases constituted the real problem of the military surgeon. An enormous percentage of all operative cases succumbed during the war as a result of these diseases.

spondence and orders from Samuel Preston Moore, Surgeon General, to Blackford better acquaints us with the battle to conquer smallpox.

May 13, 1862, from S.P. Moore, Surg. Gen'l, Richmond, Va. to Benjamin Blackford, Surg., Liberty, Va.:
Detail will be made in every army department to vaccinate the soldiers—To procure a fresh supply of pure vaccine virus the officers detailed will, when practicable, vaccinate gratis the healthy children in the vicinity.

September 22, 1862, from S. P. Moore, Surg. Gen'l., Richmond, Va. to Benjamin Blackford, Surg. Liberty, Va.:
Examine all soldiers who enter the hospital—if they do not show protection mark of vaccination, have them vaccinated at most eligible time during their stay—to procure a continuous supply of reliable virus, vaccinate the healthy children of the vicinity gratis, when opportunity offers.

November—, 1862, from S.P. Moore, Surg. Gen'l. Richmond, Circular:
To prevent the spread of smallpox and varaloid, leaves of absence or furlough on medical certificate are not to be granted to officers or men recently exposed to these diseases.

January 3, 1863, from Benjamin Blackford, Surg., Liberty, Va to S.P. Moore, Surg., Richmond, Va.:
Smallpox has appeared—I deemed it necessary to take an unoccupied building of a Mr. Miller—price $20 per month—building in a ravine—isolated and sufficiently remote from village—it will accommodate 15 or 20 patients—only building suitable—will use it until a smallpox hospital can be erected—will erect as soon as possible—disease seems to be increasing among patients recently admitted—burying ground some distance from smallpox hospital— I have secured "an uncultivated corner of an old field near the hospital"—thus will not have to carry bodies through the streets to

the general burying ground— I make this report as some object to the location of the hospital.

January 7, 1863, from S. P. Moore, Surg. Genl., Richmond, Va. to Benjamin Blackford, Surg., Liberty, Va.:
Yours received regarding transfer of smallpox patients from the army to your hospital—vaccinate all inmates and people in the vicinity.

Dec. 18, 1863, from E. N. Covey, Inspt. & Supt. of Vaccination to B. Blackford, Surgeon, Liberty, Va.:
To supply the department with vaccine virus, in addition to that procured from the men, endeavor to procure supply of scabs from healthy children of your community—forward all good crusts to this office with as little delay as possible.

January 11, 1864, from Benjamin Blackford, Surg., Liberty, Va. to S. P. Moore, Surg. Gen'l., Richmond, Va.:
Send a supply of vaccine virus as soon as practicable—several children in the neighborhood recently vaccinated with virus furnished by you—it proved worthless.

January 14, 1864, from E. N. Covey, Ofc. Inspr. & Supt., Vaccination, Dist. Va., Tenn. and Ga. to Surg. Benjamin Blackford, Liberty, Va.:
I enclose you one vaccine crust and circular to citizen practitioners—propagate the virus and circular among citizens medical friends—ask them to procure such virus as they can and forward it to this office.

March 28, 1864, from Benjamin Blackford, Surg. Liberty, Va. to Surg. E.N. Covey, Inspt. & Supt. Vaccination, Surg. Genl.'s Ofc. Richmond, Va.:
I enclose two vaccine crusts from healthy children, one three months, other six months of age.

December 8, 1864, from Benj. Blackford, Surg., Liberty, Va. to S.P. Moore, Surg. Gen., Richmond, Va.:
Am in need of more vaccine virus, supply exhausted, demand increasing here.

Correspondence Regarding Desertion

Early in the operation of the hospital, a large number of patients were transferred here by train from Lynchburg's over-crowded facilities but many never arrived. They apparently exited the train before its arrival in Liberty. To prevent patients leaving the train to desert while en route it was necessary to lock the car doors. Desertion became an increasingly large problem for the south as the war continued. So was it a problem for Blackford here in Liberty.

May 21, 1862, from Benj. Blackford, Liberty Hospital to Surg. Green, CSA, Gen. Hosp. Lynchburg, Va.:
In view of the large number of patients transferred from your hospital here, who never report, I suggest that the train doors be locked until they arrive—distance is short—I think this the only way to insure receiving the correct number sent.

May 22, 1862, from W.O. Owen, Surg., Lynchburg General Hospital to Benj. Blackford, Surg. Liberty Hospital:
I have received your letter suggesting the doors of trains be locked to prevent patients leaving the train when transferred to the Liberty Hospital—an order will be issued to that effect.

June 14, 1862, from Benj. Blackford, Surg. in charge, Liberty Hospital, to Dr. S. P. Moore, Surg. Gen., Richmond, Va.:
For sometime past large numbers of soldiers have passed on the Virginia and Tennessee Railroad without proper leave. They are from Johnston's and Jackson's armies. I think it is my duty to report it. The commandant of the post has arrested a number. I suggest that sentinels be placed on the cars in Lynchburg to examine

the papers of soldiers who enter. Conductors have become careless. Many "run the blockade" without trouble. Suggest appointment of a guard here to assist in arresting deserters.

Aug. 9, 1862, from Benj. Blackford, Liberty Hospital to Gen. S. Cooper, A & I Genl. CSA:

I beg to suggest a guard on the trains at Lynchburg to arrest deserters and stragglers. The post commandant here has arrested and remanded about 500 in the past 6 weeks. Deem it my duty to report and assist in preventing desertion. Compliments to Capt. Buford, Post Commandant.[5]

Febr. 26, 1864, from Benj. Blackford, Liberty Hosp. to Surgeon Woodall:

I have received your list of 55 men transferred—only 4 or 5 reported—have accommodations for nearly 500 at this time. When you transfer men, give a days notice, so that proper persons may be at the train to receive and assign them.

Correspondence Regarding Crenshaw's Warehouse

Accommodation was a continuous problem faced by Blackford at Liberty Hospital. While most were quite willing to rent their warehouses to the army for hospital use, some were not. If the owner was unwilling to rent his building, it was impressed by the army and converted into hospital use. Such was the case of John Balda Crenshaw who was not happy that the army had impounded his tobacco warehouse in May of 1862, over his objections to Benj. Blackford.

May 19, 1862, from Surg. Gen'l. S.P. Moore, Richmond, Va. to Surg. Benj. Blackford, Liberty Hospital:

---

[5] A military post appears to have been maintained at Liberty until the close of the war.

By authority of the Secretary of War, you may take possession of Crenshaw's factory to be used as general hospital for the sick of the army.

Oct. 16, 1863, from Benj. Blackford, Surg., Liberty Hosp., to W. A. Carrington, Med. Dir. Richmond, Va.:
Most, if not all, buildings were unoccupied when rented. With the exception of Crenshaw's Factory, have had no application to relinquish any of them. Crenshaw applied, Govt. refused, as it needed the building—no further application–presume this due to the fact that there is no further need for factories—the tobacco season is over.

Dec. 11, 1863, from Benj. Blackford, Surg., Liberty Hospital to S.P. Moore, Surg. Gen'l., Richmond, Va.:
Col. Crenshaw has applied for the release of his factory used as Hospital—unless there is an active campaign in the S. W. Va, and east Tenn., making it necessary to send their wounded here, I think it may be released—new buildings have been occupied for several months—are being ceiled [sealed] for the winter weather.

Dec. 15, 1863, from Wm. A. Carrington, Med. Dir. Ofc., Richmond, Va., to Surg. Benj. Blackford, Liberty Hospital:
Remove all hospital and public property from Crenshaw's warehouse—turn it over to its owner—if you do not need the bedding, send it to the purveyor at Lynchburg.

May 7, 1864, from W.A. Carrington, Med. Dir., Richmond, Va., to Benj. Blackford, Surg. Liberty Hospital:
Take Crenshaw's building, if actually required –vacate it as soon as it is not wanted—if you can procure tents, use them.

Correspondence Regarding Slaves and Hospital Staff

The Confederate Government had ordered that slaveholders provide slaves to be sent to the battlegrounds to dig trenches. It was up to the sheriff to get them on the train at the station.

In Bedford County Order Book 34, an order dated September 19, 1863, from the Governor, by Act of the General Assembly requires any person owning slaves between the ages of eighteen and sixty-five, and capable of hard labor, to deliver these to the county sheriff at the depot of the Virginia & Tennessee Railroad on October 1,1863. The sheriff will deliver them to the Confederate States Army to be employed 60 days on fortifications in Virginia. Approximately 200 male slaves were needed for this purpose.

October 31, 1862, from Surg. Benj. Blackford, Liberty Hospital to Surg. Gen. S.P. Moore, Richmond, Va.:
The sheriff has been endeavoring to take some of my Negro cooks and nurses to work on fortifications around Richmond—they are needed here—I ask order forbidding—have refused until I hear further.

On October 26, 1863, Blackford was summoned to appear in court to show cause why he had not delivered the slaves for duty. Blackford, being ordered to deliver two slaves and having failed to do so for 25 days and failing to appear in court this day, was fined $3 per slave per day for failure to deliver same. The court also ordered the slaves be seized. (O.B. 43, Pg. 355) See Chapter XIII.

In August 1864, the court granted Blackford leave to withdraw papers of a motion lately pending to rescind and reverse judgment for a fine imposed on him by the court. His letter to Surgeon General S.P. Moore dated October 31,1862, was filed by the court.

Correpondence Regarding Wayside Hospitals

A wayside hospital was established by June of 1863 for casualties arriving by railroad. This could accommodate 85 patients and acted as a clearing house or receiving area for new patients who would then be assigned to another hospital according to his need and available space. No doubt it frequently accepted overflow patients. We also see from the correspondence that it was used as a place of dispatch for sick soldiers leaving for discharge or furlough. The wayside hospital in Liberty was located at Reese's factory on the railroad track at the crossing of Grove and Plunkett Streets.

June 19, 1863, from Wm. A. Carrington, Med. Dir. Richmond, Va. to Surg. Benjamin Blackford, Liberty Hospital:
I wish to establish a Way-Hospital at Liberty where quarters, rations and attendance may be furnished sick and wounded going home on furlough or on discharge—it must be furnished with suitable bedding and provisions—regulations similar to those of other hospitals—have it convenient to RR depots—select some of smaller hospitals now in use—use them only in emergencies for regular hospital purposes—report when prepared.

June 23, 1863, from Surg. Benj. Blackford, Liberty Hospital to Surg. W. A. Carrington, Med. Dir., Richmond, Va.:
Have received letter regarding proposed Way Hospital—Can use a hospital building on RR near station—it has accommodations for 85 patients—about 60 beds occupied—will serve as Way Hospital very well—is it to be registered and regulated with other hospitals or separately?

Correspondence Regarding Suggested Shoe Factory

Bedford County had its share of cobblers and apparently this was recognized by Blackford. Late in the war he had this suggestion for his superiors.

Feb. 16, 1864, from Surg. Benj. Blackford, Liberty Hospital, to Capt. C. K. Mallory, AQM, Liberty, Va.:
Beg to suggest that the Quarter-Master General be written to regarding the establishment of a shoe factory here for men who

come to the hospital without shoes—many are shoemakers by trade–could make shoes for themselves and others during their period of convalescence—a factory could be established without much cost to the government—would be a benefit to the service if it was established only to repair shoes of those sent to the hospital.

No reply to this memo has been located.

Correspondence Regarding Hunter's Raid

General David Hunter came from Lexington, Virginia, through Bedford County with his Union Army on his way to Lynchburg on June 15. He arrived in Lynchburg on June 17, was repulsed and retreated to Liberty the morning of the 19th, but continued on toward Roanoke.

June 13, 1864, from Surg. Benj. Blackford, Liberty Hospital, to Brig. Gen. W. F. Nichols, Comdt. Post, Lynchburg, Va.:
The enemy are reported at Buchanan. I have nearly 500 men besides my hospital bedding, which requires transportation. I respectfully ask that you order a train for me without delay.

June 20, 1864, from W. J. Moore, Surg., Liberty Hospital, to Brig. Gen. W. F. Nichols, Com. Post, Lynchburg, Va.:
Because of recent occupation of this post by the enemy, the stores and supplies were sent off—hospital fast filling with sick Confederates and Yankees—impossible to feed them—I request 10 days rations for 300 men at once—vouchers, etc. will be sent.[6]

June 28, 1864, from Surg. Benj. Blackford, Liberty Hospital, to Wm. A. Carrington, Med. Dir., Richmond, Va.:

---

[6]The same message was sent to Mr. Leftwich, Agt. Q. Mtr. for tax in kind, with this note added. "Assume the rations to be one third pound of bacon and one and one half pounds of flour. The commandant is absent—have no transportation."

When the enemy left this county, I returned to my post—except in building used as Wayside hospital, nothing had been disturbed—lost about 80 shirts and bed ticks at the Wayside Hospital—minor losses of goods not removed–was informed the building caught fire accidental—I am satisfied it was set on fire—it was near the Tannery and Foundry destroyed—the medical officers left in charge were paroled, but were informed by Gen'l. Early when he occupied the Tower that the parole would not be respected—sudden approach of the enemy and lack of transportation made it impossible to remove bedding—requisitions on Lynchburg not honored for fear of losing trains—I sent about 230 men to Lynchburg who could do duty in the trenches—others able to march were ordered to Danville—many took the woods and have returned—medical officers have all returned—no medicines, commissary stores or records lost—the sick and wounded left here were not paroled—condition of railroad and mails—left Surg. Moore in charge.

July 4, 1864, from W. A. Carrington, Med. Dir., Richmond, Va, to Surg. Benj. Blackford, Liberty Hospital:

Yours of the 28th received—your action during raid of enemy on Liberty is approved "with the exception that there need be no anxiety to remove hospital property or Medical Officers from the scene of action as they are always respected by the enemy, and if any capture is made of them they are given up on demand of our Commissioner. Paroles given under such circumstances are invalid, and only when the captor can hold the captive, until offered at City Point for parole, are paroles respected." This rule was first promulgated in a General Order by the United States Government, and at once operated to lose the U. S. Govt. some 10,000 men thus paroled irregularly.[7]

---

[7] The status of surgeons was at that time an unsettled point of international law. According to custom now in vogue, medical officers and hospitals need not parole unless they so desire, and in case they refuse the captor has either to carry them to the exchange point or liberate them.

CHAPTER XII

The Diary of Henry C. Sommerville

Henry Clay Sommerville, the son of James and Elizabeth Mauzy Sommerville, lived with his family in the small town of Bloomery, Virginia, now West Virginia, before the family moved to Ray County, Missouri. They made this move by covered wagon, horseback, and riverboat before the Civil War. Henry, with his older brother, William, returned later to live at White Post, near Berryville, Virginia. On June 8, 1862, Henry entered the Confederate service as a hospital steward. A steward typically acted as a physician assistant. His tenure began at the Piedmont Hospital in Liberty, Virginia.

Sommerville's diary gives an image of wartime Liberty, the people he knew here, and his experiences while here. It is the only diary known to have recorded daily the events of a doctor working within Bedford's hospital structure.

The excerpts quoted here are only a few passages taken from the entire diary, which is now at the Library of Virginia. These excerpts relate to Liberty, its people, and events from 1862 to 1865.

LIBERTY, VA., JUNE 8, 1862: This I think is as lovely a Sabbath day as I have ever beheld. I arose just as the sun was appearing above the distant eastern ridges. Everything was so calm, so beautiful and quiet. The atmosphere has a hazy appearance enabling me to look at the sun with as little difficulty as the moon. The hills and mountains are so lovely and green. The little birds, how sweetly they sing. This place, Piedmont Hospital, is an elevated spot overlooking the little village and country surrounding. I have a grand view of the Peaks of Otter and all the neighboring hills. There is not a sound to interrupt the calmness and grandeur of the occasion. Surely nature lends her blandest smiles as if praising her creator and everything animate and inanimate seems to say, "Praise the Lord." A few miles distant how great the contrast. There we find multitudes assembled burning with malice, hatred, revenge, and death. We can imagine them hurrying and burdened with weapons of destruction—ready to crush each other into dust and make the land flow with rivers of blood and whiten our green hills with their bleached bones. Awful! Terrible thought! Would that the Almighty might interfere and stay this awful carnage. Today brings my 28th birthday. I feel sad to think I have lived so long and done so little good. For nearly four years I have been striving to prepare myself to practice the profession of medicine. I find I am far from it yet, owing to this Civil War. I was deterred from graduating this past spring and I find myself with limited supply of means, delicate health, and a very fast accumulation of gray hairs. I have been a professor of religion more than four years and I do not see that I have made any advancement in righteousness and holiness and fear that I am as far from Heaven as when I first started on the way. I know I have as many temptations and evil passions as ever and alas! too often I yield to their impulses. I trust the Lord will not leave me to myself! but will cleanse, renew and make me his own.

I hope by His Grace and guidance to live and yet do much good. Today I attended worship service at the Episcopal Church. I am now entirely alone, away from all friends and kindred—my dear aged parents are in the far west where I also have one kind sister, still living and one other who sleeps her last, long sleep—dear precious sister, how I loved her! I also have two brothers, none of whom I have seen since April 1860. One brother I left in Moorefield, Hardy County, Virginia, another in Middletown, Frederick County, Virginia.

Where they are and what their fate is all unknown to me. I hope all is well. May the Lord be with us all and all whom I love and give us grace and strength as our day may require.

JUNE 15, 1862: I have become acquainted with two or three very interesting ladies. Miss Claytor, living about 6 or 7 miles from here and Miss Tool from Charlottesville. The first was so kind as to make me a nice present of cake and wine. Miss Lowry is also very kind and respectful to me. Heaven bless the women!

JUNE 22, 1862: Today I heard the Rev. Dr. Converse preach. He is quite an old gentleman and interesting preacher. In the afternoon I rode out in the country about 5 miles and visited Miss Tool. Found her quite agreeable, refined and intelligent young lady. Enjoyed my visit greatly.

JULY 4, 1862: A very clear, pleasant day—in the morning I drew rations for this ward. In the after part of this day I called on some ladies (Miss Coppage) did not enjoy myself much. I am acting as steward at Piedmont Hospital where is usually about 70 patients. My duties are not irksome, but confining and responsible. We have 7 buildings in this place, Liberty, occupied as hospitals making one General Hospital under the superintendence of Surgeon Benjamin Blackford, who, by the way, is quite a gentleman. We accommodate about 700 sick. At this time are crowded with sick, the larger portion Georgians. Diarhea (sic), Debility, (Debilitus)[exhaustion] and Rheumatism are the prevailing complaints though we have several cases of Phthisis Pulmonalis and Dysentery—very little fever or lung disease.[1]

---

[1] Despite the frequent discharges reported because of consumption, many cases of this disease were undoubtedly cured by the open-air life of the soldiers, anticipating by a generation the modern treatment. Chronic diarrhea and its frequent concomitant, dysentery, have always been scourges for the armies. (Houck, 1986, 65)

JULY 22, 1862: I celebrated by attending the marriage of Mr. Ed Rucker to Miss Saunders about 6 miles from Liberty.[2] Rode a miserable, poor, grey, lame horse, which I got from the Livery stable for what was promised to be a fine cantering steed. However, I got in company with my friends, Hardcastle and Sinclair who had each worse charges than I. We arrived sore and tired at the bride's father's about dark and immediately prepared for the important ceremony. Some 6 or 8 crowded into one room where there were three beds and perspired and washed, it being distressingly hot, putting on our white gloves etc....

...It was announced things were ready, whereupon we all descended and found the fair ones all gaily attired in their uniforms. We united arms, each to his partner and walked out on the floor without changing position. The ceremony being short was soon over. The table was surrounded by blooming beauties, but nothing luxurious presented itself—it being the most barren feast I have ever witnessed. Supper over, the party retired to the parlor where evening was spent very happily by the majority. About 12 o'clock it was proposed that we should ride—our steeds caught, we hasted away. Our journey gave instances of inconvenience of riding when it is so dark that

Home of Littleberry Saunders.
Courtesy of Mrs. Mabel H. Saunders and Miss Carolyn Saunders

---

[2] Bedford County Clerk's Office, Marriage Book 1, Page 49 shows this to be the marriage of Edward P. Rucker, son of Anthony and Dolly Rucker to Mary E. Saunders, daughter of Littleberry Saunders. Edward Rucker was a tobacconist.

no one object was visible. Some of the party were under the necessity of dismounting to search for the path amid brush, gullies, and rocks of no unimportant character. Others availed themselves of the use of certain gentlemen having white coats whose presence immediately in front served as a faint guide. ...Through fate or good luck, all finally reached his destination well assured of the fact that every pleasure has its ills.

The house still stands and now is owned and occupied by Carolyn Saunders and family.

AUGUST 13, 1862: Today taken with dysentery and fever... treated by Dr. Letcher, our assistant surgeon. He gave morphine... seems to have had a good effect....An occasional use of morphine and diet has restored me again. The ladies have been remarkably kind to me, sending something every day. I shall never forget their generosity toward me and feel very grateful to Providence for placing me among such good Christian people.

SEPTEMBER 2, 1862: This day I had the gratification of leaving Piedmont Hospital and getting rid of the tyranny of F.M. Letcher. I hope I may never again have anything to do with such a would-be somebody. Dr. Blackford ordered me to act as Hospital Steward in the absence of R.C. Powell, the regular steward.[3] When he returned I got a leave of absence to visit my friends in Northern Virginia. I left here by railroad by way of Lynchburg, Charlottesville, and to Staunton with dinner at Harrisonburg...staid the night at Woodstock, and then began for Middletown, Frederic County by stage, my place of destination...to see my brother....Joy to find them all safe and in good health. The joy of meeting absent friends is not expressible by words....On parting, all those unenviable feelings which lie so deeply hidden in the sensitive

---

[3] Sommerville was a hospital steward, a noncommissioned soldier who handled medical supplies and assisted the physician.

heart...but part we must...all our joys have their portion of bitterness.

I again landed in the ancient village of Liberty, a town known for its refinement, gaiety, and aristocracy. I was absent 12 days.

OCTOBER 26, 1862: Frosty morning. Rode up to the Peaks of Otter with Mr. Bell. Left horses at the base of the Peaks and walked up to the top. I never have witnessed anything so grand. Dined at the hotel.[4]

DECEMBER 25, 1862: A beautiful, calm, clear evening.

JANUARY 12, 1863: This morning I had the honor and pleasure of escorting Miss Claytor and Miss Crenshaw by railroad to Mr. John Steptoe's about 15 miles distant. We stayed three days and had fine music and singing all the while. During the winter we had frequent meetings of certain young people of the town which added much to our otherwise monotonous life and proved to be bright social gems giving their richness to make joyful the worn and saddened mind.

APRIL 2, 1863: I was notified to appear before the board. Studied as time would permit...an attack of jaundice hindered my progress...

APRIL 7, 1863: This day I had the pleasure and honor of attending my friend, Miss Claytor's marriage.[5] Her devoted, on

---

[4] At this time the hotel was located $1/2$ mile from the spring and operated by Nicholas Cabell Horsely. (Viemeister, 1992, 97)

[5] Bedford County Clerk's Office, Marriage Book 1, Page 2, shows that Robert T. Aunspaugh, age 24, the son of Frederic and Elizabeth Aunspaugh married Anna M. Claytor, age 24, daughter of Robert Mitchell Claytor and Julia Graham Claytor on April 7, 1863. They lived out their years in Liberty and had a family of four daughters and six sons.

a brief leave of absence, came from the Army, as he holds a position of 1st Lt. in PACS... I, together with nine other gentlemen acted as attendants to Lt. Aunspaugh. Our partners were a very nice group of ladies. I set about to prepare myself for examination before the Army Medical Board for Assistant Surgeon in the Provisional Army, Confederate States.

~

Sommerville had formerly attended the prestigious Pennsylvania Medical Institute. We do not know exactly when he decided to raise his status from steward to physician, but from his statement here he had about two months in which to prepare himself for the Army Medical Board examination. We might speculate that his mentor, Dr. Benjamin Blackford, recognized his potential as a physician and encouraged him to take the examination at a time when the Confederacy was in need of good doctors.

Peculiar as it may seem today, a person with medical training in the mid nineteenth century could become a medical doctor without having formerly attended a medical school. The Confederate Army soon discovered that charltons and quacks were masquerading as medical officers and in 1862 established a system of removing the unqualified. The Medical Examiners Department thus became a section of the Confederate Army Medical Headquarters in Richmond. Every physician, whether schooled or not, had to pass the fearsome medical examination. Dr. J.J. Terrell of Lynchburg wrote of his nervousness in passing the exam. Perhaps Sommerville was even more anxious, since he had not been a practicing physician, but a hospital steward for only two years. (Houck, 1986, 65)

~

JUNE 1, 1863: Left Liberty (for Richmond)... arrived in Richmond the morning of June 2, 1863....The board acted favorably in my case....Ordered to report to the Surgeon General and was sent to Medical Director, Carrington, with orders to report to the General Hospital at Liberty. Got back to Liberty with a high fever.

~

The stress of passing the stringent army medical exam was compounded by an "attack of jaundice" which was probably hepatitis, a serious disease even by today's standards, but it did not deter him from the fatiguing ride to Richmond. He described the examination as a day of great mental exertion and anxiety, leaving him depressed about the results. Already convinced he had failed, he reported the next day to the Surgeon General and to his surprise, found that they had acted favorably in his case.

This was exceedingly gratifying since many more experienced doctors had been unsuccessful.

This passed exam changed his status from hospital steward to military officer. He was now promoted to Assistant Surgeon, reassigned to Liberty Hospital and given immediate responsibility upon his return. He was in charge of 140 patients but found it laborious to attend to so many. "Before I get through my morning visits I am so wearied and exhausted that I can scarcely stand."

JUNE 8, 1863: Today is my 29th birthday.

JUNE 11, 1863: In charge of a ward containing 140 patients at Liberty.

DECEMBER 9, 1863: Wednesday evening...This beautiful starlit night was celebrated by the marriage of two acquaintances, Capt. Sale and Miss Bell who were married by an Episcopal minister, Mr. Wharton.[6] 10 attendants (ladies and gentlemen)...elegant refreshments...most pleasant evening. Left at 2 o'clock with regret that the time had come so soon

---

[6] Bedford County Clerk's Office, Marriage Book 1, Page 52, indicates that Lauriston A. Sale, son of Nelson and Anna A. Sale was married to Edmonia Bell, daughter of Cobb and Florentine Hatcher Bell on December 9, 1863. Lauriston Sale was a merchant.

for me to retire to my lonely and inhospitable den....Would that the time will come that I will have the pleasure of taking one of the fair creatures....

CHRISTMAS 1863: This cold, bright winter day was spent ten miles from Liberty at Mrs. Williams' with a company of very nice ladies....

SUNDAY, DECEMBER 27, 1863: First Sunday I have missed from church for months...owing to a collection of fellow officers protracted stay in my room. In obedience to an order from the Medical Director of Hospitals in Virginia, I this day took my departure from the quiet town of Liberty, a place where I have been one year and eight months of my life, the greater part of which has been most pleasantly spent. I have formed many agreeable acquaintances and some choice friends. The people to me have been kind and hospitable. I believe I have the respect and good will of all. I congratulate myself with the good fortune of having been allowed the privilege of remaining so long at a place where I could have all the advantages of civil life and enjoy the benefits of refined and intelligent society, combined with the elevating association of pious Christian companions. For all this, I am truly thankful. I trust it may never be my lot to be excluded from such associations.

~

Sommerville reported for duty to the hospital in Danville, as ordered, on December 30, 1863. He served there less than three months when in March 1864 he was ordered to report to Surgeon General William Otway Owen in Lynchburg, Virginia.

~

MAY 1864, AT LYNCHBURG, VA.: We now commenced receiving sick in large numbers from the Army of Northern Virginia. During the entire month I have kept almost constantly employed, not only during the day but also frequently at night. We received thus far about 4,000 sick and wounded this month. These are fearful times and fill the soul with sadness to be witness to so much suffering. Surely woe and lamentation pervade this land.

~

Sommerville did not fancy Lynchburg in the least; he was bored and spent much time indoors reading until May 1864 when he described working day and night with 4,000 sick and wounded, the aftermath of the Battle of the Wilderness (Houck, 1986, 117).

Sommerville found a place to live with a Mr. James A. Meriwether and spent the next few weeks in the company of his daughter, "feasting on strawberries and cream." Even though he was sorely pressed at Wayside Hospital, Lynchburg, he found time to keep company with Meriwether's daughter, Fannie. On December 14, 1864, the 30-year-old doctor took as his bride, Miss Fannie Meriwether, age 21, in Lynchburg, Virginia.[7]

~

APRIL 9, 1865, LYNCHBURG, VA.: Sunday. The weather is so inviting and lovely, yet this is one of the saddest and most heart sickening of the whole of this terrible war. In the early morning, cannonading was distinctly heard for some time. The hope was that Gen'l. Lee was fighting and driving back the enemy, and such was reported to be the fact in town—but, oh how differently did things come to be. Late in the afternoon it was announced by stragglers from the army that

---

[7] At the Lynchburg Circuit Court Office, in Marriage Book 2, Page, 29, is shown the marriage of Miss Fannie E. Meriwether, daughter of James A. Meriwether to Henry Sommerville, on December 14, 1864. This document shows that Sommerville was born in Hampshire County, West Virginia. They were married by The Rev. Kinckle of the Episcopal Church in Lynchburg. James A. Meriwether had a large and prosperous farming operation at Forest.

Gen'l. Lee had been forced to surrender to U.S. forces at Appomattox C.H.

～

When Sommerville left Lynchburg and the army for White Post in 1865 he took home with him an increased knowledge of and experience with medicine and a young wife and baby girl to sustain him through poverty and reconstruction. It can be assumed that they were frequent visitors back to Lynchburg and Liberty throughout the years. We are grateful that he left the gift of his diary, a poignant Civil War portrayal of Liberty in his day.

CHAPTER XIII
County Court and Central War Committee

County Court Orders tell us how many war needs were prevalent in Liberty and the county between the years of 1861-1865. In order to meet these needs, so widely spread over a large area, the county court, early in the war, appointed a Central War Committee composed of twelve persons, representing different sections of the county. It was to this committee that the court delegated much of the work of carrying out court orders pertaining to the war effort.

These orders show the variety of problems with which the county had to deal, some of local concern and others thrust upon the county by the Confederate Government.

Battlefield Visits

JUNE 1862: Members of the Central War Committee went to Richmond to care for the needs of wounded Bedford County soldiers from the Battle of Seven Pines. The War Committee felt that the public conditions required such action and the court agreed to reimburse the committee members for expenses incurred while traveling to and remaining in Richmond to care for and provide means to the county soldiers. The court requested that the same committee return to the battlefield when the next engagement took place and render aid to our wounded soldiers. Member's expenses were reimbursed by the Committee. (O.B. 34, Pg. 123)

FEBRUARY 1863: The court ordered that the War Committee employ a competent agent to visit the troops in service and to transport to and from them packages to be sent. In addition, the agent will perform duties in relation to their comfort. (O.B. Pg. 323)

Support of Soldiers and Indigent Families

Equipping and clothing volunteers and enlisted soldiers occupied much of the court's time. Indigent families of wounded soldiers as well as widows and children of soldiers who died in service were provided for by the county through the War Committee. In August 1861 and throughout the war, the county issued bonds drawn upon the Bedford Savings Bank for such sums as necessary for the support of these needy persons. (See Appendix B.)

Much of the county's debt for war purposes was taken care of by the sale of county bonds. Many persons lost their life savings when the county could not honor the bonds on maturity or at the end of the war.

JUNE 1862: Because citizens, both north and south, hoarded hard money, gold, silver and copper, during the Civil War, merchants were frequently unable to make change. The General Assembly passed a law permitting counties and larger cities to issue small notes of less than a dollar. The court authorized the issuance of notes in 15 denominations of less than $1.00, i.e.: 5¢, 10¢, 15¢, 20¢, 25¢, 30¢, 35¢, 40¢, 45¢, 50¢, 55¢, 60¢, 65¢, 70¢, 75¢, and ordered that the value of these not exceed $20,000. These notes were all dated July 1862 and signed by John A. Wharton, who was appointed agent for this currency. Notes were made by the county for dollar amounts also under the same date but did not bear the signature of Wharton.

Instead of borrowing $20,000 for the support of indigent families of soldiers, it would be raised by the sale of these notes. John A. Wharton was named agent and directed to contract for the paper, printing, etc. He was also instructed to number and sign each note for the presiding Justice of the Court, and from time to time, put them in circulation. Wharton was ordered to deposit the money received for the issued notes in the Bedford Savings Bank to the credit of the county and periodically report to the court (O.B. 34, Pg. 124, 141).

Bedford County Notes

NOVEMBER 1862: An order by the County Court shows its intent to care for its own and assist the Confederate government in clothing troops from Bedford County. The court appointed commissioners were ordered to visit the armies and ascertain the needs of the troops from Bedford County, including shoes, socks, blankets, and all articles of clothing. John Goode, Jr. would then go to Richmond to confer with the Confederate government about arrangements for assistance in furnishing the clothing. The county proposed to secure, provide, and deliver the clothing for which the Confederate government would pay.

In the meantime the Justices would determine the kind and quality of clothing which could be procured in their respective districts, the availability of materials and the facilities for making or manufacturing these clothes as well as the probable cost. These Justices were to solicit voluntary contributions of clothing as well as materials and hold these until further order of the court. (O.B. 34, Pg. 187-188), Appendix B.

The court ordered that widows and minor children of indigent soldiers who have died in the service of the Confederate States should receive like support and maintenance from the county for one year as if the said soldier were living and serving. Central War Committee to provide for them. (O.B. 34, Pg. 206)

1864: Justices were summoned to court to execute an Act of the General Assembly passed on October 31, 1863, for the relief of indigent soldiers and sailors who had been disabled in military service. The court appointed one person from each magisterial district as purchasing agent with authority to purchase the needed quantity of supplies for a three-month period at prices not to exceed:

Flour	$200 per bushel	Beef	$2 per pound
Corn	$20 per bushel	Potatoes	$8 per bushel
Bacon	$5 per pound	Wheat	$30 per bushel

When and if it was impossible to purchase these supplies at lesser cost, agents were authorized to impress supplies at a price not to exceed those stated above, preferring not to impress articles in the hands of persons who had purchased these for speculation. (O.B. 34, Pg. 420)

Another order this year appointed one person in each magisterial district to ascertain the number and condition of families of soldiers in the military service who are receiving supplies and aid from the county. These appointees were to report their present condition to the court and to recommend those who would continue to be entitled to aid in whole or in part and the reason therefor. (O.B. 34, Pg. 420), Appendix B.

Gift to the Confederate Government

MAY 25, 1863: The court ordered that the leaden ornaments on the railing in front of the courthouse lot be presented to the Confederate Government by the County of Bedford for the purpose of making cartridges and that John A. Spilman, the agent of the Government at Lynchburg, be authorized to remove the said lead to be appropriated for the purpose aforesaid. (O.B. 34, Pg. 290)

Salt

Salt was a vital commodity for health and for preservation of foods.

MAY 1862: The court ordered John Buford to purchase 20,000 bushels of salt from the salt works in Smythe and Washington Counties and to contract for it to be delivered to the Liberty Depot as soon as possible. He was authorized to pay for the salt, the cost of transportation and any other necessary expenses. This money was to be raised also by negotiating a sale at par of county bonds. The court appointed Judge E. C. Burks, Rowland D. Buford (Clerk of Court), Alban A. Arthur (County Treasurer), John A. Wharton (Banker), and Charles Aunspaugh to receive the salt when delivered and to hold it until future order of the court. (O.B. 34, Pg. 114)

JUNE 1862: John Buford reported that the salt had been purchased for the use of people of Bedford County. The court proceeded to make rules and regulations for the sale and distribution of salt. John Buford was appointed Salt Commissioner, and the following persons were appointed commissioners for the magisterial districts:

Charles Aunspaugh	District 1	Liberty
Samuel G. Stewart	District 2	Stewartsville
James Wilson	District 3	Davis Mill
Elijah Cundiff	District 4	Fancy Grove
Samuel Hughes	District 5	Wade's Precinct
Dr. Hector Harris	District 6	Forest
William Almond	District 7	Charlemont
Thomas Kelso	District 8	Peaksville
Pleasant Cofer	District 9	Buford's Depot

The duties of the commissioners were to receive the salt, to transport it to the depot at Liberty, to divide the monthly installments into nine equal parts, and to deliver one part to each district commissioner at the depot.

The duties of the district commissioners were to receive the salt, transport it to the district's place of distribution promptly and to distribute and sell for cash to citizens in the district. The district commissioner would then collect the proceeds, deduct the expenses of transportation, deduct 5% on sales to retain as compensation for his trouble, and deposit the money in the Bedford Savings Bank at Liberty to the credit of the court. "The commissioner shall sell salt at $2 per bushel and 50¢ for each sack. Commissioners should take regard for the population of the district, in order to regulate sales and apportion each person nearly the same quantity. They must enter into a bond of $5,000 each." (O.B. 34, Pg. 124)

AUGUST 1862: One district commissioner deposited $100.23 for salt sales in Wade's Precinct. (O.B. 34, Pg. 161)

NOVEMBER 1862: The court fixed the price to sell salt at 6¢ per pound. By March 1863 the sale price was increased to 8¢ per pound. (O.B. 34, Pg. 206, 267)

FEBRUARY 1863: Micajah Davis was acting as salt agent for the county and advanced $10,857.40 to John C. Clarkson, State Supt. of Salt Works, due him from the county for its quota of salt. The Central War Committee was ordered to refund this sum to Davis. The committee was again authorized to sell bonds for this expenditure.

Mr. Clarkson proposed to the county to hire from Bedford County two Negro men for twelve months to labor at the salt works in manufacturing salt, for whom he would pay the county $300 a year each and pay the doctor bills. Micajah Davis proposed to the court that he hire to the county two men for this purpose. The court ordered Davis to deliver the slaves to Clarkson and take from him an obligation to the county with terms of contract. (O.B. 34, Pg. 323)

MARCH 1863: The court officially appointed Micajah Davis as its salt agent and declared that each person, white or black, bond or free, was to receive an equal amount of salt, but only after persons have filed with the distribution agent an affidavit showing the number of persons in his family entitled to receive salt. Sacks were to be retained and returned as soon as emptied to be preserved by the county agent. Micajah Davis "will act as agent for Liberty District and will receive compensation of 30¢ per sack of salt distributed." The agent's bond was set at $20,000.

Apparently in 1863, the county had more need for salt, since in March the court ordered E. C. Burks and J. F. Johnson to contract for the county the best terms for salt supply not to exceed twelve months from the expiration of their present contract with Stuart Buchanan Co. Again in September 1863, Micajah Davis was ordered to correspond with the State Supt. of Salt Works in order to stock the county as soon as possible. (O.B. 34, Pg. 268)

Slaves

An Act of the General Assembly passed in October 1862 required that each county impress 10% of its male slave population between the ages of 18 and 45 to work on fortifications at various battlefields in the state for sixty to ninety days. In order to accomplish this, the county had to first determine the names of slaveholders, the number of slaves owned by each, and the number each hired to work out. Each slaveholder was assigned a quota (10%) of his slaves to be delivered to the Virginia & Tennessee Railroad depot in Liberty from which place they would be sent out. Slaveholders who failed or refused to produce their quota of slaves were

COUNTY COURT AND CENTRAL WAR COMMITTEE 217

to be fined $3 per day late for each slave. Their quota was then ordered seized by the sheriff and delivered to the depot. The county court lost no time in responding to this Act by the General Assembly. Jesse Minter was appointed General Agent to superintend the delivery of slaves to the Confederate authorities in Liberty and accompany them to Richmond if necessary. (O.B. 34, Pg. 192). See Appendix B.

In March 1863, the county reported that 276 slaves were furnished for 60 days, commencing in November 1862. Twenty-one slaves were furnished for 90 days commencing in January 1863, for a total of 297 slaves furnished by March 1863. Sixty-nine additional slaves were exempt from Confederate authority because they had been impressed to work on the James River and Kanawha Canal and on the railroad, iron works, and other public works. One-hundred-sixty-four slaves were furnished in the fall of 1861 for 30 days service as teamsters at Huntersville.[1]

---

[1] Huntersville was a small town with an 1861 population of 100 persons: it was the first seat of Pocahontas County, located in that part of Virginia which became West Virginia. The town was situated in what was called the Northwest Passage, the lowest point of the Allegheny Mountains. During the Civil War, Huntersville was occupied by Confederate General W. W. Loring and considered strategically important, as well as being a vital supply center. When Major George Webster (Union Army) raided Huntersville on New Year's Day, 1862, it was the first time federal troops had penetrated so far south into the Confederate held territory of eastern West Virginia. They burned a large barn containing community stores and destroyed large amounts of clothing and food, including 350 barrels of flour, 150,000 pounds of salted beef, and 30,000 pounds of salt. Official correspondence shows losses estimated at:

Commissary	$ 10,227.75
Quartermaster	$ 2,063.66
Buildings owned by private individuals	$ 3,000.00
TOTAL	$15,291.41

(Southern Historical Paper, 169)

There was considerable disloyalty to the Confederate cause in Pocahontas County, many false rumors circulated, and most military

SEPTEMBER 1863: Another quota listing was presented to the court, which ordered slaves delivered to the sheriff at the Virginia & Tennessee Railroad Depot. The age limit was increased from 18-45 to 18-55. (O.B. 34, Pg. 338)

OCTOBER 1863: Justices summoned a number of persons to show cause why they should not be fined for failure to deliver their slave quota. Those persons were:

Thomas W. Leftwich	John A. Hunt
G. & C. Morgan	Abner Fuqua
Abraham Fuqua	N. H. Markham
William A. Creasy	Joseph Johnson
A. M. Ewing	Caleb Heptinstall
W. K. Lowry	H. A. Whitely

Those listed above showed sufficient cause and were excused from fine. These were slaves subject to only 60 days labor.

Stephen Peters	John M. Brosius
James Wilson	O. H. Perry
B. M. Kyle	James P. Holcombe
Mrs. Samuel Griffin	Robert Rosebrough

Those above showed sufficient cause for failing to deliver one slave each and were excused conditioned upon their slaves being delivered within a reasonable time. Mrs. Griffin's slave is a runaway and if apprehended is to be delivered. The slaves of Rosebrough and Wilson are sick and when improved are to be delivered. These only subject to 60 days service.

---

transactions at the camp were somehow communicated to the enemy. These problems obviously made Huntersville a difficult post to command. In the fall of 1861 the assumption can be made that slaves acted as teamsters taking supplies into or out of Huntersville for the Confederate Army. (Comstock, Vol. II, 1976, 2409)

James Lockridge	Samuel G. Claytor
Eleanor Merriman	Francis J. Turner
John J. Robertson	Samuel G. Stewart
Ayler and Ferguson

Those listed above showed sufficient cause, which were errors in the order making them exempt from the draft. They were excused from fines and exempted altogether.

James A. Merewether(sic)	Cha. D. McGhee
Charles Scott	Wm. H. Bowling
Wesley Peters	John F. Hawkins
James Lancaster	Editha Davis
Segar Coffee	Robert G. Scott and
	Brother, William
R. Scott & Co.	Benjamin Blackford
J. & C. A. Meriweather	Allen D. Hatcher

Each of the above was required to deliver one slave, except Scott who must deliver five and Blackford who must deliver two.

The court fined these $3.00 per slave for each day of failure to deliver slaves.

Wesley Peters $15	Jas. A. Meriweather $75
James Lancaster $75	Chas. D. McGhee $75
Charles Scott $375	Wm. H. Bowling $75
John F. Hawkins $75	Editha Davis $75
Segar Coffee $75	Robert G. Scott & Brother $75
Wm. R. Scott & Co. $75	J. & C. A. Meriweather $75
Allen D. Hatcher $75	Benjamin Blackford $150

The above persons were fined and their slaves ordered seized to meet their quota.

FEBRUARY 1864: Again by court order of February 11, 1864, slaveholders were listed in the court order book and ordered to surrender their quota. (O.B. 34, Pg. 386)

The War Committee attorney was also ordered to communicate with the Confederate authorities in Richmond to ascertain whether the recent draft on the county for slaves could be suspended. (O.B. 34, Pg. 395)

MARCH 1864: The Sheriff reported the following persons who failed or refused to deliver their quota pursuant to the order of February 11, 1864, were summoned in March 1864 to show cause why they should not be fined.

Charles B. Fizer	Harwood Major	James Metcalf
Wm. Ogden	Benjamin Walker	David Staples
A. M. Kyle	John Ogden	Joshua Reynolds

The above named had sufficient cause and were excused.

Mrs. Sophia Martin	Almond & Brothers
Estate of William A. Read	Stephen T. Peters for Elisha Peters

These have met their quotas and are excused.

Charles Scott, quota six slaves, was fined $19 per slave per day for 33 days of failure to deliver, or $1,980.

Wm. Bowling, quota one slave, was fined $3 per day for each day of failure to deliver, or $99.

The sheriff was ordered to seize the quota of these and deliver the slaves to the Confederate authorities by the Virginia & Tennessee Railroad and the James River and Kanawha Canal. (O.B. 34, Pg. 413)

SEPTEMBER 1864: The court again ordered the War Committee attorney to confer with the Secretary of War, Confederate States, to ascertain whether the slave draft on Bedford County could be suspended. (O.B. 34, Pg. 395, 464)

Meeting the slave quota for the Confederate authorities became a burden from which the county and its residents clearly wished to be relieved. For the first draft, the quota was 411 slaves. With each succeeding draft, the number decreased to 301 in 1863 and 148 in 1864, even though the acceptable age was increased to 55. Two drafts were made in 1865: January produced 132 slaves and April produced 145 with the help of 12 from the Virginia & Tennessee Railroad Co., 5 from the James River & Kanawha Canal Co., and 10 from G. K. Wetmer, Agent. We might assume that war damage to the railroad and canal limited their ability to operate at full strength, making these workers available for service at the battlefield where they were needed. (O.B. 34, Pg. 505,532).

On January 28, 1865, the court ordered it certified that Bedford County had furnished the Confederate Government since the commencement of the present war, by impressments of slaves, the following:

November 1862 for 60 days	276
January 1863 for 90 days	021
	297

Number detailed or exempted under the same draft	069
Teamsters sent to Huntersville, Va. for 30 days	164
Slaves furnished the Confederacy by March 1863	233

(O.B. 34, Pg. 267)

Impressed for defenses near Richmond, latter part of 1864, for 12 mo. service	052
Hired to the Confederate Government, for 12 months service, 1865	100
Total now in Confederate Government service for 12 months	152

Impressed under order October 1863, on Lynchburg defenses, 60 days	174
Impressed under order February 1864 on Richmond defenses, 40 days	130
Impressed for defenses near Petersburg, October 1864, 60 days	116
Impressed under State Law January 1865 for 60 days service on defenses near Richmond and Petersburg	<u>130</u>
TOTAL	1232

The court also certified the following on January 28, 1865, there were 1441 male slaves in the county between 18 and 55 years old.

That 201 male slaves between 18-45 years old and 64 male & female slaves of other ages escaped to the enemy, mainly during Hunter's Raid in June 1864. (O.B. 34, Pg. 508)

~

As the war wore down, the burden became increasingly heavy, not only in Bedford County, but in all of Virginia. One wonders how much longer the citizens could have carried a burden which increased each year, as their worth decreased. While the Court Orders give us a flavor of life during those days, it is remarkable to think of the many accomplishments of the court justices and the War Committee during a period of unrest and seemingly insurmountable obstacles.

CHAPTER XIV
Hunter's Raid

In June 1864, General David Hunter of the Union Army was advancing from Lexington, Virginia, toward Lynchburg, a vital supply center, with the intention of obtaining food and needed supplies and burning the city. When it was learned that Hunter planned to capture Lynchburg, not through Amherst as expected, but through the Peaks of Otter and Bedford County, with an invasion force of nearly 20,000, anxiety reigned supreme in Liberty. On June 15, Hunter's army arrived in Liberty and after burning, looting, and being generally destructive, eventually marched on to Lynchburg down two eastern pikes (now Routes 221 and 460). He arrived in Lynchburg on June 17, was repulsed, and retreated later that evening. Hunter's army returned to Liberty the morning of June 19 about 8 A.M. and continued west up the turnpike by Buford's and Bonsack.

Many versions of Hunter's Raid on Liberty have been given. No attempt has been made in this chapter to look at the raid from a military standpoint, but only to give the reader a glimpse of the raid from the eyes of those citizens who were affected. Included here are excerpts from letters and diaries giving individual accounts of Hunter's Raid on Liberty and showing clearly what the local residents endured.

Major General David Hunter and his staff spent the night of June 15, 1864, at Fancy Farm, at the base of the Peaks of Otter on what is now Route 43. With them was Thornton M. Hinkle, correspondent of the *Cincinnati Gazette*. Extracts from his journal show the sequence of events from the Union perspective as the raid proceeded.

The following excerpts are taken from an article by Mrs. Jack Hayes, which appeared in the *Bedford Bulletin-Democrat* of June 29, 1977.

*Robert Kelso home, Fancy Farm,
now owned by the Henry Clarke family*

WEDNESDAY, JUNE 15, 1864: We take breakfast at 3:45 this morning. I ride with Lt. Col. Ardney of the 36th. He gives me lessons on Botany and Geology. The scenery is beautiful. We are nearing the Peaks of Otter, the highest mountains in Virginia. [This was thought to be true at that time.] I mourn over the body of a dead captain, one of our advance guard. They are digging his grave by the roadside...we halt for the night at Fancy Farm. Our tents are set under the oaks in a beautiful lawn. The Peaks of Otter tower above us, the stars and silvery moon shine, while all around us the campfires and signal lights add brilliance to the scene. [General Hunter sent a cavalry unit in to occupy the town that afternoon.]

THURSDAY, JUNE 16, 1864: A dreadfully hot and tedious day. We have a long halt and wait in Liberty. We take lunch at the hotel.[1] The sun is very hot. We find our men busy destroying the railroad, burning ties, bridges, and bending rails....

---

[1] The hotel was located 1/2 mile from the spring and operated by Nicholas Cabell Horsely at this time. (Viemeister, 1992, 97.)

HUNTER'S RAID

FRIDAY, JUNE 17, 1864: We are underway at five o'clock. We are very near Lynchburg.[2] In the afternoon we are in sight and find a strong force in trenches between us and the city. One of our brigades is sent forward to attack them. They charge and we have a regular battle. I manage to get in the line of fire. I have generally a hard time trying to see what is going on and yet keep out of danger. I finally get on a hill with the Signal Corps. Night coming on compels cessation of fighting and I hear all about the day at the supper table. It has been a victory so far, but a great many of our brave boys have been killed or wounded. I put Medical Director to bed drunk. After that I join a party to help take care of the wounded. It is a beautiful moonlight night, but I cannot enjoy it. We pass along the line of the charge from group to group of the dead and dying. One little group, all the victims of only one shell, are mere boys, some of them fearfully mangled. It all appeals to my sympathies most powerfully. We travel on for a mile. I shall never be able to forget the pitiful moans and cries of the poor anguished victims, nor can I describe the scene.

---

[2] The men knew that Hunter's expectation was for them to live off the land by pillaging for food and provisions. Even though this impeded their speed, he continued burning homes and general destruction of the land and buildings along the way. The William A. Read family lived at Liberty Hall on highway 460 near New London. About 10 o'clock General Hunter and his staff rode up, tied their horses to the fence and seated themselves in the shade. Knowing of Lynchburg's hurried preparation, Mr. Read invited Hunter and his staff in for breakfast. While chickens were killed, biscuits were made, and mint juleps were served all at a leisurely pace for the purpose to delay the invaders as long as possible. After a late breakfast the group repaired to the parlor where the ladies played the piano for them. All sang and danced. While Hunter loitered, General Early reached Lynchburg and made preparation to defend the city. [This story from *New London Now and Then* states that this occurred on June 16; however a newspaper article from the *Lynchburg News* on Oct. 12, 1958, quotes the same story as occurring on June 18. Neither Hinkle or Strother mention this stop on either day in their journals.]

SATURDAY, JUNE 18, 1864: We are up very early. Gen. Crook and his division staff are off on a flanking movement. I visit one of our hospitals in a brick house. While I am there, the Rebels open up with shot and shell, which fly all around us. The Rebels are massing for a heavy attack on our center. All night last night, our advance forces heard the whistle of locomotives entering Lynchburg. The report is that General Jubal Early's Corps has been brought over from Richmond. If so, we shall have to resist, instead of making charges. I visit another hospital and spend some time favoring and otherwise comforting a poor fellow named Edward B. Wood from the 18th. Both of his legs have been cut off at the knees by one cannon ball. I comb the hair of a great many poor fellows, which seems a great comfort to them. I take dinner with Capt. Craig… raw onions and salt, water and hard crackers. Nothing has been going on all morning but scattered fire. I lie down near our artillery and have a good sound nap. The Rebels open up furiously with shot and shell and follow with a charge. Our men repulse them, but our raid is a failure. We can go no further, so the General decides we must retreat. So at 5 o'clock I leave, the retreat being commenced. Gen. Crook's division is made the rear guard. We ride on and on until 3 o'clock in the morning when a halt is made to get the command together. I lie down and fall asleep in a furrow of a plowed field thoroughly done up.

SUNDAY, JUNE 19, 1864: [Location—five miles from Liberty.] Lt. F. L. Torrence of the 12th Ohio, one of the wounded died. I awaken while he is being buried by the roadside…arise and walk with Dr. Webb to Liberty. I have a good rest in a house while he talks to a lady who is arrayed in the most highly colored dress. I dine with Col. Hayes [later President Rutherford B. Hayes] and then call on General Hunter with him and learn of the many difficulties in our way. The rebels are in hot pursuit and are trying to reach the gap in the mountains [Buford's Gap] before us. If successful, we will probably have to surrender. Our provisions are about out and powder nearly gone. We keep on all night. I sleep some in my saddle, some on the back step of an ambulance, and in the seat of the driver, some in the little ten-minute halts. We had no supper and Lieut. Herman Koenigsberger of the 28th Ohio gives me some scraps of cracker scooped out of his coat pocket.

MONDAY, JUNE 20, 1864: Thanks to Dr. Nellons of the 91st Ohio, I have two or three flapjacks for breakfast. Our headquarters is broken up for the present. Gen. Crook and his staff are actively engaged in protecting the rear. I wait by the roadside for his division. They spread out in line of battle and await a Rebel attack, but they refuse to come on, so we move forward. I have a long ride and talk with Maj. John F. Hoffman of the 2nd West Virginia and Lt. Foster. Visit Hunter's headquarters and learn all the news I can, then join Dr. Kellogg. We ride all night again without supper. I pass a little time in an ambulance, but get no rest. Dreadfully hungry and sleepy.

TUESDAY, JUNE 21, 1864: I am my own cook for breakfast. While we are all halting and endeavoring to get something to eat, the rebels suddenly send three shells right into camp. I sit on a horse near Gen. Hunter while he rapidly issues his orders to meet this unexpected attack. He seems to be unduly excited, almost panic stricken. He thumps some of his men on the back in his attempt to hurry them on the way. They are teamsters. This alarm is soon over. When we first halt for the usual five minutes rest, Dr. Nellons and I rest in a little woods. While thus lying and chatting, we hear some firing and noise and a little later learn that a strong Rebel detachment has rushed down from the mountains right into the midst of our artillery, driven off our men, spiked the guns, and captured the horses, and then retreated safely back into the mountains. [This was an operation of the so-called Rebel bushwhackers, or guerilla forces, that fell upon the Union Army at unexpected moments all during their retreat through Bedford County.] So these cannon and caissons had to be left behind. Some fool set fire to them and after awhile, they blew up, killing and wounding some of our men. At noon I have a good wash. We are now ascending the mountains. We are bushwhacked all day. After a supply of flapjacks, I find I cannot stand it any longer. I simply cannot ride horseback any further. Capt. Nash captures a buggy, puts two mules in it, and sets it apart for my use. At seven o'clock I lie down to sleep as long as I can in what I suppose is a short halt only. I go to sleep to the music of one of the bands.

WEDNESDAY, JUNE 22, 1864: I awake at seven and find that we have lain here all night. Our cavalry are in the [Buford's] Gap at last. What a glorious sleep I had all night. Our only reason for haste now is to get some food for our poor men. We start at first on the wrong road and have to retrace our steps. I ride with the 36th. We go on all day, without halting until we reach Newcastle. I ride and talk principally with Col. Ardney and share his dinner of cold flapjacks and chicken. At Newcastle a small boy is accidentally shot. I ride through town with Capt. Seymour Brownell. We are all in Headquarters together in a pretty house and yard near town. I have a good supper and sleep all night.

THURSDAY, JUNE 23, 1864: I ride all morning with Gen. Crook and have a full and free talk with him. He seems almost worn out. The bushwhackers are now troubling us again, this time up front. We captured four of them. We lunch at Kyles. I ride with Generals Hunter and Crook in the afternoon and we have a rather pleasant time. They introduce me to some new and exceedingly pleasant conundrums. We are still struggling up over mountains. It is hot, tiresome, hungry work. The poor men are starving. Some of them have even eaten all of our store of candles. We stop at Sweet

Springs, a beautiful place. We go to sleep on the parlor floor, supperless. I touch up a piano near my resting place.

FRIDAY, JUNE 24, 1864: I am awakened by "The Minuet" from "Don Juan" played by a private of the 12th Ohio. We lie all morning at Sweet Springs and I have a good, long nap. We finally start at 3 P.M. after I recover from despair over the disappearance of my horse that only turns up after a long search. I ride with Capt. Hayes who gives me a full account of his views on the fight last Saturday. Then I meet and ride with Col. Samuel D. Johnson of the 14th West Virginia, a friend of mine at Marietta. And later with Col. Duval of the 9th West Va. who tells me the story of his life. He has been away from home for fourteen years. One of his brothers had 20 years and another brother had 17 years fighting out west with the Indians. Later I ride with Cols. White and Nesbitt. At ten o'clock at night we stop at White Sulphur Springs, tired out. Go to sleep supperless, on the porch of the main building. While walking through the parlor, I see one soldier carrying off a bunch of keys as big as his hand. Not all of our men are gentlemen. Some are bummers and will steal everything, whether it is useful or not.

SATURDAY, JUNE 25, 1864: Again have a difficult time finding my horse. I spend the morning with Gen. Crook and lunch with him and Gen. Hunter at Greenbriar Ford. Our rations are all out. Couriers have been sent forward to hurry up supplies. Maj. Skinner is to go forward to expedite matters and take a dispatch that I have prepared for the *Gazette*. We stop for the night near a farmhouse. Once more supperless, I sleep on the porch, my saddle for a pillow. Hunter's staff do not impress me favorably. They seem too much Fuss and Feathers.

SUNDAY, JUNE 26, 1864: It has been fifteen days since I left my newspaper in Cincinnati, but it seems like fifteen years to me. We start early. Lt. E. Roberts of the 34th Ohio who suffers from a pistol shot wound in his mouth concluded to ride on in advance of the Army with Gen. Hunter. I determine to go with him so I take a farewell breakfast by the roadside with Gen. Crook. This over, we gallop on past the regiments wearily marching and I see the last of our brave boys. They are happy enough today for the supply train is near at hand. We dine on milk and corn bread and ride through to "Widow Jones" where we have supper of buttermilk, biscuits and poor coffee and pass the night sleeping poorly on the porch.

End of Hinkle's Journal.

~

Also traveling with General Hunter as a member of his staff was David Hunter Strother, a nephew and namesake of the general. Strother was a writer and an artist who had already published articles and drawings under the name of Porte Crayon. He has left more than thirty journals, which deal with his experiences during the war and until his death in 1888. A native Virginian, he was born in 1816 in Martinsburg, now located in West Virginia. The following excerpts are taken from the *Iron Worker*, Spring 1960 which published data as it referenced Hunter's Raid. After the burning of VMI in Lexington, the Union Army traveled to Buchanan to secure the bridge there and proceed over the mountain toward Liberty and Lynchburg, where was held a depot of supplies and a central railroad communication system with the Confederacy. Strother also left a journal of his experiences in Bedford County during this raid.

~

JUNE 14, 1864, TUESDAY:...a long, dusty but not unpleasant march brought us to Buchanan about sunset. We took quarters at the Haynes Hotel. Tomorrow's march arranged, Crook and Averill will move by the Peaks of Otter Road to Liberty. Sullivan and Duffie will follow. [The bridge had already been burned by Confederate Gen. McCausland.]

JUNE 15, 1864, WEDNESDAY: No sight of the enemy…we halted at the hotel between the Peaks, and while there our cavalry plundered the smoke house, getting a hundred pieces of bacon. Averill occupies Liberty with a brigade… We took headquarters in the house of one Kelso, an old fashioned brick, handsomely located in a grove of oaks with a full view of the Peaks of Otter.

JUNE 16, 1864, THURSDAY: The town of Liberty which we entered this morning is much improved since I saw it last. Our troops I fear are plundering the town and misbehaving terribly as women and children are besieging the General's door for protection. Averill told me he had seen a Confederate soldier's wife just from Lynchburg who gave him important intelligence. I called to see her and she told me she had left Lynchburg yesterday morning. The place is not strongly fortified and in this direction the only works were shallow rifle pits. All the sick and wounded had been organized to defend the place. …Soon horse, foot and artillery were started en route for Lynchburg. The day was very hot and the climate quite different from the Valley. Water was not plentiful and the land was poorer, and grazing not near so good or abundant. Averill sends word back he will camp beyond the Great Otter River tonight. Crook is marching on the line of the Va. & Tenn. RR destroying as he moves. We see the smoke columns from burning bridges on the left.

We halted for the night at a large deserted house, six miles from Liberty. It had been built on a stylish plan and was said to be haunted… I feel a vague uneasiness as to the result of our move. Lee will certainly relieve Lynchburg if he can. If he cannot, the Confederacy is gone up. If he does succeed in detaching a force, our situation is most hazardous.

JUNE 17, 1864, FRIDAY: Was aroused about 2 A.M. by the General. He showed me a dispatch from Averill stating that he had had a sharp fight at New London, about eight miles from here. The staff and escort were ordered to saddle and mount. I was directed to go to Sullivan and order him to move immediately on New London...we found the bridge at Great Otter not ready. Neither the artillery nor the trains could get across. This further delay will prove fatal to us.

McCain reported that a man named Leftwich had told him some stories of our troops being badly defeated both east and west. This irritated the General so much that he had Leftwich arrested and ordered his house to be burnt. It was a very pretty country residence and the man had a sweet daughter about sixteen and a nice family. The house was burnt and destroyed.[3] Halpine, Stockton and myself rode away saying nothing but did not wish to look upon the scene.

One of our couriers had been fired upon from the yard of one Col. Mosby (whether the guerilla or not I do not know).[4] The Gen'l. doomed his house to destruction but after burning Leftwich's he seemed to relent and as we passed he said to me, "I don't think I'll burn it." I advised him to spare it and thus the matter ended.

We came upon Averill's force at New London. The heat was intense.

From 6:30 to 7 P.M. Crook's Division engaged with musketry and artillery with great fury. During this engagement the General's staff arrived on the field, near enough to be under artillery fire and to witness the gallant conduct of

---

[3] This home was located across highway 460 from the site of Sunnyside on the north side of the highway and built by Col. William Leftwich in 1791. The name of the Leftwich family whose home was burned is not known.

[4] This was the home of Col. Thomas Yeatman Mosby who lived across highway 460 from the present Owen's Market. Another house now occupies this site. Mosby, whose home was on the north side of the highway, was active in county government. He was twice married, first to Elizabeth M. Callaway who died in 1863 and second to Caroline West of Westwood, in 1865.

Crook's troops driving the enemy in confusion from the field, capturing seventy prisoners and one gun.

This handsome little affair took place at Quaker Church five miles from Lynchburg and cost us forty men killed and wounded. It concluded about dark and we were much disposed to follow on into the town, but the chiefs thought it more prudent to wait for morning light. The staffs of all the generals, Hunter, Crook, and Averill took quarters at the house of one Major Hutton [Hutter], formerly paymaster in the US Army and an old acquaintance of General Hunter. A good supper and slept profoundly.

JUNE 18, 1864, SATURDAY: When I went to the front I found our troops close up to the enemy lines. The staff approached the tollgate on the Bedford Road. We saw a strong redoubt on the left of the road and the enemy actively engaged to their right. The appearance of the staff in the open ground was the signal for the opening of their batteries upon us. Ours replied and there was a rapid cannonade for twenty minutes. Duffie had been ordered to press vigorously on the Forestville line and at 12:30 his guns were heard on our extreme left. The heavy balls came whistling back among the staff, one passing between the General and Stockton as they sat talking on horseback. I called on Sullivan who was with Col. Thoburn lying on the ground on some boards. Sullivan said he had heard the railroad trains coming and going all night, also cheering and military music, which indicated the arrival of troops in the town. Since morning the lines were very much strengthened and were pressing him hard. He was sustaining himself but with difficulty. He said he was ready to attack if ordered but felt it would end in disaster. Thoburn spoke in the same strain and in much more decided language. I said I had begun to suspect they were right and that I would represent their views to the General. At the same time if an attack were ordered I wanted to know where he would advise attacking. He had no choice and would not suggest, so convinced was he that the enemy was strongly reinforced.

I reported to General Hunter Sullivan's views as I heard them. He seemed dissatisfied and at the same time hesitated to order the advance. For half an hour a battle raged when the cheers of our men indicated the enemy was checked. On the first attack the enemy drove 300 sheep into our lines, all of which were butchered and issued for supper. Five prisoners were questioned which indicated beyond doubt that Ewell's Corps commanded by Lt. Gen'l. Early was in Lynchburg. They represented the force in Lynchburg at thirty thousand men. The commanders acknowledged the position to be critical and all agreed that we must get out if possible. Crook was cool and matter of fact. Averill was excited and angry. He said to me "I would give my head this night if we could have taken Lynchburg." Gen'l. Hunter immediately ordered the trains to move on the back track toward Buford's Gap. The General and staff retired to Major Hutton's [Hutter's] from where we started in the morning. Our troops were all withdrawn in silence and our picket line remained until midnight, when it also withdrew and overtook the main body in safety. We took off everything except about 150 wounded, which Dr. Hayes had in a temporary hospital and left because he had no notice of the move. This withdrawal in the face of a superior force was well conducted and successful. We had a pleasant ride by moonlight and by 2 o'clock in the morning got back to our old quarters in the vacant house 5 miles from Liberty. Dissatisfied with Meigs, the General had Captain Martindale appointed chief engineer and the promptness with which he built the bridge over Big Otter to facilitate our return justified his selection.

JUNE 19, 1864, SUNDAY: Officers of the rear guard report that the moving of trains and music of bands were heard in Lynchburg again last night, indicating the arrival of further reinforcements. We moved through Liberty, Averill with the rear guard occupying that town. Duffie who had been sent ahead to seize Buford's Gap reports that there is an enemy in the Gap. He had orders to clear them out at all hazards. Averill reported that his rear guard was attacked. Our lines were evidently being forced back. Dinner was being served but the firing was so rapid and approaching so near that the General left the table and ordered the staff to horse. Averill was driven through the town, losing 100 men killed and wounded. At midnight we took the road again in the full moon shining gloriously. Some were in dread that we might fall into the hands of Rebel Raiders. At a railroad station we stopped and destroyed the telegraph wires, the General assisted personally.

JUNE 20, 1864, MONDAY: On the road all night and at dawn entered Buford's Gap, a rocky muddy road with numerous defensible positions. We hear nothing more of the enemy either front or rear. Our cavalry looks very much used up and demoralized.

We found headquarters established at Bonsack's Station, a short distance ahead. It was a humble house and I found the General and Stockton lying on the floor. A courier from Averill reports the enemy at 2 P.M. advancing on our rear guard in force. At 2:30 Crook reported enemy pressing him and threatening both flanks. Orders to saddle are given in haste to the cruel disappointment of many who had hoped for a good night's rest. Averill says he must prepare to fight immediately and this is the crisis of our fate, as this battle will save or ruin us. The trains move toward Salem in charge of Duffie.

We marched on the Salem road burning and destroying the railroad, stores, and station houses as we moved. The demonstration on our rear amounted to nothing. We rode all night stopping to graze our horses in a clover field. Burning bridges and railroad stations lighted our way...as soon as we entered Salem at sunrise I threw myself upon a table in the bar room and slept soundly for an hour.

~

Thus ends the part of Strother's journal that relates to Hunter's Raid or the Lynchburg Campaign. The retreat from Salem through the mountain gap would take them to Newcastle, to White Sulphur Springs, to Lewisburg, to Gauley and finally to Charleston.

Over the years many letters have surfaced to give us a vivid account of how residents fared and the feelings these new experiences evoked. Those included here are particularly descriptive.

A letter to Robert Aunspaugh in Confederate service from his brother Frederick in Liberty was written on June 23, 1864, and graphically describes the scene in Liberty after Hunter's Raid.

> Since the time I would have returned to Richmond the Yankees have occupied our town and played the d...l generally. Hunter, Crook, Averill, and Sullivan with a force estimated at 20,000 to 23,000 commenced passing through here Wednesday, 15th at 7 1/2 P.M. As soon as they landed or in 10 minutes after they arrived [at] the Depot, Hay house and Turpin's house were in flames. The steam mill was burnt[5]...also the Reese Hospital, RR tracks torn up. Little Otter and Big Otter bridges burnt, etc... Our dining room, back yard and garden were filled by them, everybody was visited. They demanded something to eat and were given all we had. They didn't ransack or pillage our house at all, except in the basement. Consequently our clothing is safe and untouched...I saw a light from Uncle

---

[5] Liberty Steam Mills, the county's only foundry, was owned and operated by W. R. Terry. It employed seven men and produced castings and parts for agricultural machinery, such as threshing machines, plow molds and points, tobacco presses, stones, sash weights, andirons, cauldrons and repaired broken equipment. Employees received a salary of $21 per month. The annual receipts were reported as $12,355 in 1860. (Daniels,1985, 87)

Caleb's at the Hay house, depot etc. extending parallel with the street as low as Reese's factory. You may imagine my feelings. The two Negro women that lived with us [Emily and Mary] and Joe (Mary's husband) left with the Yankees. They plundered the stores and destroyed everything in them, giving the goods to Negroes and everybody. Some goods were saved by some ladies in town, but many doubtless fell into foul hands even in town and will never be returned.

Mr. A. A. Bell lost quite heavily, as did O. P. Bell and Mr. Hoffman. None lost as heavily in goods however as did Col. Graves. He had a greater variety and a great many more goods than any other house. Some of the country people near town suffered heavy losses. Mr. Rosebrough was robbed of all his meat, corn, flour, and a Negro man. Ad's mill was visited and all the produce that was in it taken out. Wm. Claytor had two Negroes carried off or they went off. The enemy marched on to Lynchburg, where they met our forces, a fight ensued, the enemy commenced a retreat, in haste if not confusion and were closely pursued by our men. It is said that our men had arrived in Lynchburg only an hour or two before the enemy appeared.

Of course our forces were tired and broken down but they beat the enemy back…killed 72 at Lynchburg …a number were wounded but were taken back in their ambulances. We had 5 or 6 killed and some wounded.

As they approached Liberty [on June 19] and while in town, they did worse than when they went through. Mother ate breakfast Sunday morning but had nothing to eat until the next morning. They commenced passing back about eight A.M. and continued all day long. They had to destroy some of their wagons, killed a number of horses but took quite a number in the country. As their front approached town they formed a line of battle across Wingfield's Mountain extending to town. They also had a line formed in town. The skirmishers commenced their fire just up at Milton Lowry's and where Mr. Claytor used to live. The house is now occupied by Hamrick and about 20 balls were shot there or struck his house. He and his wife were there. The enemy was gradually driven back. I heard the musketry from Uncle Cobb's and feared they would not be driven through town by night, but they were and by the time it was dusk the firing ceased and we were again in Confederate lines in town much to the relief of all...several were killed in or near town. The firing was kept up until the line got to Dr. Otey's where it ceased until they passed through. Everybody down town went to their cellars... They had intended to hold the town Sunday night if they could for some were camped at the town branch and at other places, but when their skirmishers commenced falling back and firing got nearer they had to take up and move farther to the rear. A report says Averill was wounded ...don't know whether it is information by a reliable gentleman or whether it is actually true...at any rate, I do not place any confidence in it.

We have all sorts of reports. *The Lynchburg Republican* of yesterday has a batch of lies about incidents in and about Liberty. It says, among other lies, that several shells were thrown into the town. I hope you will not see or credit any exaggerated statements regarding casualties or severe mistreatment of ladies or citizens but a few citizens stayed in town...all were on alert, several were fired at through the woods and on the mountain but none was hurt. For the most part ladies were respected and altogether were respected here, except that the scoundrels cursed some of them. The [Masonic] Hall was threatened to be burnt because of the sign *"Bedford Sentinal."* The girls went out 6 times to plead for it and prevailed, after telling them that the newspaper had not been published since the war. They also went to the Lodge Room and tumbled things. Nothing was taken, I believe, unless the sword. Mr. Dunton and myself had been down there and carried off the jewels… I do not know that the families of any men composing your Co. were plundered or I would tell you for their information. If any lived immediately on the road from Buchanan, or on any public road which the enemy passed they doubtless lost some provisions if they did not conceal it, and this is what all did, I believe. All hid the most they had and kept only a small quantity for appearance sake. Mr. Rosebrough had most of his hid, but his Negro informed where it was and this is the way he lost it…Old Col. Holt lost heavily of corn and other things.

The enemy came across the mountain from Buchanan and returned up the Turnpike by Buford's and Bonsack, destroying the depot and Bonsack's factory, and I hear almost ruined old Capt. Buford. No mills were burnt in this county that I know of, unless Ball's was. In some places along the road the crops were damaged but not sufficiently to materially injure the abundance, though it will bear hard on the individuals.

Affectionately your brother,
(Signed) Fred'k[6]
P.S. The R.R. track is torn up below here. I learn the road will be in running order up to Big Otter in a few days. The telegraph office will probably be opened again today. I will have to send this to Lynchburg to mail by first opportunity. (Parker, 1930, 73)

---

[6] Joseph A. Graves in his "History of the Bedford Light Artillery" states that Frederic Aunspaugh was a merchant in Liberty and served several terms as Justice for the County Court. In 1864 he married Emeline S. Graves, daughter of William Graves.

Excerpts from a letter dated July 1, 1864, written by Alexander H. Logwood of Wheats Valley, Bedford County, to his son, Jack Logwood, then in the Confederate Army:

  The Yankees made a rade through here. Twenty or Twenty five Thousand come over by Lexington and on to Buchannon and over by the Peaks of Otter and on to Liberty and down by New London and down to forest depot and Burnt some houses in Liberty and tore up the track to forest depot and there we whiped them back.

  They broke up I recon a hundred familys they took all the horses and all the negroes they could get and meat and corn and flower and a great many clothes the people had to take all they had and cary them to the mountain and hide them and hide themselves too. I took all my corn and meat and flower and salt and bed and bedclothes and wearing clothes and trunks and wool and Negroes and horses and cows and waggons and gear and guns and a great many other things and carry to the mountain and hide them it took us a week to hide them and bring them back they did not any of them come here but they come all round us... Jack I hope when you get these few lines they may find you well and enjoying good health as soon as you get this write and let us hear from you...We all send love to you be sure to rite Soon...

           A.H. Logwood

Excerpts from a letter to Cabell Moseley of Ingleside, then serving in the Confederate Army, dated June 22, 1864, from his older sister, Elizabeth Winston Moseley of Ingleside.[7]

---

[7] Ingleside, a few miles west of Fancy Farm, was built by George Cabell Moseley in 1835 and is still standing. Having grown up together, great love and friendship existed between the Kelso and Moseley families their entire lives. George Cabell Moseley met and courted his future

Dear Cabell,

Mother is writing to you and I hardly think it is worth while for me to write at all but you know how I love to talk even with a pen. I can't enjoy this talk though for I fear you will never get my letter. If I had known Jimmie Hopkins was going a little sooner I would have written to Sue Kelso by him.

Have you heard of the Yankee invasion? We have thought and talked of very little else for the past ten days. It was reported Sunday week that the Yankees would cross the mountains next day but nobody believed it. Late Monday evening Robert met Coz Tom[8] who told him to tell father to get his property out of the way. He thought next day would be soon enough so we went quietly to bed. About two o'clock up rode Messrs. Penick, Junkin, and Withrow with horses etc. The Yankees were here. Father got his horses, Negroes and at sunrise they went to the mountains. In the evening they found out that the army [which] camped at the Farm [Fancy Farm] was ours. Coz Tom and Wm. Hopkins and others had gone to the south side and so that night Uncle Nat (Nathaniel Whitlock) took Burke, Davy, George, Albert, and the horses and went off. Father took Robert, Ben, cows, and sheep and took to the mountain.

Then for four days we were in a state of suspense, hearing first that the Yankees were at Mrs. Allen's,[9]

---

wife, Mary Whitlock, who was a first cousin of Mrs. Kelso, while a visitor at Fancy Farm. See references to this family in Lettie Burwell's journal, *Our War*.

[8] Thomas Kelso (son of Robert Kelso) enlisted in the Confederate Army and was detailed as a tanner serving through the war.

[9] Mrs. Allen was the wife of Col. Robert Allen, a Revolutionary officer. They purchased a farm, Mt. Prospect near Fancy Farm, in 1839, from the Isaac Otey estate. Their son, Robert Allen, Jr., was a Confederate officer killed at Gettysburg. See Lettie Burwell's journal for references to the Allens.

then at Mr. Burnet's and to make a long tale short, Thursday at 1 o'clock a squad of ten cavalry, horrid looking fellows came pushing in at the back and front doors, inquired where the men, horses and firearms were and while one asked the questions the rest pitched at the safe and eat as if starved. Mother, [Mary D. Whitlock Moseley, wife of George Cabell Moseley, Sr.] told them that Gen. McCausland had given notice of their coming and the men had gone to a place of safety with their stock. They said they must search the house, she replied, "Very well." "Don't be afraid, we'll not hurt women and children" they say. "I am not at all afraid," said she. They stalked upstairs, in the dining room, and then in my room and then to the smoke house, rummaged two or three trunks and took nothing at all except what they ate and did not come in mother's room at all.

Compared with their actions at other places, they were quite respectful to us. They went from here to Dr. Arrington's and took meat and clothes from there. Only stayed here half hour. It was trying to see them stalking about and talking so grand about what they were going to do. They camped at the Farm, spoiled the flourmill but didn't hurt the corn mill, ruined the orchard and garden by turning horses in, stole what they could find to eat and killed some hogs belonging to the servants. Father wanted Coz F. Prior to come here but she thought it best to stay at home. Uncle Henry [Henry Winston Moseley, a physician who lived at Moseley's Bridge] lost five Negro men, five horses and almost all his provisions. Injured Mrs. Allen a good deal, (a neighbor who lived at Mt. Prospect), stripped Mrs. McGhee, captured Mr. Hopkins' horses...six, and most of his provisions and so on.

I can't tell you anymore about it all now. Uncle Nat got back with our boys and horses all safe on Sunday[10] and General Early chased the Yankees back through this country the same day. We heard musketry distinctly... they have gone in the direction of Salem, our forces pressing them closely. Willy[11] got here Friday, wound his way 'round the Yankee army... is looking badly. Mr. Brown [Rev. Henry Clay Brown who married Martha R. Moseley, daughter of G. Cabell Moseley, Sr.] stayed here last night...left today. He is with General Early. Willy will stay til next week. We are all well and surely we will be grateful to our covenant God who has so wonderfully preserved us. Father is cutting wheat. He rode round yesterday to see what he could do for Uncle H. [Henry Winston Moseley, brother of G. Cabell Moseley, Sr.], the farm servants and some others. Coz Tom was not at home but I expect he got there tonight. He has been in the Meadows of Goose Creek... some of Coz R's Negro men went off and he cannot find out certainly which. I have to write in such a hurry that I hardly know what I am saying and fear you will find it unsatisfactory... but you will be relieved to know we are all safe and have been scarcely injured at all... May our Father in heaven lead and guide you and comfort my darling brother and enable him to be a holy man, prays your loving sister.

Cabell Moseley, the recipient of this letter and a former student of VMI was born Oct. 6, 1846, and went into the Confederate Army where he was wounded. He was in a hospital in Richmond when he died on August 24, 1864. His father, George Cabell Moseley, was with him at his death and

---

[10] The granddaughter of George Cabell Moseley, Miss Alice Moseley, remembered hearing it said that a bedspread was hung on the clothesline after the Yankees had gone to let the men know all was clear.
[11] William H. Moseley, a brother of Elizabeth, came home to get fresh horses.

Ingleside, old home of the Moseley family

brought his body back to Ingleside where he was buried in the family cemetery.

Mr. S. A. Buford wrote his memories in *War Time Recollections of Liberty*, portions of which were printed in an undated Bedford newspaper from which excerpts are quoted here.

> The Clerks of the two Courts, anticipating the federal army under Hunter, feared disaster to the records and packed them in boxes. Each with a four-horse team fled under cover of night in different directions with the records of the county and secreted them away for safety. After the retreat of the enemy all of the records were returned in good condition and replaced in the county offices from whence they had been taken. Thus all were preserved.
>
> Nearly all the males (old men) left home and went to the woods fearing they would be taken prisoner unless they took the oath of allegiance to the U.S. Government.

HUNTER'S RAID

When the Yankees entered the town the ladies, stricken with terror, fled to the upper rooms of their dwellings after closing the doors and shutters below. They watched, peeping through the shutters at the soldiers who occupied the town. They saw them visit graveyards and thrust a bayonet into a new grave to ascertain whether a new grave or a buried treasure.

By dark the Yankees set fire to the depot, railroad buildings, Reese's factory, Terry's saw mill and gristmill, the iron factory and large storehouses used for commissary storage in town. As darkness set in, the plundering began. During these years the prices of food, clothing, and necessities ran very high.

General Hunter had his headquarters at the Bedford Hotel, later known as the Windsor Hotel.[12] General Averill had his headquarters at the home of John Crenshaw on East Main Street and General Crook had his headquarters at the Ferguson Home where stood the Masonic Temple."[13]

Mrs. R. B. Claytor wrote her memories in Personal Recollections, a portion of which were printed in an undated Bedford newspaper from which these excerpts are quoted.

Uniforms for soldiers were cut by the tailor and ladies of the town held sewing bees to make the uniforms. Every woman, young and old, who could sew

---

[12] It has already been established that General Hunter had his headquarters at Fancy Farm when he was in that area. It appears he also must have established headquarters at the hotel for the short time he stayed in town. The Bedford House was built in 1856 on the site of the old Bell Tavern on the southwest corner of East Main and South Streets across Main Street from the courthouse. An 1886 deed references this as being called the Windsor House.

[13] This may have later been the brick home of H. W. [Peg] Wildman at 309 East Main Street which was owned by the Masonic Lodge from 1829 to 1895. Bedford Mutual Insurance Company now occupies this site.

was pressed into service. Women and children were left in a helpless condition. My father, in a delicate condition with lung problems, was forced to lie out at night in the bushes on a nearby mountain.

When the enemy came our houses were closed up, window blinds tightly fastened, we stayed huddled in one room. We finally peeped out of the shutters to see the rear of an ambulance filled with our towns people as prisoners.

While some wrote their recollections of Hunter's Raid, many did not. But those stories which have been passed down through Bedford families are worthy of attention here. Some of these stories were published in the Bedford papers as was the following story from Mrs. J. W. Hayes' collection.

Clarence Agee's recollections of Hunter's Union forces coming down the road between the Peaks of Otter were told to him by his grandmother, Mildred Coleman, who married Fleman Wood. They lived on this road near the old dam. Mrs. Wood said the Union soldiers took every bite of food on the place while she stood in the long spring house and poured milk into each soldier's tin cup until every drop was gone. The men searched for the cows which had produced this cool, delicious milk but did not find them because Mrs. Wood had sent her livestock high up into the mountain to hide them after she was warned that enemy troops were approaching.

Mrs. Wood's little dog was accustomed to the quiet of this mountain home and all the hustle and bustle of so many men tearing around the property excited him and he barked furiously at the Yankees. One of them shot the dog on the spot.

As night came on Mrs. Wood and her family did not dare have a light in the house for fear of attracting other soldiers. As long as she lived she remembered lying on her bed in the dark and listening to the sound of heavy ammunition wagons coming down the mountainside. The squeaking and

HUNTER'S RAID

grinding of the brakes as the teamsters struggled to keep the wagons from over running the mules and horses down the steep rocky grade could be heard for miles.

Mr. Agee was told that some of Hunter's forces camped along the creek on what is now the E. A. Overstreet farm on Route 43 North.

The following day three or four frightened old hens made their appearance, having escaped the hungry Yankees. For a while their eggs sustained the family until it was considered safe to return the livestock from their hiding places. The neighbors beyond Kelso Mill road [Northside Supply] came to their rescue with a generous share of their food.

Another episode that has been passed down, of unknown origin, is about Madame Henricus, head mistress of the girl's school located in the house now occupied by Carder Tharp Funeral Home. Fearing the Yankees would steal her clothes she donned as many as she could wear at one time for Hunter's Raid.

Still another story from Peg Maupin centers around a wounded Yankee soldier who died in the horse drawn ambulance coming over the mountain toward Liberty at the time of Hunter's Raid. As they approached Avenel, two soldiers prepared to dig his grave by the side of the road. Mrs. Burwell was concerned about his being buried like an animal and insisted they bury him in her garden by the carriage house. She found a letter to his mother and other personal things on his body and these she sent to his mother. This soldier's body remains buried at Avenel today.

Woodford was the home of Edward Callohill Burks on Burks Hill, located on the west side of Route 122 South. Judge Burks was a Justice of the Virginia Court of Appeals and editor of the Virginia Law Register. At the time of the Civil War he was a member of the Legislature. When he heard that Hunter was coming, he left home, knowing he would be captured by the enemy if he remained, so his wife and small children were unprotected except by slaves. Even though the Yankees did not find Judge Burks at home, they found his underwear and after knotting the arms and legs, filled them with flour, meal, and sugar and placed them in front on their horses. Those supplies they could not take were piled in the cellar floor with molasses and kerosene oil poured over them.

Several women and children on the south side of town fled to Woodford for protection. They were driven from the house and out in front of the enemy, which placed them between the two firing lines with the Confederates on Piedmont Hill [near Piedmont Hospital] and the Yankee raider on Burks Hill. The women and children were made to lift their skirts so the Confederate soldiers could see their petticoats and know they were women and children and thus put an end to the firing. Mrs. Burks could not go back into her house to sleep that night and went with her children to a neighbor asking to be taken in for the night. Her request was denied and she spent the night on the porch with her children.

Another story from Mrs. J. W. Hayes' collection, passed on to her from the descendants of A. B. Nichols of Three Otters tells of the bravery of his wife in protecting her home in his absence.

At the time of the war all the young men had left for service and Mr. Nichols, a prosperous merchant, was too old to join them, but he played a valuable part in contracting for Army provisions. When he learned that Hunter was headed toward Bedford from the Peaks he knew they would pass his plantation. He packed up the large stores of provisions in his custody for the Confederate Army as well as some of his own cattle, sheep, and hogs. He set out for the dense hiding place in the Dismal Swamp where he camped for several

Three Otters, home of A. B. Nichols, built in 1837
Photo courtesy Kim & Garry Howard

months until danger was past. His son George did active service in the Second Virginia Cavalry.

At the time of Hunter's Raid only the ladies were left at Three Otters. They had been warned that the invaders were on their way down the mountain. Mrs. George Nichols took a spyglass up on the deck of the roof to watch for their approach. As soon as she saw anyone approach she rushed down, mounted her waiting horse and rode to meet the Union officer in charge. Her persuasive and charming personality combined with her beauty, are credited with touching the gentlemanly heart of the officer and he posted a guard to protect the property. Later one of the Federal officers came to the house and asked permission to go up on the roof to see where the Confederate troops were. Mrs. Nichols accompanied him to the attic herself. He ascended to the deck on the roof and Mrs. Nichols promptly closed and locked the trap door, keeping him on top of the house.

Questions remain as to whether the officer was alone, did he call for help, how long did she keep him up there, and why he wasn't mad enough to burn the house down. They burned many more for less reason. Since these will never be answered we might imagine our own ending to this delightful story.

The Nichols family was noted for its generous hospitality and Mr. A. B. Nichols[14] set the standard with large hunting parties to the Peaks of Otter, followed by barbecues and dances in the spacious double parlors at Three Otters.

Lettie Burwell's sister, Kate Burwell Bowyer, preserved for us a vivid picture of the trials and tribulations endured during Hunter's Raid on Liberty in June 1864. She wrote her memories in "A Woman's Story of the War," which was published after the war in a book entitled *Our Women in the War* by the *Weekly News and Courier*, Charleston, S.C.,1885.

It was in the summer of 1864 when our beautiful Piedmont, Virginia began to be threatened with its first invasion. We heard ominous mention of Hunter and his celebrated twenty thousand, and of the preparations to move upon Lynchburg, but felt almost too secure behind our wall of big blue mountains to realize that danger could await us. But events thickened. Day by day accounts reached us that Hunter assuredly approached, while McCausland's cavalry brigade retreated, until the excitement rose to fever heat. Couriers rode swiftly past from hour to hour, reporting the enemy near and nearer.

Every family fell actively to hiding away its valuables and belongings in the most possible and impossible places. In our own case it seemed like getting ready for the entertainment of some horrible company,

---

[14] A. B. Nichols came to Bedford County from Bridgeport, Connecticut. In addition to his lovely brick home, Three Otters, he built a brick house downtown, which was used for many years as the offices of *The Bedford Democrat*. He was active with the James River and Kanawha Canal and a member of the committee, which laid the route out for it to be built between Richmond and Lynchburg. After the canal was completed his merchandise came all the way from New York by water except the short distance from Lynchburg to Liberty where oxen pulled the loaded carts.

who must have tremendous preparations made for their reception, no matter how terrible the anticipation. Servants ran in all directions. A dozen orders were given in a breath as we dashed excitedly from one point to another. Of course we never desisted from hiding our things by day or night, being, as I say, ably assisted in this by our faithful servants, who seemed as much interested for us as we for ourselves. Finding time left after all arrangements were complete, we knew so well where our valuables, our beloved white sugar, and tea, brandy etc. (for we still preserved remnants of these treasures for desperate straits) had been bestowed, that it seemed impossible others could not also divine their places of concealment. So we constantly devised newer and deeper hiding places, and were going on in this way indefinitely when the last courier swept by like a streak, his very coat tail straight behind him, calling aloud as he passed, "THEY'RE HERE! THEY'RE HERE!"

Now my sister had, in her own peculiar case, reached such a state of readiness to receive the Yankees that she became restless with leisure and just at the last said: "I haven't seen a neighbor for all these dreadful days. Think I must run over to Mr. Davis' and see what they are doing with their things." So over she went and was confused to see standing in the doorway, George Davis, a slender lad of the week before, now assumed unnatural dropsical proportions and having a swollen, helpless look.

"Why! What's the matter with George?"[15] Sister exclaimed, when his mother whispered imploringly: "Don't say anything to George. He's got on all the

---

[15] George, about eleven years old at this time, was the youngest son of Judge and Mrs. Micajah Davis. Later, in 1878 he married Clara Hoffman and they in time had six children.

clothes he possesses. I had the greatest trial to make him put them on, and if you say a word he'll take them off."

Sister had proceeded only this far in her investigations of the Davis family, when the last wild cry of the last courier rent the air. She heard "They're here! They're here!" and had but sped across the road and in our gate when the head of the Yankee column moved slowly in view amid flaunting banners and ear piercing strains of "Yankee Doodle"... that most trying of airs. May I be delivered from ever hearing another measure even akin to it, after the associations of that day.

Now as soon as this raid was found to be inevitable, I resolved that we must gather ourselves up and adopt some regular system of female tactics with which to meet it and after due reflection concluded thus...we shall owe our deliverance to personal influence on the Yankee soldiery, there being no other defense to look to, with our men all gone and every appliance relating to firearms hidden out of sight.

Plainly we could not hope, unaided, to exert this electric influence over unknown masses of impracticable Yankees, Dutch, Italians, Irish, Russians, Prussians, Poles, Austrians, and Hottentots, for the motley collection represented all nations upon the earth, mixed up with a hundred day men. Evidently we could not expect to sway this multitude without powerful support of our new black alpacas.

We did in actual fact array ourselves in the black alpacas, arranged our several hairs with exact nicety, and, in lieu of breast pins, which we feared the rapacity of the combined nationalities might not be able to withstand, we wore neat black bows, embroidered for the occasion, in white, and not calculated to excite the cupidity of any.

Attached to our persons were long pockets each containing one spoon, one fork, and a mug in case of being driven into the woods, for none knew what to expect from the brute Hunter.

A large basket, containing ham, biscuits and other necessaries of life was next prepared, like an awful picnic, secreted under Mama's bed as being the most sacred spot known to us, and one that must be respected by the Yankees, if any in the confines of the Confederacy could be. Divers lesser lunches were made ready and placed conveniently where, in any emergency, they might be produced without a moments delay. And thus was our raid studied deeply systematized, and all our tactics settled upon before the enemy appeared.

All this done, just at nightfall on the evening of June 15th, Hunter's advance moved in. Immediately a half dozen horsemen dashed down to our back porch, where our good "mammy" who never flinched from us for one moment, was waiting outside to see what would happen and whether the heavens would fall. She hurried in where we were huddled together by a dim light, and said, in an awe-stricken whisper: "They are here at the door and say they must have something to eat."

For an instant we sat paralyzed with the dreadful realization. Then I arose, taking a lighted lamp in my hand and feeling the dignity of my black alpaca arise within me, majestically moved forward, gained the door, beheld the Yankees, and making an elegant bow, stood still, lamp in hand, awaiting what might follow.

Really, at that moment, I felt nerved beyond what could have been conceived possible, actually seemed to rise several inches taller than ever before in my life (five feet one, exactly) until being always aided and abetted by exalted garment aforesaid, I absolutely towered. The soldier nearest at hand began, insolently, "Can we find anything to eat here?" The alpaca and myself, drawn up to our full height, replied by turning to a servant and saying grandly, "Jordan, can you hand this gentleman a lunch?" We would not have descended from our throne to touch it.

At once several of those exceedingly ready lunches were brought out, while the Yankee spokesman went on: "This is the first time our troops have passed here I believe." "The first time," I tersely answered. "What did you expect to see us look like?" he pursued. I drew up to a greater altitude than ever and answered, "I was perfectly prepared for the color of your skins."

With this the man, bending down upon his saddle bowed and giving me a searching look when, I shall ever believe, he first felt the full force of the black alpaca, instantly changed his whole manner and saying quite courteously, "Madam, we are much obliged to you," moved quietly away.

Almost immediately another detachment appeared, and I was wondering whether our next encounter would not end so successfully, when the leader of the second party, evidently an officer, accosted me. "Is this the home of Major Bowyer?" Amazed, I said "It is, sir." Still further amazed I heard, "I am detailed by General Powell to guard the premises for the night." And now I recalled what had been forgotten in connection with the Wytheville fight... how Col. Powell, threatened with violence as he lay a wounded prisoner, when Major B[16] dressed his wounds and assured him of protection, had said, "This shall not be forgotten, and if you or yours ever

---

[16] This is Major Thomas Bowyer, husband of Kate Burwell Bowyer, and an accomplished surgeon in civil life.

need protection which I can render, rely upon receiving it." Now behold the need, and the promised help was not forgotten. Col. Powell, recovered and restored to his command had the advance cavalry in Hunter's movement. We thanked God for His timely deliverance, and sat all night around the little bed in which our baby calmly slept away the hours so full of horror and dread to ourselves. For though the guard was faithful, it was hard to feel secure with the clang of Yankee swords and the tramp of heavy boots around us, amid camp fires at our very doors, and crash after crash telling how our enclosure were being laid to waste amid the yells and curses of many voices.

Day dawned at last and with it the division camped about us for the night moved off. A lull succeeded. We ventured to open a shutter and peep out. Could it be that this dreaded raid was over? Certainly the host we saw last night had departed and if this were indeed all, how could we ever be sufficiently thankful? But even while this blessed hope fluttered before us an indistinct roar was borne on the breeze, and lo, the yard became blue with all types of humanity! After the stretch of sunny road beyond us, a halt was always ordered under our grand old oaks, and with this the men scattered in every direction…climbing trees to peep in the upper windows and burrowing under the house to search for treasure that might be hidden there. We could hear innumerable heads bumping beneath our feet as the ventilators were torn out and this rummaging went on.

At one time when our trees and our garden and the very air seemed blue with the creatures, and the heavy doors about yielding to their bombardment, I rushed frantically into the line and appealed for help to the best imitation of a gentleman I saw there, being inspired with confidence by his clean duster. This officer at once dismounted, followed me and cleared our grounds in five minutes time, showing that the soldiers were under control and might readily have been made to respect persons and property had the officers so willed. When this regiment moved on and the same destruction threatened us again, I cast a hurried look at a fine looking man actually riding into the back porch where we were now all assembled...the other doors being barricaded...and exclaimed, "Sir, you seem a gentleman, may I ask your protection for ourselves as ladies?" He instantly rode out of the porch, stepped upon the ground, and with one wave of his sword cleared the premises. This officer gave his name as Major McCain of Kentucky, and spent several hours in conversation with us, inquired about our former lives, thought ours looked like a house where we "had a good time," approved it as a place for headquarters when they returned from Lynchburg and held the country etc. Upon this, our confederate ire waxed hot. And we indulged in many patriotic pleasantries, which of course, could only have been hazarded with one like Major McCain, of culture and intelligence.

This officer seemed really to have conceived some regard for us during his "visit," and presently his command being far ahead, he evinced by saying "Ladies, I can't bear to leave you unprotected, when I think of the army followers you will soon be exposed to, far, far worse than anything you have yet seen."

We shuttered at this and felt almost as if we must cling to this particular Yankee, and could not permit him to leave us. He called up a footsore, poor creature, who seemed to have lost his very identity. To this man Major M. handed a written order to the effect that he, the man, was detailed to guard these premises.

The individual, Charlie, left with a scrap of paper, was now become our salvation, and upon him then, our whole female battery was turned. He looked hopeless indeed. Finally I ventured: "Have you a mother?" He looked leaden eyed and said "Yes." Again, "Have you any sister?" "Yes" as before. "Well, wouldn't you be sorry to think they are having as much trouble today as we are…surrounded by as many people who were trying to destroy them?"

This seemed dimly to penetrate the boy. At last Hunter had passed, and our guard moved off as the twilight came down. I must ever believe that Charlie's whole moral tone had been elevated by these hours of association with myself, for when I said at parting, "Well, Charlie, you've done us all the good you could, I would like to do something for you in return. We poor Confederates have not much, but if there is anything you particularly need I would like to bestow it on you. What do you want most of everything in the world, Charlie?" And he hoarsely answered "SOAP!"

All these experiences, personal to ourselves, were of course varied in a thousand ways in other households, and for weeks nothing was heard among us except comparing notes, interchange of incidents, etc. One old woman nearby unable in the hurley-burley of times to get help for secreting her meat, made requisition upon her well developed Confederate ingenuity, which was better than a battalion of men. Flinging the large middlings[17] on the grass before her house, she sprinkled small particles of flour over the whole, and standing in her door, arms akimbo when the Yankees swarmed up, she called out: "You can take that meat if you want it. McCausland's been along here

---

[17] Middlings were pork from between the ham and shoulder, of medium quality, grade, and size.

and done something to it...I don't know what!" There was at once closer inspection made, specs of flour discerned, and the meat left undisturbed.

But to come back to my narrative...the night succeeding this awful day, June 16, 1864, for it was more like the day of judgement than anything I ever expected to pass through in this mortal existence...as again we sat encircling baby's bed, who should suddenly appear like an apparition among us but Major Bowyer! He knew the country perfectly, was a good woodsman...and simply could not resist flanking the pickets to see whether we were living or dead. The guard of forty men left to hold our town while Hunter made his march to Lynchburg, lay all around us, and when with a whispered greeting Major Bowyer dropped down into the darkness from the door, can anybody tell how tenfold more miserable it left us? But next day a faithful old servant brought us messages of his safe return through the lines to rejoin Breckinridge's command not however without a little irresistible bushwhacking and sharp shooting at detached parties of the enemy, as they roamed over the country on missions of destruction.

When three more days had passed, during which time we had never disrobed ourselves for sleep, our servants came in a tumult one morning at daylight and said: "They've come back! The town is full of 'em." Which latter collective pronoun was now always understood to refer generally and particularly to Yankees. And the town was full of "em"! They literally poured in, though this time moving by a different road, which gave us the miserable stragglers to contend with, without the opportunity for appealing to the better class for protection.

We were indeed in despair when two young men with pleasant faces and wearing the insignia of the regular guard presented themselves, and said they were Philadelphians, that they could not bear to see the ruin which their army spread through the land; that they could only select one house at each point over which to constitute themselves guard and would today preserve ours.

These gallant Philadelphians sat with us during the whole day, often driving off hordes who would otherwise have torn us to pieces. Many times did our distracted neighbors, informed of our good fortune, send to "borrow our guard," and we were always neighborly enough to lend one for a short while!

Houses about us were ravished from attic to cellar and their inmates treated with gross indignity, while when our destruction seemed inevitable a timely hand was ever stretched forth in our defense and who shall say how far the potent spell of the "black alpacas" may not have achieved this great result?

But all things have an end, even the wild Yankee stampede, which poured through our town like a cataract until sundown, when the welcome guns of Early's and Breckinridge's advance were heard over the hills! What a day of triumph and deliverance! What an evening of thanksgiving to God!

We tried to stay in the cellar, while a sharp skirmish took place across our house and balls rattled on the roof, but the excitement proved irresistible! No longer able to endure our imprisonment we rushed up to the yard again, and found ourselves surrounded by our dear, dear Confederates, whom we knew so well, when there were handshaking, tears, and cheers and the wildest enthusiasm on both sides. At once our doors were flung wide open and so remained during the night, while officers and men poured into and throughout the house; slept on the porches and cooked in the kitchen, and thus surrounded we lay down and slept the first sweet sleep of security for many nights.

There were some features about the loss of friends in Confederate times which, taken in conjunction with the stern necessities of those times, had to be met with sad practicality. As soon as one was known to mourn the death of a friend, and this alas! was but too often, it became the imperative custom to send to the stricken house any articles of mourning apparel not then in use, and request an exchange for the colored habiliments which might be there discarded. Thus in this indiscriminate barter did all sorts of incongruities arise.

Any lingering tendency towards following a fashion had long since been beaten out of the female mind, and women now aspired to nothing beyond the mere wearing of clothes, irrespective of style, shape or texture. Large women appeared squeezed into garments of smallest proportion, small women floating about in almost limitless space; while women of tall stature dangled below circumscribed skirts, and others trailed about in fathoms of useless material. To all these eccentricities of costume the confederate eye had become inured, as well as to the striking effect of blue bonnets with green plumes, red dresses with purple mantles, &c. until these extraordinary modes failed to offend even the most fastidious.

Indeed, expedients of the most desperate sort had now to be resorted to in all directions. The flooring of our country meat houses, saturated with the salt drippings of years, was dug up and prized as a salt substitute in horse food. The ashes of corn cobs was much esteemed in lieu of soda. Sorghum was the substitute for sugar, while wheat, rye, chestnuts, sweet potatoes, in short, anything in the vegetable kingdom was found to supply the place of coffee, and so on ad infinitum.

For a Virginian of the old regime, who had always lived on the choicest of edibles, to smack his lips and relish a decoction of burnt chestnuts, sweetened with sorghum, was considered as highly patriotic.

When General Lee's exhausted remnant of an army was delivered up to Grant at Appomattox the great Confederate heart ceased to beat. There may have been some twitching and a little quivering about the extremities, but soon all settled into that stiff and soulless body which has now, for so many years, lain in state in our Southern hearts.

Now did confusion reign, as Lee's disbanded men, without money or provision, individually and without organization, tried to reach their distant homes. The roads were alive with men riding and on foot, horses, wagons and ambulances...all rushing pell-mell through the country, and yet there were no deeds of violence committed or fear of disturbance within our houses. These facts at once speak the element of which our Southern army was composed, for if ever there was temptation goading men on to deeds of wrong, it was in the want and misery of these disbanded soldiers, left to their own devices and finding themselves in a country without law or restraint of any kind.

Yes, we are a law abiding and magnanimous people, and these dreadful days proved us so. In the midst of the turmoil described above, my husband, with some brother officers, passed along to North Carolina, believing that Johnston's army survived and that the struggle for our Confederacy must still go on, but before many days they returned, convinced that all was indeed over.

Ah, who can tell the darkness of that hour! "Now sunk the sun, the general pulse of life stood still" and if the war in its opening had hung like a pall over the land, how trebly was this so in its close! Then "hope beckoned with a delusive smile." Now the very midnight of despair was come! We knew not where to pick up the broken threads of existence. Our homes laid waste, the very superstructure of our social system was gone and its graces, joys, comforts dashed into fragments and cast out to the winds!

APPENDIX A

Samuel Harris and His Gun

Samuel H. Harris was 31 years old when he enlisted in Company C. of the 28th Virginia Infantry, on May 15, 1861. He was living in Liberty and supporting his wife and a four-year-old son Charles while working as a carpenter.

The 28th Virginia Infantry was also known as the Old Dominion Rifles and saw action in May 1861 at the first Battle of Manassas. They were later assigned to Hunter's Brigade, Pickett's Division and spent the winter of 1861-2 at Centerville in Fairfax County, Virginia. In 1862 they were at Richmond and participated in the Battle of Williamsburg.

In the latter part of May they fought at the Battle of Fair Oaks (Seven Pines). It was at this battle on May 31, 1862, that the "secret weapon" of the South was first used. This weapon was the Williams Machine Gun, invented by Captain R. S. Williams, CSA, of Covington, Kentucky, the first machine gun ever used in combat.

Used as a test in action under the direction of the inventor, the results were so satisfactory that the Confederate Government ordered seven batteries of six guns each. A single barrel breechloader, with a two-inch bore, it fired 65 rounds per minute for a range of 2000 yards, a forerunner of the Gatling Gun.

Two of these batteries were made at Lynchburg, four at Tredegar in Richmond and one at Mobile. The limitation of this gun was soon discovered and it was later discontinued. When hot, the breech was prone to expand causing jamming and failure to relock.

Apparently Samuel enlisted just in time to see action at First Manassas for tradition passed down in the family says that he learned to operate the Williams Machine Gun. After one of the later battles when the gun's weakness was known and its use discontinued, Samuel hid his gun in a swamp near the battlefield, before his unit was ordered to move on. He had first greased it well and wrapped it in oilcloth before he sunk it into the swamp. Perhaps he was ordered to dispose of it or perhaps he had just become attached to it, we do not know. But we do know that the gun was obsolete by the end of the war.

When the war was over Samuel kept thinking about that gun and one day he returned to the swamp to retrieve it. He remembered where he hid it and soon found it. He loaded it on a wagon and returned to Liberty with it. It wasn't long before he put it in working order once more, and each year thereafter Samuel celebrated July 4th by shooting a round from his machine gun for the whole town to enjoy.

After his death, the gun lay idle, unattended and unused in his garage on Bedford Avenue. His grandson, Bully Harris, finally gave it to Edwin Hoffman, a Bedford native and a weapon specialist, who identified it and made a carriage for it by Army specifications. Mr. Hoffman lived in Woodstock, Virginia, where he made a portion of his home into a weapons museum. He displayed the gun there for many years.

Before his death Mr. Hoffman sold the gun with several other items to the New Market Battlefield Museum. There are only a few of the Williams Machine Guns in existence today. Of the three known ones, one is reported to be in the Museum at West Point, New York, and one is reported to be in the possession of the U.S. War Department. I believe Samuel would be proud today to know that his gun is well cared for at the New Market Battlefield Museum.

APPENDIX B

Court Order: To identify slaveholders and the number of slaves owned by each in order to requisition manpower for the public defence. (Order Book 34, Page 192)

At a Court of Monthly Sessions continued and held for Bedford County at the Courthouse, thereof, on Thursday, the 31st day of October, eighteen hundred and sixty two. PRESENT: A. Donald, Hezekiah T. Jordan, Samuel H. Quarles, Jesse Minter, John M. Jones, Gent. Justices.

The Justices appointed at a special session of this Court held on the 17th of October, 1862, to ascertain and report amongst other things to the Court at this term the names of the several slaveholders in their respective districts, the aggregate number of slaves owned by each, the number thus owned between the ages of 18 and 45 years, having made their several reports and the court having inspected, examined and corrected the same and having further considered the requisition of the Governor of this Commonwealth upon this County for 450 slaves between the ages of 18 and 45 made in pursuance of an Act of the General Assembly passed October 3rd, 1862, entitled "An Act Further to Provide for the Public Defence."

Name of Slaveholder	Quota	Name of Slaveholder	Quota
District 1		Mrs. Lucy Davis	1
Wm. Leftwich	3	Micajah Davis	2
John Q. Dickinson	2	Dr. James Saunders	2
Thos. M. Wilkinson	1	Nelson Lowry	1
Col. John Crenshaw	1	Mrs. Mary McGhee	2
Ro. C. Mitchell	1	John W. Holt	1
Wm. M. Burwell	1	A. B. Nichols	2

Edward C. Burks	2
Richard Crenshaw	1
Dr. John W. Sale	1
Mrs. Jane R. Tinsley	1
W. A. Staples	1
Jesse T. Hopkins	1
Edward F. Walker	1
Mrs. A. D. Mitchell	1
Wm. Witt	1
Mrs. Elizab. McDaniel	1
Mrs. Wm. P. Holt	1
Jesse H. Miller	1
Wilson C. Hewitt	1
S. P. Walker	1
Alex Jordan	1
George Fizer	1
William Terry	1
Peter eeks (?)	1
Mrs. D. Aunspaugh	1
William Graves	1
Kemp G. Holland	1
George L. Kenzer	1
Misses S.&A. Witt	1
Miss Sally Fuqua	1
John Buford	2
Gustavus A. Wingfield	2
Rives S. Scruggs	1
Thos. P. Mitchell	1
Henry W. Moseley	1
Mrs. Martha Stone	1
William T. Campbell	1

John F. Sale	1
Abram Fuqua	1
Elliott Lowry	1
Judith Lowry	1
Walker McDaniel	1
Charles W. Gill	1

District 2

Henry Stiff	2
Ro. Miller	2
James C. Kasey	1
Joel Wright	1
Henry P. Compton, Est.	1
Temperance Payne	1
Joel Dent	1
Thomas Nelson	1
John Gibbs, Est.	1
David Newsom	1
Elizabeth Newsom	1
Joel Gibbs	1
William Johnson	1
Joseph P. Wright	1
James Saunders	1
Anthony Wright	1
Nancy Wright	1
Maria Board	1
Isaac Wigginton	1
H. S. Sinks, Est.	1
William Huddleston	1
B. R. Jeter	1
John Q. A. Wright	1

APPENDIX B

District 3	1	Elijah Garrett	1
John Hancock	1	Caroline Leftwich	1
David Hannabass	1	Wm. McClain	1
Mrs. Polly Hurt	1	Nathaniel Newsom	1
George Johnson	1	Thomas J. Preston	1
Mrs. Permelia Moorman	1	E. C. Jones	1
Thaddeus Nance	1		
Wilson Meador	1	**District 4**	
Thos. C. Overstreet	1	Sophia Martin	3
Eben Nelms	1	Emelia Anthony	1
Thos. W. Robertson	1	Samuel G. Tinsley	1
Joel L. Hurt	1	John P. Preston	1
Christopher Hancock	1	William Payne	1
Jordan Lipscomb	1	Matthew Hall	1
Obediah Meador	1	Jonathan Goard	1
C. C. Peters	1	Martha D. Parker	1
Martha Scruggs	1	James H. Keatts	1
Mrs. Rucker	1	Lewis C. Arthur	1
Green B. Martin	1	John H. Turner	1
Benj. B. Turner	2	William Austin	1
Stephen P. Smith	1	Dan'l Tompkins	1
Mrs. A. Morgan	1	Sophia Thurman	1
Reuben Guthrie	2	Julia Saunders	1
John Board	2	James Lancaster	1
Christopher Cundiff	1	John B. Witt	1
Henry Loyd	1	Elizabeth Fields	1
John Compton	1	William English	1
Mrs. Martha Huddleston	1	Stephen English	1
Mrs. Elizabeth Hopkins	1	James O. Hensley	1
Josephus Hurt	1	Mrs. F. L. Saunders	1
John Jordan	1	Alex Leftwich	5

Thos. Saunders, Est.	1	Eleanor Merriman	1
Elijah Swain, Est.	1	Henry Jones	1
		Avy Hicks	1
District 5		John B. Irvine	1
William L. Goggin	1	Wm. H. Irvine	1
John J. Robertson	1	William Steptoe	1
Thomas Creasy	1	John Everett	1
Ammon H. Parker	1	Spot Brown, Gdn.	1
Hannibal Harris	1	Thos. Y. Mosby	1
John West	1	Tilghman Cobbs, Jr.	1
Jas. McG. Kent	1	John William Jones	1
Mrs. Lucy Penn	1	John Downing	2
David J. Wells	1	Ro. W. Callaway	1
S. P. Robertson	1	J. J. Farris	1
Thomas Fuqua	1	Richard M. Wells	2
Mrs. F. S. Chalmers	1	Mrs. Frances Hudnall	2
S. J. Wade	1	Tilghman A. Cobbs, Jr.	2
George W. Leftwich	1	Richard Callaway	3
Lafayette Leo	1	William A. Read	3
Charles Andrews	1	Wm. H. Leftwich	3
Mrs. Rives Scruggs	1	R. B. Thomson	3
Miss C.M.C. Irvine	1	Granville L. Brown	2
Edward Callaway	1	John Goode, Jr.	3
Spot Brown	1	Thomas T. Saunders	1
William C. Mitchell	1	Henry P. Brown	2
David Austin	1	Ralph Callaway	1
Thomas J. Phelps	1	Read & Jett	2
Miss Bettie Walker	1	Dr. Thos. Nelson, Est.	1
E. M. Claytor	1	Mrs. Alex Irvine	1
Dr. James Saunders	1	Walter J. Hopkins	1
Archibald Wade, Jr.	1	Garnett Lee, Est.	1

APPENDIX B

S. Peters	1	Col. Thos. Munford	1
Miss R. E. Callaway	2	Nathaniel Manson	2
G. A. Burton	2	James Metcalf	2
Mrs. Joseph Wilson	1	Carlton Radford	2
John Martin	1	Hugh Scott	2
		Willis Poindexter	2
District 6		H. M. Ogden	2
Hiram Cheatwood	1	Charles Scott	3
Dr. Hector Harris	1	Mrs. T. H. Nelson	3
Richard Chappele	1	Sam'l. McGhee	2
Mrs. Emily Jones	1	Edward Hutter	2
Sam'l. McDaniel	1	Albert McDaniel	2
Mrs. E. Reid	1	M. W. Radford	2
William Monroe	1	David Kyle	2
James Armisted	1	James Harris	1
Richard Poindexter	1	Henry O. Thomas	1
D. Arth. Bolling, Est.	1	Joshua B. Ogelsby	1
Mrs. E. Davis	1	William Stevens, Est.	1
R.D. Dawson	1	William Radford	1
John J. Knight	1	Joseph Speece, MD	1
Eliza Poindexter	1	Robert Buckner	1
Lodowick Moorman	1	William Merino	1
Mayo Davis	1	Mrs. Amy Radford	1
John M. Anderson	1	Samuel Griffin	1
Jesse B. Jeter	1	J.H. Mattox	1
James Younger	1	Benj. Wigginton	1
J.A. Meriweather	1	John Armistead	1
Lodowick Ogelsby	1		
Charles Meriweather	1		
Allen Hatcher	1		
Mrs. Lucy Logwood	1		

District 7

Howard Major	1
Joshua Reynolds	1
Sally Douglas	1
Jesse S. Burks	1
John Turpin	2
James M. Rucker	3
Charles B. Reynolds	1
Sarah Wharton	1
Uriah Hatcher	1
Mary Turpin	1
Philip Turpin	1
Thomas N. Turpin	1
Judith/Jas. Elliott Est.	1
Davis Poindexter	1
H. A. Whitely	1
Benjamin N. Hobson	1
Thomas Hatcher	1
Patsy Bellamy	1
J. D. Turpin	1
S. C. Arthur	1
Dr. R.A. Sale	1
G.W. Noell	1
John C. Noell	1
Nelson A. Thompson	2
John D. Burks	1
Beverly Padgett	1
A. S. Thompson	1
Benjamin Wilkes	1
Thomas B. Joplin	2
Samuel Hobson	4
Martin P. Burks	2
William E. Sledd	3
R. N. Douglas	1
John Ogden	1
Elisha G. Turpin	1
John S. Poindexter	3

District 8

William L. Wilkinson	1
Jesse Jeter, Est.	1
Frances H. Bell	1
Frances R. Allen	1
Robert N. Kelso	3
William Harris	1
William Powell	1
Judith Hurt	1
Richard Davis	1
William Hobson	1
A. M. Ewing	1
Mildred Brown	1
Thomas Kelso	1
James Jennings, Jr.	1
William J. Ferrell	1
William G. Joplin	1
Thomas Campbell	1
John C. Hopkins	1
Joseph S. Hardy	1
Thomas Marsh	1
John H. Lowry	1
William Jeter	1
Charles B. Lowry	1

APPENDIX B

District 9

Ro. C. Jones	1	Cornelius Pate	1
David Thaxton	1	John Wilson	1
Paschal Buford	2	Jeremiah G. Hatcher	1
Nathaniel Thaxton	2	Henry C. Ferrell	1
George P. Luck	1	Mary C. Otey	1
Hampton Arrington	1	John Smelser	1
Matilda Williams	1	Goodrich Moore	1
James L. Campbell	1	Daniel K. Forgie	1
Nancy Campbell	1	William G. Rieley	1
William H. Bilbro	1	Fountain M. Hawkins	1
Isabella Jones	1	John W. Andrews	1
James A. Holley	1	Martha Layne, Est.	1

And the Court doth order that such of the slaveholders above mentioned as shall not have sooner delivered their respective quotas above specified to the Confederate authorities, shall deliver the same to the Sheriff of the County at the depot of the Virginian and Tennessee Railroad in the town of Liberty on Tuesday, the 11th day of November, next to be by the said Sheriff delivered to an agent or officer of the Confederate States and the Court doth appoint Jesse Minter, Esq. a General Agent for the County to superintend the delivery of said Negroes to the Confederate authorities, take a proper receipt and vouchers for the same, attend the valuation of the same, accompany the said Negroes to Richmond if necessary, and do whatever may be necessary and proper in the premises. And that agent report his proceedings to this Court at its next term. And the Court doth further order that the Clerk furnish without delay to the Sheriff of this county a sufficient number of copies of this order to be by the said Sheriff at the earliest day practicable delivered one to each of the acting Justices. And it shall be the duty of the said Justices with all possible dispatch to give notice to the said slaveholders in their respective districts of this order and if necessary associate any fit persons with them in giving such notice. And it shall moreover be the duty of the said Justices to attend in their respective districts to the collection and delivery of the said quotas to all proper receiving officers and agents and if need be take proper receipts and vouchers for the same and report the same to this Court at the next term with the names of such slaveholders as fail or refuse to deliver their respective quotas. Ordered that this Court be adjourned until the next Court in course. Signed: Benjamin Donald.

Court Order Re: Clothing Soldiers of Bedford County. (Order Book 34, Page 187, 1862)

On the motion of Edward C. Burks, Esq. the following order was unanimously entered.

The court with the propriety of aiding the Government as far as practicable in clothing the troops in this county in the Confederate service, doth order that William A. Wingfield, Thomas Y. Mosby, James I. Noell and Jesse Minter be hereby appointed as Commissioners whose duty it shall be to visit our armies in northern Virginia, and the Honorable John Goode, Jr. to visit the army near Richmond and ascertain as accurately as possible the necessities of the troops from this county in respect to clothing, including shoes, socks, blankets and every article embraced in a soldiers apparel and outfit. That John Goode also repair to Richmond and confer with the proper authorities of the Confederate Government and ascertain what arrangements, if any, can be made with the Government to cooperate with it in furnishing said clothing to the troops from this county, proposing to the said authorities at the cost of the Government to cooperate with it in the procuring, providing, making up and forwarding such clothing as may be necessary for the purpose aforesaid.

APPENDIX B

Court Order Re: Relief for Indigent Soldiers, Sailors and Their Families. (Order Book 34, Page 420, 1864)

In pursuance of an Act of the General Assembly passed on October 31, 1863, entitled An Act for the Relief of the Indigent Soldiers and Sailors of Virginia who have been or may be disabled in military service, the Court considers the propriety of appointing purchasing and impressing agents in the County. The Court doth appoint Charles M. Gill in Magisterial District 1, James M. Matthews in District 2, William A. Wingfield in District 3, Elijah Cundiff in District 4, Thomas Y. Mosby in District 5, Sam'l McDaniel in District 6, John D. Burks in District 7, James S. Woolfolk in District 8, and George P. Luck in District 9, agents on behalf of this court with authority to purchase such quantity of supplies of provisions as may be deemed necessary for the months of May, June, and July for the support of indigent families of soldiers in the county, the military services of the Confederate States at prices not to exceed the following: Flour $200 per barrel, corn $20 per bushel, bacon $5 per lb., beef $2 per lb., potatoes $8 per bushel, and wheat $30 per bushel, when it is possible to purchase said supplies of provisions herein stated at prices not to exceed those prescribed by the Commissioner appointed by the State of Virginia under the Act of Congress of the Confederate States regulating Impressments.

Ordered that the following persons be and are hereby appointed to ascertain the number and condition of the families of soldiers in military service who are receiving supplies and aid from this county and report to the committeeman in the district the names and conditions of such families as in their opinion are not entitled to aid with their reasons, therefor to Court: Wilson M. Wheeler to act in District 1, Josiah H. Nimmo in District 2, William A. Wingfield in District 3, John H. Turner in District 4, Tilghman A. Cobbs in District 5, Lewis E. Campbell in District 6, James O. Noell in District 7, John M. Jones in District 8, and Jesse Minter in District 9.

BIBLIOGRAPHY

Ackerly, Mary Denham & Parker, Lula Jeter. *Our Kin*. Harrisonburg, VA: C.J. Carrier Co., 1981.

Bagby, George W. *Old Virginia Gentleman & Other Sketches*. Richmond, VA: The Dietz Press, 1948.

Bedford Democrat newspaper: June 12, 16, 1857. September 11, 1857.

Blunt, Ruth A. *Sketches & Recollections of Lynchburg with Places and People with Addition*. Lynchburg, VA: J.P. Bell Company, (For Lynchburg Historical Foundation, Inc.) 1974.

Breckenridge, Lucy and edited by Mary D. Robertson. *Lucy Breckenridge of Grove Hill, Journal of a Virginia Girl, 1862-1864*. Kent, OH: Kent State University Press, 1979.

Brock, R.A. *Hardesty's Historical and Geographical Encyclopedia, Special Va. Edition*. NY, Chicago, Toledo: H. H. Hardesty & Co., 1884.

Catton, Bruce. *The Coming Fury*. Garden City, NY: Doubleday & Co., 1961.

Catton, Bruce. *Terrible Swift Sword*. Garden City, NY: Doubleday and Co., 1963.

Christian, W. Asbury. *Lynchburg and Its People*. Lynchburg, VA: J.P. Bell Company, 1900.

DAR, Peaks of Otter Chapter. *Echoes of Olde Liberty*. Lynchburg, VA: Progress Publishing Corporation, 1976.

Daniel, Harrison. *Bedford County, 1840-1860; The History of an Upper Piedmont County in the Late Antebellum Era.* Bedford, VA: The Print Shop, 1985.

Driver, Robert, Jr. & Howard, H.E. *2nd Virginia Cavalry.* Lynchburg, VA: H. E. Howard, Inc., 1995.

Goldman, Bobby. *The Goldman Brothers Civil War Letters.* Published material, compiled and transcribed by Bobby Goldman.

Fields, Frank E. *28th Virginia Infantry.* Lynchburg, VA: H. E. Howard, Inc., 1985.

Goode, John. *Recollections of a Lifetime.* NY & Washington, DC: Neale Publishing Co., 1906.

Graves, Rev. Joseph A. "The Bedford Light Artillery, 1861-1865." *Bedford Democrat,* 1903.

Hardesty, H. H. *Historical, Geographic Encyclopedia.* NY., Chicago, Richmond, and Toledo: H. H. Hardesty & Co., 1884.

Houck, Peter W. *A Prototype of a Confederate Hospital Center in Lynchburg.* Lynchburg, VA: Warwick House Publishing Co., 1986.

Marshall, Virginia Foster. *St. Thomas Protestant Episcopal Church.* Bedford, VA: The Print Shop, 1976.

McMurray, Richard M. *Two Great Rebel Armies.* Chapel Hill, NC: UNC Press, 1989.

Parker, Lula Jeter. *The History of Bedford County, VA.* Bedford, VA: Bedford Democrat, 1st edition, 1954.

Pierce, Mary Berry. *The Berrys of Virginia*. New York: Family History Article, 1985.

Comstock, Jim. *Southern Historical Society Papers, Vol. 11 and Vol. 17. West Virginia Heritage*. Richwood, WV. 1976.

Stevenson, Estelle Moseley. *George Cabell Moseley of Ingleside, Bedford County*. Compiled by Estelle Moseley Stevenson.

The Conservation Fund. *Civil War Battlefield Guide*. Edited by Frances H. Kennedy. Houghlin Mifflin Co., 1990.

Viemeister, Peter. *The Peaks of Otter, Life and Times*. Bedford, VA: Hamilton's, 1992.

INDEX

Symbols

11th Regiment 44
11th Regiment, Mississippi 45
11th Virginia Infantry 174
12th Ohio 229
14th West Virginia 229
21st Virginia Cavalry 18
28th Ohio 227
28th Va. Infantry, Pickett's Division 21
28th Virginia Infantry 19, 174
28th Virginia Volunteers 17
2nd Virginia Cavalry 49, 175
2nd West Virginia 227
34th Ohio 230
3rd S.C. 179
4th Mississippi Regiment 40
4th Va. Hvy Arty. 181
58th Virginia Regiment 133
6th Va. Cav. 181
7th New York Regiment 21
7th Regiment of New York 16
91st Ohio 227
9th West Va. 229

A

Adams, Thomas 178
Agee, Clarence 246
Albemarle Military Institute 4
Alexander, Sallie 21
Alexandria 64, 66, 88, 95
Alice 27, 37, 41, 63, 70, 84, 96, 97, 101, 104, 105, 106, 108, 114, 123, 127, 129, 133, 137, 158, 163
Allen, Fanny 85, 106, 107, 108, 140, 166
Allen, Frances R. 270
Allen, James 14, 97, 161
Allen, Julia 87
Allen, Major 85
Allen, Mary Wingfield 52
Allen, Mr. 32, 55, 56, 78
Allen, Mrs. 98, 241, 242
Allen, Robert 20, 48, 55, 56, 69, 241
Allen, Robert, Jr. 241
Almond, William 214
Altizer, E. D. 178
Anderson, John M. 269
Anderson, John N. 9
Anderson, Mr. 45
Andrews, Charles 268
Andrews, John W. 271
Angle, D. 178
Anthony, Emelia 267
Ardney, Col. 224, 228
Armistead, John 269
Armistead, Mrs. 175, 177
Armisted, James 269
Armstrong, W. 178
Arrington, Dr. 242
Arrington, Hampton 271
Arrington, S. E. 178
Arthur, Alban A. 214
Arthur, Lewis C. 10, 267
Arthur, S. C. 270
Aunspaugh, Charles 214
Aunspaugh, Daniel 2
Aunspaugh, Elizabeth 204
Aunspaugh, Frederic 204, 239
Aunspaugh, Lt. 205
Aunspaugh, Mrs. 6
Aunspaugh, Mrs. D. 266
Aunspaugh, Robert T. 7, 204, 236
Austin, David 268
Austin, William 267
Avenel 12, 13, 18, 34, 43, 58, 64, 65, 81, 82, 83, 92, 98, 155, 160, 167, 168, 247
Averill 230, 231, 232, 234, 235, 236, 245
Ayler 219

B

Bagby, Dr. George W. 43
Baker, R. J. 178
Baker, T.R. 188
Barker, Colonel 103
Barnett, F. 178
Barnett, Josephine 71
Barrett, James F. 178
Barton, Cousin 166
Barton, J. M. 178
Battle at Richmond 161, 164
Battle of Bull Run 17
Battle of Fair Oaks (Seven Pines) 263
Battle of First Manassas 99
Battle of Gaines Mill 163
Battle of Manassas 133, 263
Battle of New Market 21
Battle of Seven Pines 210
Battle of the Wilderness 208
Beale, Willie 130, 131
Beauregard, General 60, 66, 78, 93
Bedford House 1
Bedford Letcher Grays 8
Bedford Light Artillery 7, 174
Bedford Rangers 8
Bedford Volunteers 23
Belfrey, Josiah 178
Bell, A. A. 237
Bell, Cobb 206
Bell, Edmonia 206
Bell, Florentine Hatcher 206
Bell, Frances H. 270
Bell, Miss 206
Bell, Mr. 204
Bell, Mrs. 69, 89, 92, 97, 158
Bell, O. P. 9, 237
Bell, William I. 9
Bellamy, Patsy 270
Belle, Mrs. 157
Belleview 21, 167
Berry, Annis 55

Berry, Mr. 19, 57, 63, 78, 79, 93, 94, 127, 129
Berry, Mrs. 106
Berry, William Wallace 17
Bethel 62, 63
Beveridge, R. 179
Bilbro, William H. 271
Binns, J. A. 178
Bist, J. M. 178
Blackford, Ben 124
Blackford, Benjamin 124, 147, 152, 157, 162, 168, 174, 177, 183, 185, 188, 201, 205, 219
Blackman, S. 178
Blackwell, E. G. 178
Board, Charles A. 174, 175
Board, John 267
Board, Maria 266
Bolling, D. Arth. 269
Boon, Mr. 45
Bowling, Wm. 220
Bowling, Wm. H. 219
Bowyer, Dr. James 22, 24, 96, 140
Bowyer, Dr. Thomas Michie 7, 15, 16, 18, 19, 20, 21, 23, 26, 31, 32, 37, 39, 42, 51, 52, 55, 60, 67, 70, 80, 82, 85, 91, 93, 115, 116, 121, 123, 125, 139, 143, 145, 157, 159, 162, 167, 174, 254
Bowyer, Eliza 139
Bowyer, H. M. 15
Bowyer, Henry 15
Bowyer, James 52
Bowyer, Kate Burwell 58, 168, 250, 254
Bowyer, Lillian 111, 121
Bowyer, Lulie 36, 57
Bowyer, Major 254, 258
Bowyer, Mr. (Dr. Bowyer's father) 26, 120, 121
Bowyer, Mrs. Dr. James 95
Bowyer, William 157
Bowyer's Battery 156

INDEX 281

Bramblett, Mrs. 135
Bramlett, Becky 85
Breckenridge, Cary 35, 130, 162
Breckenridge, Eliza 131, 168
Breckenridge, Emma 130, 168
Breckenridge, General I.C. 103
Breckenridge, Gilmer 35, 154
Breckenridge, James 28, 35, 70, 95, 115, 122, 130, 137, 141, 143, 162, 164, 167
Breckenridge, John 35, 154
Breckenridge, Lucy 159, 168
Breckenridge, Matilda 15
Breckenridge, Mrs. 129
Breckenridge, Tom 164
Breckinridge, Jimmie 56
Brinkley, John 56, 69
Brinkley, Lou 70
Bristol, Virginia 4
Broadwater, Thos. 178
Brosius, John M. 218
Brown, Granville L. 268
Brown, Henry Clay 243
Brown, Henry P. 268
Brown, Mildred 270
Brown, Spottswood 9, 268
Brownell, Seymour 228
Buchanan, James 22
Buckner, Robert 269
Buckwalter, E. J. 2
Buena Vista 102
Buford, Capt. 239
Buford, John 214, 266
Buford, Paschal 271
Buford, Rowland D. 214
Buford, S. A. 10, 244
Bull Run 73, 184
Burks, Edward C. 214, 216, 247, 266, 272
Burks, Jesse S. 6, 270
Burks, John D. 270, 273
Burks, Martin P. 270
Burks, Mrs. 65

Burnet, Mr. 242
Burrough, J. 178
Burton, G. A. 269
Burwell, Armistead 33, 110
Burwell, Fan 13, 14, 15, 24, 28, 33, 35, 39, 40, 44, 54, 56, 58, 60, 70, 89, 92, 94, 95, 98, 100, 102, 104, 110, 112, 113, 114, 115, 121, 122, 123, 124, 126, 128, 129, 130, 131, 132, 139, 140, 141, 143, 148, 167
Burwell, Frances Steptoe 12, 13, 15, 33, 35, 37, 38, 39, 48, 50, 54, 58, 61, 64, 67, 69, 72, 78, 82, 83, 91, 94, 95, 100, 106, 108, 111, 122, 126, 127, 132, 137, 139, 140, 141, 143, 144, 145, 146, 148, 149, 152, 154, 157, 163, 164, 165, 166
Burwell, James 13
Burwell, Kate "Sister" 13, 15, 16, 17, 18, 21, 22, 23, 35, 36, 37, 38, 42, 43, 46, 47, 48, 49, 50, 51, 52, 54, 55, 59, 60, 61, 67, 69, 71, 72, 74, 79, 80, 82, 84, 85, 87, 91, 92, 93, 94, 95, 96, 105, 111, 112, 113, 115, 116, 121, 126, 132, 137, 139, 140, 144, 146, 149, 158, 161, 163, 164, 167, 252
Burwell, Letitia 12, 14, 167, 168, 170
Burwell, Mary 67
Burwell, Mary Frances "Fan" 130
Burwell, Mrs. 247
Burwell, Nat, Jr. 104
Burwell, Rosa 13, 15, 37, 39, 40, 44, 52, 53, 54, 56, 58, 60, 71, 80, 81, 89, 92, 95, 96, 100, 111, 112, 114, 116, 122, 124, 126, 127, 128, 131, 132, 136, 138, 143, 145, 146, 148, 151, 156, 157, 160, 165, 166, 168

Burwell, William Armistead 92
Burwell, William McCreary 12,
    13, 15, 16, 18, 22, 23, 26, 27,
    32, 37, 40, 44, 45, 48, 50, 51,
    52, 53, 54, 56, 57, 58, 60, 63,
    66, 69, 70, 73, 74, 75, 76, 77,
    83, 84, 88, 91, 102, 103, 106,
    107, 108, 110, 114, 115, 116,
    120, 122, 125, 126, 127, 128,
    129, 135, 137, 138, 140, 144,
    145, 146, 155, 157, 163, 164,
    166, 265
Bush, William 9
Butler, T. J. 178
Byrd, Robt. J. 178
Byrd, Wm. 178

C

C. F. Rifles 7
C. R. Rifles 7
Cain, W. T. 179
Caldwell, Mr. 146
Caldwell, Mrs. 145, 146
Callaway, Edward 268
Callaway, Elizabeth M. 232
Callaway, R. E. 269
Callaway, Ralph 268
Callaway, Richard 268
Callaway, Ro. W. 268
Calnan, Frank 179
Camm, Midshipman 129
Camm, Sallie 22
Campbell, Bowyer 12
Campbell House 2
Campbell, James L. 271
Campbell, James Lawrence 111
Campbell, Lewis E. 273
Campbell, Mr. 62, 63, 67, 73, 76,
    77, 78
Campbell, Mrs. 61, 63, 64, 77
Campbell, Nancy 271
Campbell, Thomas 270
Campbell, William T. 4, 62, 76,
    170, 185, 266
Captain Jordan's Artillery 40
Caroline 163
Carr, Emma 104
Carr, J. W. 179
Carrington 205
Carrington, W. A. 189, 194
Carroll, Wm. 179
Carter, John 179
Carver, Willis 179
Cedar Hill 41, 172
Chalmers, Dr. 138
Chalmers, Mr. 27, 93
Chalmers, Mrs. F. S. 268
Chappele, Richard 269
Charlottesville 4
Cheatwood, Hiram 269
Chestnut Hill 18, 19
Childers, J. 179
Chilton, Mr. 41
Christian, Magdalen 79, 97, 166
Christian, Marcellus P. 18, 158
Claggett, Dr. 174
Clark, Captain 159, 160, 163
Clark, I.N. 173, 185
Clarke, Frank 168
Clarkson, John C. 215
Clay Dragoon Co. A 42
Clay Dragoons 7
Claytor, Anna M. 204
Claytor, David M. 175
Claytor, E. M. 268
Claytor, Julia Graham 204
Claytor, Miss 201, 204
Claytor, Mrs. R. B. 7, 245
Claytor, Robert Mitchell 204
Claytor, Samuel G. 219
Claytor, Wm. 237
Clusky, Captain 45
Co. A, 12th Ga. 178
Co. A, 18th Ga. 180
Co. A, 21st Ga. 179
Co. A, 2nd Virginia Cavalry 53

INDEX 283

Co. A, 32nd Va. 181
Co. A, 44th Ala. 178
Co. A, 49th Va. 179
Co. A, 4th Texans 180
Co. A, 6th NC 181
Co. A or K, 47th Ala. 178
Co. A, Tenn Cavalry 179
Co. A. 180
Co. B, 14th Ga. 182
Co. B, 1st La. 179
Co. B, 28th N.C. 181
Co. B, 30th NC 182
Co. B, 34th N.C. 179
Co. B, 39th Ga. 179
Co. B, 42nd Va. 180
Co. B, 61st Ga. 179
Co. B, 8th Fla. 180
Co. B, Cobb's Ga. Legion 178
Co. B, of Wise Troop, 2nd Virginia Cavalry 93
Co. C, 16th Ga. 180
Co. C, 19th Miss. 181
Co. C, 26th Ga. 181
Co. C, 30th N.C. 180
Co. C, 3rd N.C. 180
Co. C, 59th Ga. 181
Co. C, 9th La. 180
Co. C of the 2nd Virginia Cavalry 35, 167
Co. C. of the 28th Virginia Infantry 263
Co. D, 11th Va. 179
Co. D, 12th Ga. 180
Co. D, 13th Ga. 180
Co. D, 14th Ga. 182
Co. D, 14th N.C. 178
Co. D, 16 GA. 178
Co. D, 1st S.C. 178
Co. D, 22nd Va. 179
Co. D, 30th N.C. 180
Co. D, 33rd N.C. 178, 179
Co. D, 41st Ala. 180
Co. D, 6th S.C. 179

Co. D, 7th S.C. 180
Co. E, 14th La. 179
Co. E, 15th Ala. 179
Co. E, 1st Ala. 180
Co. E, 23rd S.C. 180
Co. E, 27th Va. 181
Co. E, 2nd Fla. 182
Co. E, 31st Ga. 181
Co. E, 34th Infantry 41
Co. E, 3rd Bn., S.C. Inf. 181
Co. E, 44th Ga. 179
Co. E, 48th Ala. 181
Co. E, 4th Ala. Btn. 179
Co. E, 4th Texans 180
Co. E, 6th Ga. 181
Co. E, 8th S.C. 181
Co. E, 9th Ala. 180
Co. F, 10th Ala. 180
Co. F, 10th Tenn. Cav. 182
Co. F, 13th Ga. 180
Co. F, 15th N.C. 180
Co. F, 16th Miss. 179
Co. F, 21st Ga. 180
Co. F, 22nd Reg. Ga. Vol 183
Co. F, 23rd N.C. 181
Co. F, 2nd S.C. Battn. 180
Co. F, 2nd Va. 178
Co. F, 45th Ga. 180
Co. F, 61st Ala. 180
Co. F of the 28th Va. Infantry 8
Co. F, of the 5th Louisiana Infantry 168
Co. G, 13th Ala. 179
Co. G, 15th Ga. 181
Co. G, 20th Ga. 180
Co. G, 24th Ga. 178, 179
Co. G, 2nd S.C. Rifles 181
Co. G, 34th Infantry 41
Co. G, 38th Ga. 178
Co. G, 3rd S.C. 179
Co. G, 3rd,Tenn. 179
Co. G, 41st Ala. 181
Co. G, 43rd Ala. 178

Co. G, 44th Ga. 181
Co. G, 47th Ala. 178
Co. G, 50th Ga. 181
Co. G, 53rd N.C. 181
Co. G, 57th Va. 178
Co. G, 6th N.C. 179
Co. G, 8th Va. 182
Co. G., 9th La. 181
Co. H, 15th Ala. 178, 180
Co. H, 15th La. 181
Co. H, 15th NC 182
Co. H, 28th N.C. 180
Co. H, 44th Va. 181
Co. H, 48th Ga. 182
Co. H, 55 Va. 181
Co. H, 60th Va. 181
Co. H, 8th La. 181
Co. H, Va. Cavalry 179
Co. I, 11th NC 181
Co. I, 15th Ala. 180
Co. I, 1st Md. 179
Co. I, 24th Ga. 178
Co. I, 35th Ga. 181
Co. I, 3rd Ark. 180
Co. I, 48th Miss. 182
Co. I, 48th Va. 182
Co. I, 55th Va. 181
Co. I, 62nd Va. 179
Co. I, 6th N.C. 179
Co. I, 6th S.C. 179
Co. I, 7th S.C. 178
Co. I, 9th La. 179, 180, 181
Co. I, La. 181
Co. K, 12th S.C. 178, 181
Co. K, 16th Ga. 181
Co. K, 21st Ga. 180, 181
Co. K, 26th Ala. 179
Co. K, 31st Va. 182
Co. K, 3rd Va. 179
Co. K, 41st Va. 179
Co. K, 4th Ala. 179
Co. K, 54th Va. 178
Co. K, 5th N.C. 179

Co. K, 7th SC 182
Co. L, 2nd Miss. 180
Co. L, 3rd Ga. 179
Co. L, Palmetto Sharp Shooters, SC 182
Co. M, Phillips Ga. Legion 181
Cobbs, Sandy 36
Cobbs, Step 95
Cobbs, Tilghman A. 273
Cobbs, Tilghman, Jr. 268
Cofer, Pleasant 214
Coffee, Segar 219
Coleman, Mildred 246
Colonel Preston's regiment 55, 56, 70, 73, 74
Compton, Henry P. 266
Compton, John 267
Converse, Rev. Dr. 201
Coppage, Miss 201
Covey, E. N. 191
Covington, J. W. 179
Craig, Capt. 226
Craig, James 179
Creasy, Thomas 268
Creasy, William A. 218
Crenshaw, Eliza M. 41, 172
Crenshaw, John 5, 9, 41, 171, 172, 245, 265
Crenshaw, John Balda 4, 172, 185, 193
Crenshaw, Lucy 172
Crenshaw, Miss 204
Crenshaw, Richard 9, 266
Crockett, Captain 46, 47, 48, 50, 68
Croly, Miss 79
Crook, General 226, 227, 228, 230, 231, 232, 234, 235, 236, 245
Cross Lanes 90
Culpeper 173
Culpeper Courthouse 66, 67
Cundiff, Christopher 267
Cundiff, Elijah C. 9, 214, 273

INDEX

D

Davis, Annis 55
Davis, Editha 219
Davis, Ellen 18, 106, 111, 112, 131, 155, 269
Davis, George 251
Davis, Jefferson 7, 23
Davis, John 17, 19, 159, 164
Davis, Lucy 175, 265
Davis, Maggie 65, 88
Davis, Mary Annis 17
Davis, Mayo 269
Davis, Micajah 2, 4, 18, 70, 73, 171, 185, 215, 216, 251, 265
Davis, Mollie 18
Davis, Mr. 67, 75, 79, 85, 129, 251
Davis, Mrs. 56, 61, 87
Davis, Mrs. Micajah 34
Davis, Nannie 17, 19, 55, 56, 65, 85, 88, 110, 131, 143, 158
Davis, Richard 270
Davis, Sam 19, 20, 22, 31, 34, 36, 57, 100
Davis, Samuel P. 17
Davis, Thomas 18
Davis, Thomas Edward 17
Davis, Tom 20, 21, 22, 24, 26, 27, 31, 33, 40, 42, 44, 59, 65, 159, 164
Dawson, R.D. 269
Day, J. W. 179
Delbridge, George 45
Dent, Joel 266
Dickenson, Mr. 83, 112
Dickinson, John Q. 265
Dillard, Lucy 21
Dillon, Ned 139
Doctor 26, 41, 53, 54, 61, 80, 81, 89, 90, 114, 133, 156, 157, 158
Donald, Alexander Jr. & Sr. 22
Donald, Andrew 22, 99, 265
Donald, Benjamin 22, 24
Donald, James 22

Donald, Mr. 22, 24, 26, 65, 67, 82, 89, 90, 99, 110, 112, 114, 141, 164, 166
Donald, Mrs. 24, 25, 26, 27, 61, 89, 90, 98, 110, 114, 129, 141
Donald, Robert, Sr. 22
Donald, Thomas, Jr. 22
Douglas, Dr. 68
Douglas, Lulie 57, 156
Douglas, R. N. 270
Douglas, Sally 270
Downing, John 268
Duffie 230, 233, 235
Duke, Dan'l 179
Dunton, S. L. 2, 3, 37, 62, 170, 239
Duval, Col. 229
Dykes, W. 179

E

Eads, Dr. 174
Eagle, Alexander 179
Early, General Jubal 225, 226, 234, 243
Ellen 27, 37, 41, 63, 70, 84, 96, 97, 108, 114, 123, 127, 129, 133, 137, 151, 158, 159, 163
Elliott, Judith/Jas. 270
English and Classical School at Timberidge 4
English, Stephen 267
English, William 267
Ettinger, Mr. 41
Eubank, Alexander 4
Everett, Edward 33, 57, 59, 68
Everett, John 268
Eves, Dr. 147, 148, 151, 155
Ewell's Division 162
Ewing, A. M. 218, 270

F

Fagan, Colonel 46, 47, 48, 51, 68
Fagan, Mrs. 52
Fairfax Courthouse 61, 88, 93

Fancy Farm 22, 98, 99, 223, 224, 241
Farris, J. J. 268
Faulkner, Colonel 45
Federal Hill 42
Ferguson 219
Ferrell, Henry C. 271
Ferrell, William J. 270
Fields, Dr. 174
Fields, Elizabeth 267
Fink, John M. 179
Fizer, Charles B. 220
Fizer, Charlie 176
Fizer, George 266
Fizer, Mary B. 176
Fizer, Mary Oney 175, 176
Fizer, Mrs. 177
Fizer, William 176
Forbes, J. N. 179
Forgie, Daniel K. 271
Fort Donaldson 127, 128, 137
Fortress Monroe 16
Fort Sumter 7
Foster, Lt. 227
Franklin Hotel 47
Frederick, Mrs. 175
Freeman, J. M. 179
Freeman, J. S. 179
Frierson, Dr. 174
Fuqua, Abner 9, 218
Fuqua, Abraham 218
Fuqua, Abram 266
Fuqua, Sally 266
Fuqua, Thomas 268

G

Gaillard, E.S. 188
Galloway, L. 179
Gamble, J. S. 179
Garner, T. (?) J. 179
Garrett, Elijah 267
Gay, John 111
Getty, L. G. 179

Gibbs, Jesse R. 10
Gibbs, Joel 266
Gibbs, John 266
Gibson, Lieutenant 46, 47, 50
Gill, Charles M. 273
Gill, Charles W. 9, 266
Gilliam, Mrs. 114, 133, 165
Gilmer, William 162
Gilmore, Dr. 26
Gish, Sarah 175, 177
Gish, William 1, 54
Goard, Jonathan 267
Godfrey 26
Godfrey, Lewis 179
Goggin, William L. 268
Goldman, Jasper 182
Goldman, Marion 183, 184
Goode, Edmond 133
Goode, John 133
Goode, John, Jr. 53, 54, 212, 268, 272
Goode, Mrs. 56, 76, 77, 78, 94, 152, 156, 162
Gordonsville 167
Grattan, Sallie 48
Graves, Col. 237
Graves, Emeline S. 239
Graves, Emma 110, 111, 112, 143, 162
Graves, Joseph A. 239
Graves, William 5, 239, 266
Gregory, J.F. 1
Griffin, Charlie 48, 132
Griffin, Charlotte 23
Griffin, Elizabeth 23
Griffin, Mrs. Samuel 218
Griffin, Samuel 218, 269
Grooms, John H. 179
Grove Hill 35
Guthridge, J. M. 179
Guthrie, Reuben 267
Gwathmey, Anne 70, 104, 105
Gwathmey, Cary 91

INDEX

Gwathmey, Mary 104
Gwathmey, Mollie 154

H

Hall, Matthew 267
Hall, W. 179
Halsey, Don 51
Hampton 53
Hamrick 238
Hamrick, Andrew J. 180
Hancock, Christopher 267
Hancock, John 267
Hannabass, David 267
Hanson (Hinson), J.L. 179
Hardcastle 202
Hardy, Joseph S. 270
Harper, Dr. 174
Harpers Ferry 14, 16, 53, 63
Harris, Bully 264
Harris, Captain 130, 131
Harris, Charles 263
Harris, Hannibal 268
Harris, Hector 9, 214, 269
Harris, J.B. 180
Harris, James 269
Harris, Mrs. Samuel 175
Harris, S. A. 4
Harris, Samuel H. 263
Harris, William 270
Harvey, Charles 166
Harvey, Jane D. 99, 140, 161
Harvey, John 145
Harvey, Mr. 162
Harvey, William 23
Hatcher, Allen D. 219, 269
Hatcher, Jeremiah G. 271
Hatcher, Thomas 270
Hatcher, Uriah 270
Hawkins, Fountain M. 271
Hawkins, John F. 219
Hayes, Capt. 229
Hayes, Mrs. J. W. 246
Hayes, Rutherford B. 226

Haynes, Mrs. Jacob 175
Head, W.J.E. 179
Hemphill, W.C. 179
Henderson, Mr. 47, 49, 50, 105, 109, 123, 124, 125, 126, 154
Henricus, Madame 247
Hensley, James O. 7, 267
Heptinstall, Caleb 218
Herndon, A.S. 179
Hewitt, Wilson C. 34, 124, 266
Hicks, Avy 268
Hilts, J.R. 180
Hinkle, Thornton M. 223
Hobson, Benjamin N. 10, 270
Hobson, Samuel 270
Hobson, Sue 25, 63
Hobson, William 270
Hoffman, Clara 251
Hoffman, Edwin 264
Hoffman, John F. 227
Hoffman, Mr. 67, 135, 237
Hoffman, Mrs. John 175
Holcomb, Mary 48, 52
Holcombe, James P. 218
Holcombe, Mary 125
Holiday, Lulie 156
Holland, Kemp G. 266
Holland, W. O. 179
Holley, James A. 271
Holmes, J. S. 179
Holt, Col. 239
Holt, David 59
Holt, J. H. 180
Holt, John W. 265
Holt, Wm. P. 266
Hooper, Mr. 75
Hopkins, Elizabeth 267
Hopkins, Jesse Turner 9, 34, 266
Hopkins, Jimmie 241
Hopkins, John C. 10, 270
Hopkins, Mr. 242
Hopkins, Walter J. 268
Horsely, Nicholas Cabell 204, 224

Housemann, Mr. 45
Howard, R. 179
Huddleston, Martha 267
Huddleston, William 266
Hudnall, Frances 268
Hudson, W.W. 179
Hughes, Samuel 214
Hunt, Chas. N. 179
Hunt, John A. 218
Hunter 236, 244, 253
Hunter, David 197, 223, 234, 245
Hunter's Brigade, Pickett's Division 263
Hurley, Fannie 175
Hurt, Joel L. 267
Hurt, John P. 10
Hurt, Josephus 267
Hurt, Judith 270
Hurt, Polly 267
Hurt, William O. 10
Hutter, Edward 269
Hutter, Lieutenant 142
Hutton [Hutter], Major 233
Hutton's [Hutter's], Major 234

I

Ingleside 98, 240, 244
Irvine, Alex 268
Irvine, C.M.C. 268
Irvine, John B. 268
Irvine, Wm. H. 268
Irwin, T.P. 180

J

Jackson, J. 180
Jackson's Division 162
Jacobs, Ellis 180
Jacobs, M. 180
Jenkins, James 180
Jennings, James, Jr. 270
Jeter, B. R. 266
Jeter, Fielding H. 9
Jeter, Jesse 270

Jeter, Jesse B. 269
Jeter, William 270
Johnson, George 9, 267
Johnson, J. F. 216
Johnson, Jesse 180
Johnson, Joseph 218
Johnson, Mr. 54, 59, 62, 67, 73
Johnson, Mrs. 62, 63, 64, 78, 82
Johnson, Samuel D. 229
Johnson, William 266
Johnston, Charles 101
Johnston, Fanny 33
Johnston, Frederick 81, 83, 101
Johnston, James 168
Johnston, Jane Wood 23
Johnston, Joseph E. 23, 70
Johnston, Nancy 81, 83
Jones, E. C. 267
Jones, Emily 269
Jones, Henry 268
Jones, Isabella 271
Jones, John M. 265, 273
Jones, John William 268
Jones, Ro. C. 271
Jones, Robert 6
Jones, Robert E. 9
Joplin, Thomas B. 270
Joplin, William G. 270
Joplin, Wm. Y. 180
Jordan 64, 87, 138, 254
Jordan, Alexander 40, 172, 266
Jordan, Hezekiah T. 265
Jordan, John 40, 147, 267
Jordan, John Y.M. 174
Jordan, Jubal IV 40
Jordan, Mrs. 143
Jordan, Pricilla 40
Jordan, Tyler 1, 7, 40
Jordan, William 40, 80, 172

K

Kasey, James C. 266
Kasey, Jericho 21

INDEX 289

Keatts, James H. 267
Keisler, H. 180
Kellogg, Dr. 227
Kelso 231
Kelso, Robert N. 10, 99, 241, 270
Kelso, Sue 241
Kelso, Thomas 99, 214, 241, 270
Kent, Dr. James McGavock 7, 8, 268
Kenzer, George L. 266
Key, W.A. 180
Kinkle, W. H. 94, 208
Knight, John J. 269
Koenigsberger, Herman 227
Kroutner, Mr. 158
Kyle, A. M. 220
Kyle, B. M. 218
Kyle, David 9, 269

L

Ladiner, E. B. 180
Lamar Rifles, 11th Mississippi Regiment 44
Lancaster, James 219, 267
Land, R. J. 180
Lands, B. Patrick 180
Langhorne, Anne 51
Langhorne, George 126
Langhorne, William 72, 105
Layne, Martha 271
Lee, Garnett 268
Leesburg 97
Leftwich 232
Leftwich, Alexander 9, 267
Leftwich, Caroline 267
Leftwich, George W. 268
Leftwich, I.T. 125
Leftwich, James T. 87
Leftwich, Mr. 197
Leftwich, Mrs. 62, 84, 94, 152
Leftwich, Mrs. James 87
Leftwich, Thomas 7

Leftwich, Thomas W. 218
Leftwich, William 232
Leftwich, Wm. 265
Leftwich, Wm. H. 268
Leo, Lafayette 268
Letcher, Dr. 147, 161, 164, 168, 174, 203
Letcher, Governor 7, 14, 18, 47
Leyburn, Dr. 174
Leyburn, Eliza 86
Leyburn, Mr. 100, 106, 110
Leyburn, Mr. and Mrs. 85
Leyburn, Mrs. 100, 106, 112
Light, J. W. 180
Ligon, W. B. 180
Liles, James 180
Linbarger, J. R. 180
Lincoln, Abraham 7, 10
Lines, J. P. 180
Linus, Clarissa Baldwin 99
Lipscomb, Jordan 267
Lockridge, James 219
Logwood, Alexander H. 240
Logwood, Jack 240
Logwood, Lucy 269
Loring, W. W. 217
Lovelace, Wm. A. or O. 180
Lowry, Charles B. 270
Lowry, Elliott 266
Lowry, J. M. 4
Lowry, John H. 270
Lowry, Judith 266
Lowry, Milton 238
Lowry, Miss 201
Lowry, Nelson 265
Lowry, Triplett E. 175
Lowry, W. K. 218
Loyd, Henry 267
Luck, George P. 10, 271, 273
Lucy 122
Lunsford, J. L. 180

M

Mahoney, M. 181
Major, Harwood 220
Major, Howard 270
Mallory, C. K. 196
Mallory, Colonel 157
Mallory, Edward 161
Manassas 63, 74, 75, 76, 78, 80, 82, 84, 111
Manassas Gap 53
Manassas Junction 57, 59
Mannering, J. A. 181
Manson, Nathaniel 269
Maria 108, 112, 113, 114, 115, 116, 117, 118, 119, 146
Markham, N. H. 218
Marsh, Thomas 270
Marshall, E. Wm. 181
Martha 122
Martha (servant) 88, 89
Martin, Green B. 267
Martin, John 269
Martin, Sophia 220, 267
Martindale, Captain 234
Martinsburg 70
Mary, Cousin 124
Mason, F. F. 181
Mason, James 107
Matthews & Wright 5
Matthews, James M. 5, 9, 273
Matthews, William 37, 132, 141
Mattox, J.H. 269
Maupin, Miss 131
Maupin, Peg 247
McCain, Major 256
McCanby, Wm. 181
McCausland, Gen. 242
McClain, Sam'l. J. 180
McClain, Wm. 267
McDaniel, Albert 269
McDaniel, Elizab. 266
McDaniel, Sam'l 269, 273
McDaniel, Walker 266
McDonald, J. A. 180
McGee, G. 180
McGhee, Chas. D. 219
McGhee, Mary 265
McGhee, Mrs. 242
McGhee, Sam'l. 269
McGowan, J. A. 180
McKee, A. T. 180
McKee, H. E. 181
McNair, Rbt. 180
McNeese, Mrs. 106, 112
Meador, Obediah 267
Meador, Wilson 267
Means, Jinny 131, 155, 156
Meem, Lawrence 154
Meredith, Dr. 36, 49, 50
Meredith, Dr. Samuel 36
Meredith, Lulie 57, 61, 63
Meredith, Samuel 156
Merewether, James A. 208, 219, 269
Merino, William 269
Meriweather, Charles 269
Meriweather, J. & C. A. 219
Meriwether, Fannie E. 208
Merriman, Eleanor 219, 268
Metcalf, James 220, 269
Miley, Dan'l 180
Miller & Wilson 5
Miller, Edwin 180
Miller, Jesse H. 266
Miller, Mr. 190
Miller, N. A. 181
Miller, Ro. 266
Milum, Geo. Wm. 180
Minter, Augustus L. 8
Minter, Jesse 217, 265, 271, 272, 273
Mitchell, A. D. 266
Mitchell, Charlotte 23
Mitchell, Harvey 23, 33, 42, 69
Mitchell, Jacob 48, 125
Mitchell, Jane Johnston 56, 72, 81

Mitchell, Katherine 23
Mitchell, Lou 56
Mitchell, Lucy 48, 50
Mitchell, Mary Louise 23, 56
Mitchell, Mildred 112
Mitchell, Mr. 47, 125
Mitchell, Mrs. Harvey 71
Mitchell, Ro. C. 265
Mitchell, Robert 23, 34, 42, 57, 70, 81, 83, 91, 95, 117, 131, 146, 157, 168
Mitchell, Sue 71
Mitchell, Sue Henry 23, 56
Mitchell, Thos. P. 7, 266
Mitchell, Tom 60, 64, 68, 71, 112, 131, 166
Mitchell, Willie 23, 56, 71, 113, 121, 166, 168, 268
Mizell, Wm. 181
Monroe, William 269
Moore, Dr. 174
Moore, Dr. John 18
Moore, Goodrich 271
Moore, John 181
Moore, Mary Evelyn 18
Moore, Samuel Preston 186, 190, 193, 195
Moorill, F. A. 180
Moorman & Peters 5
Moorman, A. F. 180
Moorman, Lodowick 269
Moorman, Permelia 267
Moorman, S. P. R. 9
Morgan, A. 267
Morgan, G. & C. 218
Morris, Alice 129, 132, 151
Morrison, J. M. 180
Mosby, Charles L. 42
Mosby, Eliza 127
Mosby, Leslie 130, 131
Mosby, Lizzie 45, 47, 49, 64, 72, 77, 124, 126, 127, 143, 151
Mosby, Mary 132, 143

Mosby, Mr. 42, 43, 44, 46, 50, 87, 123, 126, 143, 147, 232
Mosby, Thomas Yeatman 232, 268, 272, 273
Mosby, Thos. Y. 268
Mosby, William 45, 46, 49, 51, 54, 64, 72, 73, 77, 87, 105, 123, 124, 126, 147, 164
Moseley, George Cabell, Sr. 98, 240, 242
Moseley, Alice 98, 240, 243
Moseley, Cabell 98, 240, 243
Moseley, Elizabeth Winston 240
Moseley, Henry Winston 242, 243, 266
Moseley, Martha R. 243
Moseley, Mary D. Whitlock 242
Moseley, William H. 243
Moses, Dr. 160, 162, 164, 168, 174
Mount Pleasant 55
Mt. Prospect 241, 242
Munford, Mr. 26, 71
Munford, Mrs. 91
Munford, Thos. 269
Munson's Hill 88, 91

N

Nance, Thaddeus 267
Nash, Capt. 228
Nellons, Dr. 227
Nelm, Mrs. 66
Nelms, Eben 267
Nelms, Lieutenant 40, 44, 45
Nelson, Helen 63
Nelson, John A. 175
Nelson, Mrs. T. H. 269
Nelson, Thos. 266, 268
Nesbitt, Dr. 174
Newsom & Wright 5
Newsom, David 266
Newsom, Elizabeth 266
Newsom, Nathaniel 267
Nichol, Mr. 99

Nichols, A. B. 9, 248, 249, 265
Nichols, Abel 99
Nichols, George 99, 249
Nichols, J. M. 181
Nichols, W. F. 197
Nimmo, Josiah H. 9, 273
Noell, G.W. 270
Noell, James I. 272
Noell, James O. 273
Noell, John C. 270
Norfolk 134
Norman, Alfred E. 181
Northern, W. G. 181
Norton, R. T. 181
Norvell House 47, 52

O

Oaklands 105, 165, 167
Odomill, F. 181
Ogden, H. M. 269
Ogden, John 220, 270
Ogden, Wm. 220
Ogelsby, Joshua B. 269
Ogelsby, Lodowick 269
Old Dominion Rifles 7, 17, 263
Old Dominion Volunteers 25
Oney, James W. 176
Oney, Mary E. Thomas 176
Osborne, H. S. 4
Otey, Dr. J. A. 2, 9, 238
Otey, Isaac 241
Otey, Mary C. 271
Otey, Mrs. 124
Otterburn 22, 24, 90
Overstreet, E. A. 247
Overstreet, Thos. C. 267
Owen, William Otway 192, 207

P

Pace, Mrs. 112
Padgett, Beverly 270
Page, Dr. 87

Parker, Ammon H. 268
Parker, Caleb D. 9
Parker, Martha D. 267
Pate, Cornelius 271
Pate, Mrs. 88, 143
Patterson, General 75
Patterson, John Ed 100
Patterson, Mr. 115
Patton, Mr. 166
Payne, Ella 125
Payne, Temperance 266
Payne, William 267
Pelfrey, T. Josiah 181
Pendleton, Mr. 77
Penn, Lucy 268
Perry, O. H. 218
Peters, C. C. 267
Peters, Elisha 220
Peters, S. 269
Peters, Stephen T. 218, 220
Peters, T. S. 181
Peters, Wesley 219
Peyton, F. 181
Phelps, Charles 1
Phelps, Thomas J. 268
Phillips Ga. Legion 180
Phillips, Lucy 34, 81
Phillips, Virginia Phinney 19
Pican, Raymond 181
Piedmont Institute 4, 185
Pierceville, Virginia 8
Pike, Albert 137
Pike, Luther Hamilton 116, 117, 121, 139, 168
Pike, Walter 94, 118, 138, 155
Pitchford, John 181
Poindexter, Davis 270
Poindexter, Eliza 269
Poindexter, John S. 270
Poindexter, Richard 269
Poindexter, Willis 269
Pollard, Susan 99
Posey, E. F. 181

INDEX 293

Powell, General 254
Powell, Mr. 71
Powell, R.C. 203
Powell, William 270
Preston, Colonel 48, 49, 51, 53, 64, 66, 155, 156
Preston, Jimmie 72, 130, 131
Preston, John P. 267
Preston, Robert 45
Preston, Sarah 15
Preston, Thomas J. 267
Price, N. W. 181
Prior, F. 242

Q

Quarles, Betty 68, 110, 135, 160
Quarles, Samuel H. 265

R

Radford, Amy 269
Radford, Captain 8
Radford, Carlton 22, 269
Radford, Colonel 49
Radford, M. W. 269
Radford, Mr. 85, 120, 121, 154
Radford, R. C. W. 49
Radford, William 269
Ragland, James M. 172
Raines, Richard 172
Ransom, H. G. 181
Read & Jett 268
Read, William A. 220, 225, 268
Redding, Elhannan 181
Redman, F. S. 181
Reed, Geo. 181
Reese, John M. 171, 185
Reid, Mr. 47
Reid, Mrs. E. 269
Reilly, William 10
Reinhardt, Chas. 181
Reynolds, Charles B. 270
Reynolds, Joshua 220, 270

Rice, D. H. 181
Richardson, Frederick 168
Richmond 163
Rieley, William G. 271
Rifle Grays 7
Roanoke Island 126, 128, 136
Roberts, E. 230
Robertson, John J. 219, 268
Robertson, S. P. 268
Robertson, Thomas W. 9, 267
Robinson, Dr. 160
Robinson, Tonie 29
Rodes, Fanny 132
Roemer, Major 133
Rooks, Hezekiah 181
Rosebrough, Mr. 237, 239
Rosebrough, Robert 218
Rothsay 49
Round Hill 105
Rousseau, Captain 103
Royall, Fanny 49, 79, 80, 81, 83
Rucker, Ed 202
Rucker, James M. 270
Rucker, Mrs. 267
Rudd, Ben 46, 47
Rudd, Bev 49, 50
Rudd, Fanny 125
Rudd, Mrs. 50, 125

S

Sale, Anna A. 206
Sale, Capt. 206
Sale, Dr. 73, 76, 114, 151
Sale, John F. 6, 266
Sale, John W. 266
Sale, L. A. 2
Sale, Lauriston A. 206
Sale, Mr. 37, 95, 108
Sale, Mrs. 25, 69, 91, 152, 157
Sale, Nelson 206
Sale, R.A. 270
Sale, Rev. Nelson 31
Samuel Hoffman 1

Saunders, Carolyn 203
Saunders, H. G. 181
Saunders, James 265, 266, 268
Saunders, Julia 267
Saunders, Miss 202
Saunders, Mrs. F. L. 267
Saunders, Thomas T. 268
Saunders, Thos. 268
Scott, Charles 219, 220, 269
Scott, General 76
Scott, Hugh 269
Scott, R. & Co. 219
Scott, Robert G. 219
Scott, Wm. R. 219
Scruggs, Martha 267
Scruggs, Rives S. 266, 268
Scruggs, Theophilus 10
Selden, Dr. 174
Shelton, George W. 9
Shilling, John J. 181
Sikes (Sykes), Wilson L. 181
Sinclair 202
Sinks, H. S. 266
Skinner, Maj. 229
Sledd, William E. 270
Slidell, John 107
Slidell, Mr. 107
Sloat, A. 4, 80, 108, 141
Smelser, John 271
Smith, Charlie 29
Smith, J. M. 181
Smith, Mrs. 160
Smith, Stephen P. 267
Smith, Vinal 3
Sommerville, Dr. 174
Sommerville, Elizabeth Mauzy 199
Sommerville, Henry Clay 199, 208
Sommerville, James 199
Sommerville, William 199
Southside Dragoons 7
Speece, Joseph 269
Speed, John 120

Speed, Mr. 47, 50, 120, 125, 126, 147
Speed, Mrs. 125
Spilman, John A. 213
Staples, David 220
Staples, W. A. 266
Stephens, Alexander H. 23
Steptoe, James C. II 23
Steptoe, John 204
Steptoe, Katherine Mitchell 34
Steptoe, Marion 110
Steptoe, William 97, 147, 268
Stevens, Mr. 23
Stevens, William 269
Stewart, B. F. 181
Stewart Brothers 5
Stewart, Samuel G. 214, 219
Stiff, Henry 266
Stockton 233, 235
Stone, E.B. 170
Stone, J. F. 2
Stone, Martha 266
Strother, David Hunter 230
Suggs, J. B. 181
Sullivan 230, 232, 233, 236
Sunnyside School 4
Surls, Martin L. 181
Swain, Elijah 268
Sweet Springs 228

T

Talbot, Elbert A. 9
Taliaferro, William 56
Talley, P. F. 182
Tayloe, Colonel 154
Tayloe, George 154
Tayloe, Ginnie 70, 104
Tayloe, Jimmie 134, 135, 139, 142
Tayloe, Mr. 70
Tayloe, Nannie 91, 101, 102, 104, 115, 137
Tayloe, Rosa 70, 101, 104, 131

Tayloe, Thornton 101, 102, 104, 115, 122
Tayloe, Willie 104
Taylor, R.K. 188
Taylor's Brigade 159, 162
Terrell, J.J. 205
Terry, Captain 53
Terry, Charlie 154
Terry, Jane 172
Terry, Mr. 66
Terry, William R. 7, 42, 236, 266
Thaxton, David 271
Thaxton, Nathaniel 271
Thoburn, Col. 233
Thomas, Henry O. 269
Thomas, Colvin M. 181
Thompson, A. S. 270
Thompson, Major 46, 47, 48, 51
Thompson, Nelson A. 270
Thomson, R. B. 268
Three Otters 99, 248, 249, 250
Thurman, William P. 174
Thurman, August L. 9
Thurman, Sophia 267
Tinsley, Jane R. 266
Tinsley, Samuel G. 267
Todd, Dr. Charles H. 147, 160, 161, 164, 165, 168, 174
Toler, William D. 172, 185
Tompkins, Dan'l 267
Tool, Miss 201
Toombs, Mrs. Robert 59
Toombs, Robert 38, 81, 84, 126
Torrence, F. L. 226
Tucker, W. T. 182
Turner, A. W. 182
Turner, Benj. B. 267
Turner, Francis J. 219
Turner, John H. 267, 273
Turpin, Elisha G. 270
Turpin, J. D. 270
Turpin, John 270
Turpin, Mary 270

Turpin, Philip 270
Turpin, Thomas N. 270
Tuton, Wm. G. 182

U

Uncle Mat 92

V

Vienna 65
Virginia and Tennessee Collegiate Institute 4
Virginia Military Institute 8, 9, 230, 243

W

Wade, Archibald, Jr. 268
Wade, S. J. 268
Wade, Samuel I. 9
Walker, Benjamin 220
Walker, Bettie 268
Walker, Edward F. 266
Walker, S. P. 266
Wallace, G. W. 182
Wallace, W. F. 182
Waller, E. B. 182
Watkins, Raymond W. 178
Watts, Alice 167
Watts, Allen 108
Watts, Emma 167
Watts, Mrs. 104, 105
Watts, Mrs. General 165
Watts, William 104, 105
Webb, Dr. 226
Webster, George 217
Weere, Wiley 182
Welch, David 182
Wells, David J. 268
Wells, Richard M. 268
West, Caroline 232
West, John 268
West, John W. 9
West, Laura Virginia 19

Wetmer, G. K. 221
Wharton, Lymon 68, 72, 114
Wharton, Mrs. 62
Wharton, Rev. John A. 3, 31, 41, 65, 67, 72, 78, 82, 85, 87, 88, 89, 97, 120, 121, 128, 132, 143, 147, 151, 161, 206, 212, 214
Wharton, Sarah 270
Wheatly 34, 35
Wheeler, Wilson 9
Wheeler, Wilson M. 273
White, Samuel M. 10
Whitely, H. A. 218, 270
Whitesides, Samuel C. 1
Whitlock, Mary Daniel 98, 99, 241
Whitlock, Mrs. 77
Whitlock, Nathaniel 241
Wigginton, Benj. 269
Wigginton, Isaac 266
Wildman, H. W. [Peg] 245
Wilkerson, William L. 10
Wilkes, Benjamin 270
Wilkes, Charles 107
Wilkinson, Thos. M. 265
Wilkinson, William L. 270
Williams, Matilda 271
Williams, Mrs. 207
Williams, P. 182
Williams, R. S. 263
Wilson, D. B. F. 182
Wilson, James 7, 214, 218
Wilson, John 271
Wilson, Mrs. Joseph 269
Wilson, W. M. 182
Wingfield, Cass 32, 141
Wingfield, Charlotte 20, 21, 23
Wingfield, Charlotte Griffin 20
Wingfield, Gustavas Adolphus 20, 23, 32, 266
Wingfield, James Frank 21
Wingfield, Judge 165
Wingfield, Katherine S. 21
Wingfield, Mary 20, 56
Wingfield, Mr. 32
Wingfield, Mrs. 69, 72
Wingfield, Nannie 21, 141
Wingfield, Samuel G. 21
Wingfield, Sarah 21
Wingfield, Sis 16, 20, 87, 92, 95, 141, 142, 167
Wingfield, William A. 9, 272, 273
Wingfield, William Lewis 7, 21
Winkler, Mr. 98
Winkler, Mrs. 40, 56
Wise Troop of Lynchburg 27
Witherspoon, Mr. 45
Witt, John B. 267
Witt, Misses S. & A. 266
Witt, Wm. 266
Wood, Edward B. 226
Wood, Fleman 246
Wood, Wm. B. 182
Woodbridge, Mr. 114
Woodford 247
Woods, Rbt. 182
Woolfolk, James S. 273
Wordly, J. 182
Worsham, Raleigh 54
Wright, Anthony 266
Wright, Joel 266
Wright, John Mays 5
Wright, John Q. A. 266
Wright, Joseph P. 266
Wright, Nancy 266
Wright, William 151

Y

Yancey, Louisa 175
Yorktown 144
Younger, James 269